PADRE PEDRO

Apostle of
Hope

The Story of Father Peter Opeka

JESÚS MARÍA SILVEYRA

Foreword by Cardinal Franc Rode

Interior design, layout, and editing: Claudia Volkman, Creative Editorial Solutions

Graphics assistance by Tim Percic, www.perciccreative.com

Cover design: Claudia Volkman and Tim Percic

Project Coordination by Edward and Milena Gobetz

"Padre Pedro, Apostle of Hope. The Story of Father Peter Opeka," by Jesús María Silveyra. ISBN 978-1-60264-986-6.

Library of Congress Control Number: 2012902339.

ACKNOWLEDGMENTS

I wish to express my heartfelt gratitude to:

Pedro Pablo (Peter Paul) Opeka for opening the doors to his life and offering me the testimony of his love in the midst of the marginalized and excluded.

All the people of Akamasoa, especially to Father Roque (Rok Gajsek), Marie Odette, Teresa, Honorine, Pierrette, Fideline, Tojo, Viviane, Emma, Patrice, Guy, Jean-Jacques, Marcial, and Maurice, for their kindness and cooperation.

All the boys and girls of Akamasoa, especially to those in the dining room, for their continuous show of affection which filled me with joy.

Julieta, my wife, and every one of my children: *Julieta, Jesús, Felipe, Andrés, Catalina, and Pedro,* for their unconditional support for this journey, and in particular Felipe, for transcribing all the recorded interviews.

Bernardo Olivera, for helping me for over twenty years in my spiritual journey of discernment, and especially for encouraging me to write this book.

Martín Serantes, friend and confessor, who, like Father Peter, opted for the poor a long time ago.

The Opeka family: Alojz and Marija (who passed away in 2006), Bernarda, Helena, Mariana, Luis, Luba, Lucia, and Isabel, for opening their homes and their feelings.

Elena Feeney, for her translation, and *Marko Petrovic,* for his editorial assistance.

His Eminence, Cardinal Franc Rode, for kindly agreeing to write a Foreword to the book.

Professor Edward and Milena Gobetz, without whose persistent efforts this book would never have been translated and published in English.

Peter and Sue Osenar, Rudolph and Victoria Kolaric, Anna Nemec, and Ivan and Paula Hauptman, for their financial support.

Rudy and Anna Knez and Marica Lavrisa of the Slovenian Catholic Mission Aid (Misijonska znamkarska akcija), for their sponsorship of the translation project.

Terezka Znidar, for all her enthusiasm and help.

Marta Cinollo, for her French lessons before my departure.

Marcelo Serantes, for his medical advice.

All the *friends and relatives* who prayed for the success of this project.

Tim Percic of PercicCreative.com for the appealing book cover design.

And especially *Claudia Volkman* for her knowledge, leadership, and patience in bringing to fruition this first English-language edition on the marvelous work of Father Opeka.

TABLE OF CONTENTS

FOREWORD

When I met Peter (Pedro) Opeka during a visit to Madagascar in 1977, I wrote in my diary: "Arriving in the courtyard of the mission center in Vangaindrano, we were surrounded by a swarm of chattering, inquisitive children. Out of the crowd there came forward, like a young Moses in the midst of his people, the warm and personable Peter Opeka. There is something indestructibly young and refreshing about him. It is of such stuff that heroes are made."

When now, over thirty years later, I remember the expression "a young Moses in the midst of his people," I realize how prophetic that comparison had been. After fifteen years of service in Vangaindrano, in southeast Madagascar, Opeka came to the capital Antananarivo, where he was confronted with the unspeakable poverty of the people living in the city's slums, or even worse—in tunnels dug under the heaps of rubbish. Seeing thousands of children and adults scavenging the rubbish dumps in order to find something to eat or sell, he was horrified.

He said to himself: "I must do something for these people. I must first of all awaken the sense of hope in them." He befriended and encouraged the poorest of the poor who were devoid of hope, telling them, "Even if everyone has neglected you, God has not forgotten you." He was convinced that Christianity's essential message was to provide hope for each and every person.

"When I began visiting these incredibly poor people on the streets and rubbish dumps, I had no idea what would come out of this," says Peter. Then, in 1989, he founded the association Akamasoa—meaning Good Friends—which has worked ever since to unite the poor in the desire to rise above the humiliation and despair of poverty and to achieve the dignity of a life worthy of a human being.

A bricklayer's son, he began teaching the poor how to work hard, to make bricks and build family homes, and in this way strengthened in the people the consciousness of their own worth. Today, the Akamasoa boasts seventeen impressive villages. Almost every family has its own home (which it gradually pays for in small installments), while working hard and following the rules democratically established by the delegates of the entire Akamasoa community. The settlements have all the necessary infrastructure: schools (which, according to the most recent report, are attended by over 9,000 children, from kindergartens to high schools and lyceums), dispensaries, shops, churches and a huge multipurpose sports hall where on Sundays and holidays from four to six thousand worshippers gather to pray and sing.

The inhabitants of these new communities hope to become self-sufficient and independent of foreign aid as soon as possible, while multitudes of other poor are waiting to take part in this unique journey to hope, with dignity and hard work. They work in a quarry and on construction projects. There are many different enterprises, including woodworking, metalworking, and mechanical and tailoring workshops, which produce items necessary for domestic use, as well as for sale. By now, the Akamasoa Welcome Center has also provided food, clothing, counseling, or emergency medical aid about 200,000 transient destitute visitors; in 2007 alone 7,739 families and a total of 28,584 individuals were helped.

So daring and large-scale an undertaking by the missionary Opeka could not go unnoticed. Books and articles in French, German, Spanish, Slovenian, and other languages were written and film documentaries were produced about his and, as he constantly reminds us, his people's amazing accomplishments. In 1994, he was voted Madagascar's Man of the Year. In 1998, he received the French National Order of Merit (Ordre National du Mérite). In 2001, the ambassador of the United States of America to Madagascar presented him the recognition by the Habitat for Humanity International. The Kiwanis World Service Medal was awarded to him in 2005 by the Kiwanis International, headquartered in Indianapolis, Indiana.

In January, 2008, France named him the Knight of the Legion of Honor (Chevalier de la Legion d'Honneur), and in December of the same year Pope Benedict XVI and the St. Mathews Foundation recognized Father Opeka's splendid work by presenting him with the Cardinal Van Thuan's Award, while the Slovenian Catholic Conference honored him with the St. Cyril and Methodius Medal, its very highest form of recognition. In addition, the representatives of Madagascar and of Slovenia, together with Prince Albert of Monaco (now His Royal Highness Albert II), a friend and benefactor of Father Peter, are among those who support him for the Nobel Peace Prize. His many friends in the United States also hope he may soon be recognized as the CNN Hero, or Hero of the Year, a role model of immensely dedicated and exceptionally successful humanitarian work.

Peter Opeka, born in Argentina of Slovenian refugee parents, the spiritual child of St. Vincent de Paul, having saved thousands of people from the bondage of poverty and despair, has become internationally known and has often been compared to Mother Teresa whom he deeply admires.

9

It is only fitting that the English-speaking world, too, should become acquainted with him. That is why I welcome with great pleasure the English translation of the book *Un Viaje a la Esperanza (A Journey to Hope)*, which has been written by Opeka's Argentinean friend, Jesús María Silveyra. I hope it will reach a wide audience, and that through it as many people as possible will come to realize that the spiritual dynamism of Jesus' words, "Whatever you did for one of the least of these brothers of mine, you did for me" (Mt 25:40), continues to inspire heroic deeds. The missionary Peter Opeka is a witness to this.

CARDINAL FRANC RODE

Prefect - Emeritus of the Congregation for Institutes of Consecrated Life

and Societies of Apostolic Life, Vatican

PART ONE

ONE

LANDING IN MADAGASCAR

I am on the plane that is taking me from South Africa to Madagascar. When the captain informs us that we are about to land and we descend to an altitude of ten thousand feet, I can see through the window the landscape of the "Great Island" (the fourth largest island in the world), whose name was mentioned by Marco Polo in the chronicles of his travels. My first impression, while flying over the central high plateau where the capital is situated, is that I am arriving in a well-known place that is engraved in my memory: green hills colored red by the soil, sinuous roads disappearing from sight, flooded brown rivers, lagoons of different shapes, rice paddies that become greener in the valleys, scarce or no forestation.

My fears rise to the surface once again. First, concerns about my health—I had the hepatitis B vaccination before leaving home in Argentina, and yesterday in the hotel in Johannesburg, I took the weekly pills to prevent malaria. In addition, I carry the recommended antibiotics in case of cholera, but I am still worried about yellow fever. "Vaccination is only required for people who travel from an infected country," the specialist in infectious diseases told me. However, the fear of catching something still prevails because a few days before my departure, Peter's sisters mentioned the case of a Slovenian relative who had visited him some time before and had suffered the first attacks of malaria only after he had already returned to Europe.

My other fear, even more profound and visceral, haunts me: that of descending into the world of poverty, with all the prejudices I have created for myself before my departure—especially whether I will be able to put up with twenty-one days in close contact with it. It is true, there is poverty everywhere, and today it is Argentina's greatest problem, with figures soaring—but I have always been an external observer, never getting personally involved. I do not know if this is due to lack of opportunities, fear, indifference, helplessness, or a mixture of all these.

We land at the Ivato airport, situated on the outskirts of this capital that has such a difficult name, Antananarivo ("The Thousand Towns"), which the Malagasy simply call "Tana." The aircraft taxis on the asphalt runway, the tires and the brakes screech, the aircraft shakes. I leave my fears behind; it is too late to back out now. As Father Peter said in his first email, when we decided to go ahead with this book: "Once you step into the boat, there's no turning back."

We have arrived. "The Divine Adventure," as Father Peter referred to my trip, is beginning. I look for my backpack. I am hopeful that I will not encounter any problems, either with the visa I must request upon arrival or with customs on account of all the medication (and candy!) I am carrying with me. I go down the steps. It is not as hot as I imagined it would be, and it's not raining either, which I thought would be the case at this time of year. We walk to the arrivals area. For the time being, I do not wish to look ahead into the distance to see if Father Peter is waiting for me, as he promised.

First step: join the queue for those still needing to buy visas, with the letter of invitation from the Akamasoa humanitarian organization in hand. I buy the stamp for the visa. "Twenty dollars," a dark man says.

I'm thankful that I had the foresight to bring cash. A lady with Asian features next to him hands me my change—one dollar—and stamps my document. Voilá! It is strange, the people here look like a mixture of Asians and Africans, but it is understandable: this Indian Ocean island, two hundred fifty miles off the East African coast, received its first inhabitants of Malayo-Indonesian origin at the beginning of the Christian Era, followed by Arab merchants bringing slaves from Africa. It is a unique place, amalgamating these different races into its unusual island environment.

"Le billet d'avion, s'il vous plait." The man is simply asking for my airplane ticket, but in accelerated French I do not understand immediately, despite the ten hurried lessons I took in the hope of being able to communicate with the people of the island. He realizes I have not understood and repeats in English: "Ticket. Plane ticket." I hand it over. My passport and ticket pass from one hand to another. I follow the procedure from the other side of the small window, surrounded by people of diverse physical features, predominantly from the Merina ethnic group. This group is the most Asian-looking and their features are the most common in this part of the high plateau.

Having retrieved my passport, I go to look for my suitcase as I would in any other airport in the world, a world recently shaken by the terrorist attacks in Madrid. While I'm waiting by the conveyor belt, I listen to Malagasy being spoken, which I suppose comes from Indonesia but is mixed with Arabic words and tribal sounds of the northeast coast of Africa.

The customs officer asks for my passport and tells me to open my suitcase but not the backpack in which I am carrying candy for the children of Akamasoa and the jumble of medication to protect me from so many potential dangers. As the man begins his inspection, I hear the unmistakable voice of Father Peter telling him there is no need for that. "He is one of ours," he says, referring to the inhabitants of the Akamasoa villages (which in Malagasy means "Good Friends"). I watch him as he comes over to meet me, with the bushy gray beard which makes him stand out and gives him a prophetic aura, the blue eyes under a creased forehead due to the years that weigh on his shoulders, the very white skin with reddish blemishes typical of Slavs, his athletic build, and those long arms which I recognize from our first encounter in Buenos Aires.

"Oui, Mompera," the man answers, closing the suitcase. "Mompera" ("My Father") is how all Malagasy refer to priests. I suddenly realize that he must have recognized him because Father Peter is not wearing any vestments, with the exception of the large distinctive cross that hangs from his neck.

TWO

FATHER PETER

This Vincentian missionary, an Argentinean of Slovenian origin, was born in 1948 in the San Martín province of Buenos Aires and baptized Pedro Pablo Opeka. I met him in Buenos Aires when he came to celebrate the ninetieth birthday of his father, Alojz Opeka, with his family.

It all began on Sunday, July 21, 2003. I opened the newspaper *La Nación* and noticed an article entitled "The Priest Who Has Rescued 17,000 Africans from the Streets." I devoured the good news about Father Peter. We are so used to bad news that when something good appears, it is worth pausing for a minute. And that is exactly what I did. My spirit soared when I read the subtitle: "In what was formerly a rubbish dump, he has created a small city." Some details about his life and work appeared in front of my eyes. When I read that Father Peter "approached men on the streets and explained to them that there was a way out of that kind of life: work," it was as if a thunderbolt crashed in front of me that Sunday morning.

"Faced with extreme poverty, Peter suggested they could create a new life of work and solidarity for themselves," the article read. "This is exactly what needs to be done!" I exclaimed to myself. This is true in Argentina, and everywhere in the world where marginalization and misery devastate

17

man's dignity. "Give a man a fish, and you will feed him for a day. Teach a man to fish, and you will feed him for a lifetime," the proverb says. The article added the following remark by the priest: "Poverty isn't a consequence of our destiny; it's something caused by men, especially by politicians who make promises and don't keep them."

Powerful words pronounced by a man with a beard and curly hair… words that touched my heart, as I thought of the political novel I had published the year before entitled To Die with Glory. In it, I imagined a president of the republic who, as soon as he had taken office, began building houses himself, inviting the outcasts and the deprived to join him in his project, thus creating "Centers of Hope" all over the country. Of course, that was fiction and the president was killed five months after taking office. Father Peter, on the other hand, was a real character who was alive and, moreover, visiting Argentina.

The next day, I made up my mind to find him and invite him to do an interview on the weekly radio program I host with my wife and some of our children. But how to track him down? I knew from the article that his parents lived in Ramos Mejía and that he was a member of "The Congregation of the Mission," founded by St. Vincent de Paul (whose priests are called "Vincentians" or "Lazarists" after the hospital of St. Lazarus in Paris, which was their first priory). First, I contacted the Vincentians. Everyone knew Father Peter, but no one knew his telephone number. Finally, thanks to directory assistance, I found the numbers of the only two Opekas living in the Ramos Mejía district. I dialed the first number, and Marija Marolt, Father Pedro's mother, answered. "Yes, he's here. Please wait a minute," she said in Spanish with a foreign accent.

Father Peter's simplicity and good disposition became obvious as soon as we started talking. We arranged a meeting for the following day. Afterwards came the interview, full of emotion and that magnetism which emanates from his personality, transforming my fantasy world into reality and making it possible to discuss those ideals in a practical and concrete way.

After the first radio interview, we had several meetings during which he told me about his life and the Akamasoa project. It was in October, after a farewell Mass together with his friends and relatives, that I proposed writing a book in Spanish. "I agree, but let's put it in God's hands. What will be, will be," was his answer. So I started trawling the world of publishing companies, looking for one that would be interested in the project.

Finally, at the end of February 2004, a possibility appeared, and then another one. I wrote Father Pedro an email to which he replied: "If you could meet with me in mid-March, it would be better because I have to go to Europe to look for donations for the hospital we are building." And he added: "It would be a good idea if you could stay at least until Palm Sunday." As simple and down to earth as that, even though I had not anticipated traveling so soon.

I analyzed how best I could arrange any pending business; I examined the pros and cons of making such a big trip so soon; I talked it over with certain people; and eventually I made up my mind to travel, despite the fact that I had decided a few months before to devote some time to financially more profitable activities. But the proposal also gave me an opportunity that I considered unique: that of immersing myself in the life of an exemplary man and in a great humanitarian project in this world so void of content and examples. Bearing that in mind, it was impossible to be overcome by doubts.

❧

The life of Father Opeka (in the Slovenian language, "Opeka" means "brick" or "tile") was marked from before his birth by his parents' sacrifice, suffering, and effort. The lives of Marija and Alojz must be taken into account in order to gain a better understanding of their son. To do this, we must revisit Slovenia at the end of the World War II, but not without first mentioning something about this nation which has only recently joined the European Union.

Slovenia, a small country in central Europe, began consolidating its ethnic identity with the arrival of the Slavs in the sixth century AD during the Carantanian dukedom. In 1335 the dukedom became part of the Hapsburg Empire (which later became the Austro-Hungarian Empire). During the economic crisis at the end of the nineteenth century, some of the inhabitants of what is today known as Slovenia emigrated to the Americas, especially to the United States, and the first Slovenian immigrants to Argentina date back to those times (even though it was a very small group). At the end of the World War I, the Austro-Hungarian Empire was dismembered and a third of the Slovenian territory went to Italy (including the great port of Trieste). The rest became part of the kingdom of Serbs, Croatians and Slovenians, which in 1929, under King Alexander's dictatorship, became known as Yugoslavia.

Alexander was murdered in Marseilles in 1934, and in 1941 Germany and Italy invaded Yugoslavia. At that time, several resistance groups sprouted up in the Balkans; the most prominent ones were the communist partisans of Josie Broz (better known as Tito) and the monarchists (or "chetniks") commanded by Mihajlovic. In Slovenia, the domobranci (the Home Guards) did not align themselves with either party, hoping for independence from any foreign power. When the war ended, Slovenia recovered most of its territory that was under Italian rule, except for the port of Trieste and Gorizia. At that moment, the territory of the former Kingdom of Yugoslavia fell into the hands of Tito, who established a socialist economy and subordinated and persecuted all noncommunists. Finally, after the fall of the Berlin wall and the dismemberment of the former Soviet Union, the new world framework encouraged the outpouring of independence movements within Yugoslavia. Slovenia declared its independence on June 24, 1991, and became a sovereign country.

THREE

DISCOVERING ANTANANARIVO

Back to the present and my trip. Father Peter walks towards me and we give each other a warm hug. "So it's true. You've arrived! It's true. You are here," he says, happy to see me. Jean-Jacques, a twenty-one-year-old young man who works with him in Akamasoa, helps me with my luggage. Peter repeats the same greeting over and over again, happy to see that an Argentinean writer, a fellow countryman, is interested in his humanitarian project. I cannot believe it either. I have arrived. I'm actually in Madagascar after having overcome so many doubts and fears, ready to immerse myself in this poverty-stricken country.

According to the World Bank's frightening data, out of a total of 208 countries, Madagascar is one of the seventeen countries with the smallest income per capita. Sixty-four percent of its inhabitants live on less than $240 USD per year. If the purchasing power of the population is taken into account, it ranks 201st (Argentina, post-devaluation, comes in 74th). The average life expectancy is fifty-five; in Argentina, it is seventy-four. Forty percent of Malagasy children are undernourished, with an infant mortality rate of thirty-six per thousand, compared to Argentina where it is nineteen per thousand; and 53 percent of the population does not have access to clean drinking water.

Peter takes me by the arm and leads me to a white pickup, a gift of the Slovenian Missionary Center, all the while turning away peddlers offering all types of souvenirs—from drums to cigarettes. I pass on to him regards from his family. We advance along the small highway that later becomes a street in the city, then a highway again. I gaze at the green vegetation and the red soil, now nearer, more intense, raging, making the countryside more beautiful. "It's very green now because it's the rainy season, but it's not the same in winter," he explains.

I tell him that Alojz, his father, when I called him to say good-bye, had said: "May God protect you on the way." And that Marija cried on the phone and promised to pray every single day for me until my return. He is deeply moved and shakes my arm with his strong hand, to repeat yet again: "So you are here. I still can't believe it."

We continue advancing but at a slower pace because the traffic becomes heavier as we go deeper into the suburbs of the city. "Tananariva" was what they called the capital during French colonial rule. After the country gained independence in 1960 it regained its old name of Antananarivo. With a population of almost 1.5 million inhabitants, it is the most important city in this country. In the distance, what used to be the king's castle and the prime minister's palace stand on the top of a hill, flanked by Catholic and Protestant cathedrals.

Poverty is here, before my very eyes, announcing that the descent has begun. The highway becomes a street, with sidewalks about twelve inches wide, interrupted every now and then by a stairway which leads to the upper floor of a house, or a store which juts out of the row of buildings. This means that everyone has to walk in the street—pedestrians risking life and limb and the traffic getting delayed. People of all kinds—some with big, wide-open eyes, others with small, slanted ones; black, dark, or copper-colored skin; pedestrians and peddlers; women with buckets full of water on their heads; men piling up bags of coal; and children, hundreds of barefoot children. Now the houses have become hovels, and stores offer all kinds of things to passersby. From meat hanging outdoors, turning purple at this time of day, and piles of bananas teeming with flies to dresses and trousers swaying in the air, polluted by exhaust fumes and counters packed with electronic goods. "They are Chinese products, most of which are smuggled in," Father Peter explains.

I am in Antananarivo, the capital city of a country where the vast majority of people have no running water (on some corners, it is even sold in cans), electricity (something I discover later on while moving around at night in the different neighborhoods), or gas (cooking is still done using charcoal, contributing to the deforestation of the island). This is a city with many cobbled streets that go up and down the different hills, where clothes hang from the balconies and there is filth everywhere. Barefoot children, women rummaging through garbage containers, small buses packed with people (where you have to push your way in during rush hour), wheelbarrows with bags of rice or beans transported by human power—while the sun bakes fruit and vegetables on the stalls as if nothing unusual were happening.

This is Madagascar: a country of seventeen million inhabitants, with a surface area of almost 373,000 square miles (larger than France and Belgium put together). Here 70 percent of the population still lives in the countryside and both Malagasy and French are spoken. Fifty-one percent of the population is Christian (divided almost in half between Catholics and Protestants), 3 percent is Muslim, and the rest continues to practice native cults. The population grows at an annual rate of 3 percent; the flag has the same colors as the Italian one (although they are arranged differently), and the country's currency is the ariary.

In terms of resources, Madagascar exports coffee, cotton, shell-fish, vanilla (it is the world's number one producer), and spices such as cloves, but the amount imported in capital assets, fuels, and food products is much larger, so there is always a deficit in the balance of trade. Its main commercial client continues to be France.

✧

Peter mentions that Bernarda, his eldest sister, sent him an email telling him about our meeting before my departure. I met his six sisters: Bernarda, Helena, Mariana, Luba, Lucia, and Isabel, as well as his brother, Luis. This was an incredible and necessary meeting, in which they all gave me their opinions of their brother, a priest who has been living in Madagascar for the last thirty years, struggling against poverty. Gathered around a table, we reviewed his biography and the life they had all shared together. They gave me a family history written by their father, Alojz Opeka, describing how he miraculously escaped from Slovenia where he was almost executed by the communists. His story deserves to be told here.

FOUR

ALOJZ OPEKA'S STORY

"In May 1945, persecuted by communism, a great number of soldiers and civilians were forced to abandon Slovenia and move to other countries. From the refugee camp in Vetrinj (Viktring, Austria), the British sent us back to Slovenia and handed us over to the Slovenian partisans. The British deceived us, since we were told that we would be taken to Italy. They transported us in cargo trains, stacked together like cattle. At the time, we didn't mind because we thought we were being taken to Italy where we would be safe. When we realized the train was heading for Slovenia, we became very afraid. In that train, my whole family was traveling: my parents, a sister, and a brother. My mother had said: 'Wherever one goes, we all go.'

"When we arrived in Slovenia, the communist partisans took charge of us. They greeted us with swearing and cursing and told us to leave all our belongings in the carriages. They loaded us onto another train headed for the city of Maribor, where we stayed for several hours under the scorching sun without food or water. The following day, we were transported to the city of Celje, where they hid us in some woods so the locals wouldn't see us. From there, they made us walk barefoot, under a siege of blows from the butts of their rifles, as far as Teharje. Many died on the way, overcome by exhaustion and the blows they had received. When we reached the concentration camp, exhausted, hungry, and thirsty, they put us in small barracks that were dirty, foul-smelling, and full of lice and fleas. Once a day, they would give us a small stew (if you were lucky, you might find one noodle) and a mug of water. They kept us like this for several days. Our exhaustion was such that we were unable to feel anything—not even when they struck us. A few feet away from our barracks, there was a much larger building where they took groups of our people at night. We didn't know why they were doing that, until we heard screams and crying. It was the barracks of torture and death.

"One night, they took my sister Maria away (she was only twenty-five), and we never saw her again. The following night, while I was by the washbasins, I was surprised to see my mother. She looked me in the eye and, between sobs, she said: 'Son, this is the last time we will see each other.' She dipped her fingers in the water, made the sign of the cross on my forehead, and entrusted me to the Holy Family. That was the last time I ever saw my mother, because the next day they took her to the barracks of death.

"My father had been left behind in Celje. After having beaten and tortured him, they sent him home, where shortly afterwards he died as a result of all the blows he had received. My brother, who was twenty-eight years old at the time, tried to escape with three other young men from our group, but he was discovered and returned to the barracks. After being tortured by his own companions (who were forced to do so by the partisans to serve as a lesson so nobody else would try to escape), he was executed.

"Finally, it was my turn. As the large barrack was already full of corpses, they took us to a nearby hill (Bernica) to put us to death there. They tied us up in twos with telephone cables and loaded us onto trucks. In our truck, there were forty-four men of all ages. Many had sustained broken bones or compound fractures due to under-nourishment, exhaustion, and the beatings they had received. During the journey, some moaned, others cried, and still others prayed—and some even sang. We all knew where we were going.

"I was lucky to have been placed in a corner towards the front of the truck. A thousand ideas of how I could untie myself crossed my mind. Thanks to the movement of the truck and the effort I made to free my hands, I did manage to untie myself, but I could do nothing because I had a fellow prisoner on top of me and a guard was lean-ing his legs on mine. We reached the hill at midnight. They made us crouch down, striking us with the butts of their rifles. Before I knelt down, a young partisan tried to poke his fingers into my eyes (be-cause they were very blue), but as I was bathed in sweat and covered in dust, his fingers slipped without hurting me. Infuriated, he began shouting all kinds of insults and hitting me with a cane. When I jumped off the truck, he realized I had become untied and started to shout: 'He untied himself, he untied himself.' Instantly, I had three partisans on top of me. They tied me up again—but with barbed wire this time. I thought they would kill me then and there, but instead they sat me down with those who were being guarded more rigor-ously than the rest.

"Then we were divided into three groups. They removed all the clothes of those in the first and second groups and then took them away. We started hearing the shots; we knew what was happening. As I was still wearing clothes, I tried to untie myself again and succeeded in doing so. I told my companion in a low voice that I had untied myself. Then we received the order to undress. As I got up, I leaned the palm of my hand on the ground, and a guard who was behind us noticed, gave the alert and, immediately, four partisans lunged towards me. They separated me from my companion and took me about 150 feet farther away. There, about ten soldiers, who stood guard over me and insulted me, laughed at my feat, saying that I had only a very little time left to live.

"They forced me to go back to the initial place, where they tied me up with my companion, Joseph. Two men guarded us, one on either side. One of them shone his flashlight on my hands so that I couldn't untie myself again. When he got tired of holding it, he hung it from my shirt. I never gave up on the idea of running away, although I knew that this time it would be more difficult. After a while, we started walking towards the top of the hill. The silence was deadly. All we could hear were the gunshots, nearer each time. When we got to the top, we could see that the place was lit up and that they were throwing the wounded and dying into a common grave.

"Joseph and I were the first ones to be called forward when they decided to proceed with the executions. At that moment, I thought: 'It's now or never.' I remembered my mother's last words by the wash-basins: 'May the Holy Family accompany you.' I entrusted myself to them. I summoned all my strength, managed to untie myself, took the guard by surprise, and hit him; he lost his balance and fell. I jumped over him and hurled myself down the hill, managing to hide in a neighboring wheat field. The bullets passed near me. They searched for me for a long time, but when they saw no further movement, they gave up, thinking I was dead.

"I waited there until daybreak. I could tell exactly where I was since I knew the place well, and I planned an escape route. During the day I hid in the woods, and at night I walked to places where I would be safe. I ate what I found in the small vegetable patches.

When I saw a road that was safe, I would approach a house and ask for food, even though the people were frightened at my appearance because I looked like a beggar. On a beautiful, sunny day, while I was crossing a meadow, I saw a small shrine at the side of the road. It was of Jesus crucified and it was completely destroyed. In front of that broken Christ, I promised I would return some day to rebuild it.

"Under these terrible conditions, I was on the road for thirty days before I reached my home. My aunt, who was at home, didn't recognize me and wouldn't let me in. I had to mention different anecdotes from my childhood to convince her that it was really me. She fed me and hid me in the barn. The partisans came by every night, so I had to hide in the woods. There I met other domobranci (anticommunist soldiers), and together we planned how to escape from Slovenia to Italy.

"I had to overcome new dangers, but God wanted me to live and gave me the opportunity to meet with my compatriots in the Red Cross refugee camp of Senigallia, in the province of Ancona, Italy."

⚜

In the refugee camp, Alojz Opeka, thirty-two years old at the time, would meet his future wife, Marija Marolt, aged twenty-six.

FIVE

ARRIVING IN AKAMASOA

Father Peter toots the horn. I imagine he does so to complain about a cart pulled by two oxen that is obstructing the traffic, but I am wrong. Peter has just spotted Father Rok walking along another streetside market. Father Rok turns around and recognizes the pickup. Peter asks me to move to the middle of the seat and invites him to get in. He introduces us. "Father Rok. Jésus Marie, the Argentine writer."

Father Rok smiles. At first, I think it is because of my name, but as the days go by, I realize he always has a smile on his face, at least whenever he is with me. We get on well immediately. The cart moves along and we can advance again. I try out my French on Father Rok. Avoir. Etre. Le passé composé. I make an effort to remember what I have learned, and I try not to make any mistakes, especially when I speak about the future using the auxiliary tense. Every now and then, Peter or Rok kindly correct me.

I find it incredible that we have been in the pickup for over an hour and I have not heard Peter complain at all about the traffic. Is it the custom, or simply his good nature? We pass yet more markets, houses, hovels, meat covered with flies, charcoal being transported, smoke, people carrying water, some wearing shoes but the majority "pieds nus," as the French say. What surprises me most is the number of children on the roadside, sitting or playing on the narrow sidewalks—so vulnerable. I can imagine what would happen if there was a crash and a car careened off the highway. Instant death for sure, adding to the several thousands who die each day as a result of the extreme poverty on this island.

Father Rok is also Slovenian; he is a missionary of the Congregation of St. Vincent de Paul. He has been in Madagascar for thirty-four years and has been helping Father Peter for seven years in Akamasoa, especially with catechism and Sunday Masses in the organization's different towns. He knows Argentina because he spent some months there, and I am surprised at how well he remembers Buenos Aires and some of the country's provinces, even Bariloche in southern Argentina.

At a certain point, Peter stops the pickup truck and Father Rok gets out. He does not live with Peter but in the house of the Vincentians, halfway between the center of Antananarivo and the town of Andralanitra—our final destination. "He only stays overnight on Thursdays, but he comes to the Akamasoa offices every day to give me a hand," Peter tells me.

We have to make a detour along a dirt road to get away from the traffic which is only letting us advance at a snail's pace. We go up a small hill, one of the many that are to be found in the capital—a capital that includes, unbelievably, some rice fields in its very center, owned by farmers who never sold their plots even as the city grew and so remained stranded in the middle of the city. I imagine small soybean farms next to the Obelisk in Buenos Aires! The owners would be millionaires if they sold them by the square meter. "Rice here is like bread; it's the staple diet of the Malagasy," Peter remarks. As the days go by, I will become truly conscious of this during every meal.

Peter tells me that Carole (a French writer) arrived two days before and that her companion, Gregoire, will arrive on Thursday. "I hope we will be able to cope," he says. My visit happens to coincide with that of a young French couple who are planning to write a biography of Father Peter. When he mentioned this in an email, I said I did not mind. First of all, I would be staying a week longer, and secondly, rather than being a hindrance to each other, it could be mutually beneficial. The question was whether Peter would be able to cope. Spending the mornings with them and holding meetings with me in the afternoons, talking, telling stories, explaining, answering the many questions which both the French couple and I want to ask, not only about his life but also about the Akamasoa project. Talk, talk, and more talk... Knowing that Peter is a man of action, he must grow weary at the prospect of so many words.

We leave behind the meteorological station and the huge plot of land surrounded by walls and pine trees owned by the Adventists. It looks like the street will once more become a free road. However, houses and markets appear again instantly. I suppose that in every poor country there are plenty of small stores because people buy only what is strictly necessary for each day. And now I observe firsthand how they do so—the seller uses a small empty condensed milk can as a measuring cup: two cans of rice, one can of white beans, half a can of sugar, four bananas, three small tomatoes. Supermarkets are in the city center where the very few people who can afford to buy a week's worth of groceries live.

We continue our conversation. I mention the topics I would like to cover with him, but I do not want to talk much longer, because I don't want to have to pull out my tape recorder right away. Peter, as I will come to realize, has an immediate, simple, and profound answer for every question, as his heart is wide open, without any trace of deceit or duplicity.

"We are almost there," he says. We climb a slope. I can see the countryside once again, with those rich shades of green cut through by the red soil. Small streams where the women wash clothes and then spread them out on the grass in the sunshine; men working with their long spades in the rice fields; teams of oxen plowing the small plots. "Manantenasoa is over there," he says, pointing at a hill that can be seen beyond the valley. This is another Akamasoa village, the largest, with rows of precisely aligned brick houses facing the afternoon sun, which is just beginning to set.

We turn right onto an asphalt road. We have arrived at Andralanitra, the village founded in April 1991 by Akamasoa. It borders the municipal landfill site that emits large columns of smoke to welcome me. The redbrick houses are pretty—they have reddish tiled roofs and the windows, balconies, and doors are painted light blue. There are neat vegetable patches on the side, bordering impeccably clean stone streets. What a contrast to all I have seen along the road! There are even trees by the sidewalks and irrigation ditches so the water can circulate during the rainy season. No wonder so many visitors are praising Akamasoa's work.

A small round plaza rules over the area next to the basketball court, bearing a sign that reads: "Cité Akamasoa" ("The Town of Good Friends"). I think of Peter's family and imagine how proud they would feel if they were here looking at everything I can see.

SIX

MARIJA MAROLT'S STORY

Yes, his family would be proud to see in person the great work of Akamasoa, in the same way Peter is proud of his parents' life stories. Proud of Alojz Opeka, who was miraculously saved from death on the hill of Bernica, and equally proud of Marija Marolt, who also had to overcome many difficulties. According to her own account, Marija was taken prisoner by the communist partisans, along with one of her sisters, in 1943.

❦

"One day the soldiers arrived at our home. I remember them pounding on the door. At that time, we were nine brothers and sisters (we were originally twelve, but three had already died). Of the five daughters, two were studying in the capital city. When we heard the pounding, one of my sisters managed to hide and then run away. The soldiers were coming for the daughters of Anton Marolt, whom everyone in the area knew because of his resistance to communism, since he was a devout Catholic.

"My sister and I had to accompany them. They kept pushing us along the road. We climbed a hill, then another, to arrive at some woods before going on to a village where the partisan brigade was stationed. Once we had reached the highest hill, I asked one of my captors to let me look at my town for the last time, since I believed they were going to kill us.

"The town of Gornje Potpoljane was there at our feet, with its lights and belfry towering above the roofs. We were detained there for four months, working in the kitchens. My father moved heaven and earth to rescue us. The domobranci had partisan prisoners and an exchange was proposed, and we were involved in that exchange. We had to defend our integrity at all costs, although there were some women that supported the communists, and they surrendered easily to them. I remember one night a shadow entered the room where several of us were sleeping. The partisan grabbed me by the ankle so as to drag me out of the room. I started screaming, so much so that the man got frightened and let me be. In the end, the soldiers set us free, and we returned to our town.

"Before the end of the war, the word spread that the Russians had entered Slovenia. They planned to kill all Catholics, whom they accused of collaborating with the Germans (even though this was rarely the case). In 1945 my father decided that five of us (four girls and one boy) would flee with him to Austria, and from there we would go on to Italy. My mother, with the four youngest children, would stay at home until our father returned for them. We prepared a cart and said good-bye. The roads were packed with people who were running away from the Russians and from the communist partisans.

"Once in Austria, my father sent me with another lady to the Red Cross camps in Italy to see if it was safe. We crossed the Alps. Fortunately, it was June and not winter. I can't even remember how many miles we covered. It took us seven days to reach Treviso and seven to return to let them know that it was safe there. The lady that spent that fortnight with me would later become my daughter's mother-in-law. We spent some time in Treviso (Veneto), and later they moved us to Forli (Emilia Romana) and finally to Senigallia (Ancona), where I met Alojz.

꧁꧂

Alojz and Marija met by chance because Anton, Marija's father, together with his brother Tone, were put up in the same barracks where Alojz was living. At that time, Marija used to mend the refugees' clothes and often visited her father in the barracks. All the camp knew the story of a certain Alojz Opeka, originally from Topol, who was the only survivor of the Bernica massacre. One day, Alojz asked her if she could mend a pair of trousers for him. While they were chatting, Marija asked which town he was from, and when he answered, she asked him if he knew the "famous" Alojz Opeka.

"I am Alojz Opeka," the tall young man with eyes blue like the sky replied. When Marija finished mending his trousers, he asked her how much he owed her. She answered: "An Our Father." And in that way, mending a pair of trousers in exchange for a prayer, the relationship which would last to the present day began. Almost sixty years have passed since then.

They got married in the refugee camp, where they lived for two years. Their first daughter, Bernarda, was born there, and Marija became pregnant again. They planned to immigrate to North America, but neither the United States nor Canada would accept married immigrants. Somebody mentioned the possibility of going to Argentina, telling them the country was undergoing a process of expansion, with rich resources and scarce population. They made up their mind and set off for Argentina, together with Marija's three sisters and brother, not knowing a word of Spanish. Anton returned to Slovenia, to his wife and the four remaining children, even though he knew that, once he entered his country, he would never be able to leave it again. Marija and Alojz arrived in Buenos Aires on January 21, 1948, on board the Santa Cruz ship, together with hundreds of Slovenians.

※

"During the first fortnight or so, we lodged at the Immigrants' Hotel next to the port. One day, a builder came looking for bricklayers to work at one of the army barracks. Since that was Alojz's trade in Slovenia, he hired him. He invited us to live at his home, and he put us up in his garage. We slept on the floor on cardboard, and Bernarda slept in the suitcase we had brought with us.

"Eventually we moved into a boardinghouse in the San Martín district. The bedroom was slightly larger, but still rundown. When we managed to save some pesos, Alojz bought a heater and a mattress that he had to carry on his back for the twenty blocks that separated the shop from the boardinghouse because it was impossible to get on a bus with it.

"Some weeks later, more Slovenians arrived at the Immigrants' Hotel (it is estimated that thousands arrived during those months). My husband went there and arranged with five other families to rent a house that had five rooms. The monthly rent would amount to 350 pesos. A few days later, we were able to move into the new house, near the Diego Thompson Hospital in the San Martín district. Meanwhile, Alojz's employer was very happy with him, so he put him in charge of the work they were carrying out.

"Peter was born on June 29, 1948. Alojz took me to hospital that day and left for work. Since it was a holiday for state employees, there were very few people working in the hospital. After examining me, they called the midwife, but they told me that the baby wasn't going to be born yet. After that, they took me to the maternity ward on a gurney. The nurse left the room and closed the door, leaving me alone. I saw a cross on the wall and started to pray. Since it was the Feast of St. Peter and St. Paul, I prayed to both saints for an easy delivery and vowed that if it was a boy, I would call him Peter Paul.

"At that precise moment, the labor pains and contractions started. I managed to get off the gurney, dragged myself to the door, and went out into the dark corridor. I saw a white figure moving in the distance so I started to shout. The nurse turned around, came towards me, and demanded that I get back on the gurney. After a while, the midwife arrived and started asking me to push. 'Come on, come on,' she said. I expected she would help me as Mrs. Stariha had done in Italy when Bernarda was born, but she didn't do anything. Finally, the baby was born, weighing about nine pounds. I thought, 'Peter, you have certainly suffered before arriving in this world!' The nurse phoned my husband's employer to let him know we had a boy.

"Alojz came running to the hospital, happy to have a son. When he saw Peter, he exclaimed, 'He will be a bishop!' because his head was large and long like that of the bishop in his town."

SEVEN

MY NEW HOME

"Welcome to Akamasoa," Father Peter exclaims. It has taken us almost an hour and a half to get from the airport to Andralanitra (which means "Grace from Heaven" in Malagasy), one of the towns built by Akamasoa. Peter parks the car next to the gate. When I get out, I am hit by the smell of putrefaction coming from the adjacent landfill site. Peter explains: "It depends which way the wind is blowing." A group of women come to greet me, and Peter introduces them to me. Among them are Marie Odette (whom everyone calls Mademoiselle Bao), Olga (who is called Maman'i Prisca, which means "Prisca's mother"), and Honorine. Some children, whose names I will learn later on, accompany them.

For a moment, I contemplate the place: a reception office adjoining the school, the warehouse where the food is stored, the green wrought-iron gate, a cobblestone patio, Peter's house (exactly the same as the others), the staircase that goes down to the chapel, and beyond, the valley with marshes and rice fields at the foot of the hills. Pretty, very pretty.

Jean-Jacques takes my suitcase. Olga brings the keys to the house where I will live for three weeks, right next to the room where the children watch television on Sundays, the security group meets with

Father Peter on Saturday mornings, and members of the Catholic youth group share their experiences on Friday nights. Peter leads me by the arm to the house. There it is, next to the jacaranda tree and the small square with the water tap from which the villagers fetch water on a daily basis.

Olga has some trouble opening the iron door. The key gives her a hard time because the house is seldom used. It has two stories and a brick facade like all the rest. I fetch my suitcase and enter my new home. There is a dining room with a table, two wooden benches, an empty refrigerator, and a little pantry for storing food. There is a corridor leading to the wooden staircase, and further on, a dark room with only one bench and another empty refrigerator. Beyond that is the bathroom with its electric boiler (which means I can have a hot shower every day).

I retrace my steps and climb the creaky staircase. There are two bedrooms: one has two beds, a small table, and a chair, with a window overlooking the jacaranda tree and the water tap; the other one has only one bed, a small table, and a chair. Its window looks out at the enclosed vegetable patch that is shared by two other houses—the one where Marcial, the Akamasoa driver, lives and the one belonging to Miss Theresa, who is in charge of the village of Manantenasoa.

I decide to stay in the bedroom with two beds—one to sleep in, the other to serve as a wardrobe. On the little table, I find a bottle of mineral water, so I have a sip. "You mustn't drink water from the tap," was the doctor's warning in Buenos Aires, and I plan to abide by it. I'm happy that I am able to take up residence so close to Peter's house, despite the smell which comes from every corner, seeping through the cracks in the window frame and assaulting my nose. I take out the bags of candy from my backpack (Lucia, Peter's sister, was the one who suggested I should bring them for the children), go down the stairs again, and out into the street where Peter is waiting for me.

We go through the gate, across the cobbled patio, down the stairs, past the Chinese rosebush and the two white wooden benches on which we will frequently sit to talk before dinner, and enter his house. In the small dining room, Peter offers me some tea, and we start talking. I give him the candy and he gives me a small book with his photograph on the front cover, which contains some of his thoughts in French. I open a page at random. "C'est à travers les coeurs des hommes de bonne volonté que travaille l'Esprit de Dieu" ("It is through the hearts of men of good will that the Holy Spirit works"). The phrase has a profound effect on me, beyond the stench and the misery that have been engraving themselves in my eyes ever since I set foot in this country. I want to devour the booklet, but Peter stops me by saying: "It's a gift." Then he announces that prayers in the chapel start at half past five. He asks me to meet him there later.

I walk home. About ten children come to greet me, clinging to my arms like grapes. I contemplate those smiling faces with their bright eyes, slanted like mine or as big as shiny stars, greeting me with "Bonjour, monsieur!" I find it difficult to get back into the house because the key gets stuck when I try to open the door, and it is impossible to lock from the inside. This annoyance, combined with the stench of the landfill, puts me in a bad mood. I was happy a moment ago, stroking the children's hands, but my mood swings suddenly, and I climb the stairs muttering to myself. I place the hanger with my trousers on a nail in the whitewashed wall. I make the bed. I feel the pillow and complain to myself about its stiffness. My heart struggles against the vulgar feelings that demand comfort, convenience, and the good things of life.

I go up to the bathroom to wash my face and brush my teeth. Looking in the mirror, fighting the smell that wafts in through the paneless windows, I tell myself: "It's just a matter of getting used to it." I go back out, but I cannot lock the door. I don't know what to do. I have my things upstairs—my camera, my passport, my tape recorder, my money. Who will rob me here? I don't know. There are so many people in the streets. My inner struggle continues, but I cannot immerse myself in this world if I don't get rid of my usual prejudices.

I leave the door unlocked. Whatever will be will be!

❧

I enter the chapel. I sit down on the floor with the children on a raffia mat that smells of grass, reeds, and earth. The tabernacle is in the shape of an Alpine house, the altar is made of a block of stone, the image of the Virgin Mary to its right and the cross behind it. Peter is seated in front, near the large open windows. There are two frescoes at the top of the back wall right above the entrance doors. One depicts people raking through the landfill site, and the other shows people working in the quarry.

My eyes continue to wander around the chapel. On the left wall, there are three more paintings depicting the world: Moses with the Ten Commandments; and Jesus talking to the people. Further on, in front of the altar, a piece of stone displays an inscription in Malagasy: "The Spirit of the Lord is upon me" (Lk 4:18). Then, my gaze wanders to the congregation, consisting of a few women, two men, several boys, and a few teenage girls, but mainly children. They begin to sing as the sun sets, embracing the hills (which I can see through the large windows) with fire, gilding the marsh and the rice paddies.

The girl beside me has a runny nose. She is black, very African, her eyes wide open like two black suns; the soles of her bare feet are by contrast as white as snow. I reach for her hand. She looks at me and smiles. Her mother, at her side, is sitting on the matting like everyone else. The smell of the landfill site mixes with the odor of perspiration, along with the characteristic smell of raffia matting. As the singing raises my spirits, I can smell wheat, bread, and renewed hope, as if I were in heaven receiving a gift by the grace of God.

❧

While I watch Peter, sitting before the image of the Virgin Mary, singing with the children, I start thinking once again about his mother's story.

EIGHT

A LARGE FAMILY

"Peter was baptized when he was fifteen days old in the cathedral of San Martín. Some time after that, my husband and twenty other colleagues were hired to go and work in Miramar, located in the southern part of the Province of Buenos Aires, about 290 miles from the capital. I stayed at home with the two children. Since the postal service was pretty slow at the time, I didn't receive much news from him. A month after his departure, he called me and told me he would come to fetch us because he had found a permanent job with a better salary, about forty-five pesos a day. Alojz arrived, and we set off, accompanied by five families from San Martín. We settled in a tourist resort and began saving up to buy a plot of land so we could build our own house."

❖

In the beginning, Alojz worked in Mar del Sur, about thirteen miles from Miramar, building the first bungalows for the seaside resort. Later, in Miramar, he put up some of the houses that are still standing today on the esplanade and continue to be a source of pride for his children. Helena was born in June of 1949 in a private clinic and as Marija said: "Without so much suffering this time." In May

1950, they settled in their own house on the corner of two streets, numbered 46 and 11.

❦

"Mr. France, who worked with my husband for six years, lived with us. We put him up in the kitchen, which we fixed up a bit so he would be comfortable. My brother Tone, the cook in the hotel in Mar del Sur, also came to live with us and soon started working on the construction sites with Alojz. We had a bed, and the children slept on the floor.

"For Mariana's birth, I was hospitalized on the same day we celebrated our fifth wedding anniversary (August 3, 1946), and she was born the following day. At that time, my husband's work began slackening because there was a scarcity of cement. Fortunately, Mr. Edi Skulj called us from Buenos Aires and asked if Alojz could travel to build a house there. My husband was more than happy to accept, so off he went with my brother Tone and Mr. France.

"Once again, I remained alone with the four children, and I was now also pregnant with my son Luis. For a whole month, I didn't receive any news, and the neighbors began to wonder if he had abandoned me. Around that time, I bought a bicycle, and every Sunday I cycled to church, even though I had to leave the children with one of the neighbors, which made me anxious. At that time, Peter was three years old, and he loved playing on the swings. One of those Sundays when I returned home from Mass, I found my husband at home. He asked me to pack up because we were returning to Buenos Aires. He had found a job that would last at least a year.

"We stayed in San Martín, renting a room from an old Slovenian immigrant, a communist, who didn't really trust us. When he left the house, he used to lock the door, so I had to climb through the window if I wanted to go shopping. Later on, we moved into another boardinghouse in Caseros, and Luis was born there. This time I had the baby at home because we asked the midwife to come to our house.

"Some time later, an acquaintance mentioned that plots of land were being allocated in the neighborhood of Don Bosco in the town of Ramos Mejía. In that district, there was a Salesian priest, a Slovenian named Father Mernik, whose parish was a focal point for the community. So we decided to buy a plot and start building a house. When a room and a kitchen had been built, we moved in. We all slept in the same bed. During all those years, we moved thirteen times and lived poorly; therefore, we learned what suffering was. Here, in Ramos Mejía, where we still live, I have always felt happy, above all because we own the house we live in."

⊰❈⊱

This is how Marija's story ends, but Peter's life continues—as does the memory of that first meeting we had in Buenos Aires. "We were a very happy, close-knit family who knew what hardship was because we spent our lives struggling to survive. We had very few possessions, but we shared whatever we had." During his first school years, Peter had to change schools three times due to his temperamental nature, until he finally settled at School Number 42 in Ramos Mejía. He attended that school up to fourth grade. At home, they spoke Slovenian, read the inspirational lives of the saints, and prayed the Rosary together every night. When they played "Mass," Peter acted as the officiating priest, the sisters as parishioners, and his brother as altar boy. According to Bernarda, by that time, wherever he went he stood out as a leader—a strong and brave leader but with a great sense of justice and solidarity, which was reflected in his trying to help the very poor.

On weekends, they got together with the Slovenian community, which was very close-knit because they sometimes found their new environment rather hostile. They suffered from the fear all immigrants experience when facing a different culture, so they tried to get together and encourage one another, knowing their survival depended on their unity. They were strengthened in this by their Catholic faith and the political persecution they had all suffered, which had forced them to escape from their home country.

The Slovenian priest brought the community together on Sundays for Mass. Choirs and folk dance groups began to form, and in time they decided to open a school to transmit their mother tongue to their children. Peter remembers those "youthful days" which began with Mass, continued with lunch and sports (volleyball and soccer), and ended in parties during which polkas were danced. Today, there are Slovenian centers in Buenos Aires City, San Justo, Ramos Mejía, San Martín, Morón, Castelar, Carapachay, Lanús, Mendoza, Miramar, and Bariloche.

When he was ten years old, Peter became a boarder at the school of the Baraga Missionary Center in Lanús (a province of Buenos Aires), directed by Slovenian priests of the congregation of Saint Vincent de Paul. He attended this institution, known as "Maria Reina" (Mary Our Queen) until his second year of secondary school. Years later, his brother Luis would attend the same school, while his sister Bernarda boarded with the Vincentian nuns in the neighborhood of Constitución in the capital.

During these years, Peter developed two great passions: soccer and a love for the Gospel. He became a fan of "Independiente," the famous club from Avellaneda, and he still remembers the forward line of that team: "Bernao, Mura, Mario Rodriguez, Suarez, and Savoy." With his strong build, tenacity, and skill, Peter was a fearsome center forward. He had good ball control with both legs and was also a great header.

His other passion was Christ and the example of his life. "My vocation was born reading the Gospels. The figure of Christ always made a profound impact on me—not so much the miracles he performed but his humility and the power of his example. I was attracted by the fact that he was always in the company of the humble, the outcasts, and the deprived—so much so that I felt that I had to imitate and follow that Christ." Perhaps for that reason, when he was fourteen years old he asked himself: "What if God is calling me to the priesthood?" However, the woman who was the school cook used to tell his father: "Before that young man becomes a priest, I will be pope!"

While he was growing up, whenever he was home on weekends or during part of the summer he began learning his father's trade, bricklaying. He first helped him to enlarge the house in Ramos Mejía, and later he accompanied him to various construction sites. By the time he was thirteen, he was able to erect a wall by himself—a skill that would prove very useful later on in life, and especially in Madagascar.

When he was sixteen years old, he decided to finish high school at the seminary run by Vincentian priests in Escobar, Buenos Aires. Peter was still struggling between his two passions. He was offered the opportunity to tryout at Velez Sarsfield soccer club. His mother gave him the following advice: "If you decide to become a soccer player, you will have the glory and vanity of men, but if you become a priest, you will have the honor and glory of God." Peter didn't understand why a priest could not be a soccer player as well, since both were compatible. However, at the Provincial Father's suggestion ("You must choose either one or the other"), and because he was so powerfully attracted by the Gospel, he chose the second option.

By that time, no doubt influenced by the life of St. Vincent de Paul (the patron saint of charity work), he was already considering becoming a missionary among the lowliest farm laborers. (St. Vincent had founded the Congregation of the Mission in 1625 with the aim of evangelizing the poor, and in 1633, together with Louise de Marrillac, he founded the Daughters of Charity to serve the needy.)

In 1966, Peter began his three-year novitiate in the San Miguel district. The work of the seventeenth century French saint had made a deep impression on him. During the summer, he traveled with Bernarda and other youths from the Argentinean Missionary Association (AMA) to a place called "El Malleo" in southern Argentina, where they did missionary work among the Mapuche Indians. The members of the group took on various responsibilities, coordinated by Father Bufano (who would later become a bishop). Peter's assignment was to go to the mountains with Father Barreto to visit poor families.

"I felt as if I were in a cinemascope film with the Lanín volcano, capped in snow, watching over us. I walked with the help of a stick and covered myself with a poncho. In that place, I acted as a godfather to a Mapuche boy. His family's marginalized situation made me indignant because they were also God's children and our brothers."

Two young architects in the group tried, without much success, to put up a model house in order that afterwards the Mapuche people could copy it. Peter said that if they let him do it "as his father had taught him," he was sure he would succeed. So, in one week they built a house, and the architects ended up being told what to do by a bricklayer! "The problem was that they didn't know how to lay the foundations," Peter remembers. He was only seventeen years old, but he already believed that the best way to help the poor was to ensure that they had decent housing.

NINE

MY FIRST DINNER

The children continue singing in the chapel, clapping to the rhythm of the song. The Malagasy language permeates my pores. From time to time, one of the children turns around and smiles at me. When I close my eyes, I return to this "grace from heaven," where the children seem like angels and we are all united in the same spirit. The lights go out and, at the same time, the singing stops. A candle is lit next to the image of the Virgin Mary. The children start praying in a spontaneous manner. I cannot believe it—even a five-year-old girl gives thanks out loud, without feeling embarrassed or afraid of what the others may say. The words flow while the twilight gives way to darkness and the evening star clings to a cloudless sky. When they finish praying, the last song is sung—the one I remember having heard in Buenos Aires while watching a video about Akamasoa.

Afterwards, Tojo's father (pronounced Tudzu) stands up and welcomes me. Father Peter translates into Spanish. The hundred or so children fix me with their steady gazes. Afterwards, Father Peter is the one who welcomes me on behalf of everyone and ends by asking me if I want to say anything. I get up, surprised and a little nervous. What should I say? "Congratulations on the singing; it has touched my heart. Christ was absolutely right when he asked his disciples to let the children come to him, because children are the best thing in this world." They applaud.

I go outside with Peter and Miss Bao. There, too, more children come to greet us. All kinds of hands: hot, warm, cold, humid, joyful, aching, dirty, and clean are placed gently in mine. "Veloma," they say in Malagasy. "See you soon." I imagine that these children are the main source of energy for Peter. Yes, the children—the 8,500 children that attend the Akamasoa schools every day. Peter fights for them. His hope lies in this new generation that has begun to live a much better life than their parents live—well-fed, provided with healthcare and education. Jean-Jacques is a good example. His father abandoned the family and his mother died when he was nine years old. This young man, brought up and educated in Akamasoa from the age of twelve, is now at university.

It's half past six in the evening. Soon the Southern Cross will appear in the starlit sky, indicating that we are in the southern hemisphere. Peter introduces me to his goddaughters: Tojo, twenty-one years old, and Viviane, who is twenty-three. They were hanging around the landfill site when he met them for the first time. Now they are teachers at the school and live together in the house just next to the dining room. They intend to devote themselves as laywomen to the work of Akamasoa.

At seven o'clock, we are joined by Carole. She's twenty-nine years old, a Parisian, and this will be her first book, written in collaboration with Gregoire—a biography in French about "le Père Pierre." We enter the dining room. At the entrance, there is a dog called Mig that has lost a leg; next to it, a small brown cat relaxes. Two tables are set for dinner. There is no oven: the food is prepared outside, next to the laundry sinks, on charcoal rings. At one table, the little girls and the teenagers sit together: Janina, Sylviane, Ando, Uny, Rina,

Natasha, Hanta, Stella, Tina, Veronique—and Balita, the only boy. The grown-ups sit at the other table—Peter at the head, Carole to his right, and myself on his left. Miss Bao, Olga, Tojo, Viviane, Felana, Claudine, and Prisca (Olga's daughter) also sit at our table. I look carefully at the food: couscous, rice, some stewed meat cut up into strips, and pea soup. In front of Peter's plate, there is some bread wrapped in a napkin. The locals drink rice water, but for us, the foreigners, there is a bottle of mineral water.

Peter blesses the meal with a prayer. The girls at the other table wish us "bon appétit," answering themselves with a "merci beaucoup." They say it in French, Spanish, Malagasy, and Slovenian—a charming gesture for their guests.

⟡

My first dinner at Akamasoa begins. Miss Bao is in charge of serving. I pass my plate. I don't say anything, but I am not at all keen on couscous. To me, it always seems rather bland and flavorless, which is why it is generally served with stew in order to bring out its taste. But here, with wheat being scarce, it is prepared only on special occasions—a gesture that my carnivorous stomach from the pampas fails to notice.

Next Miss Bao serves me a portion of rice soaked in the pea soup, to which she adds a small quantity of meat. We begin eating. Peter speaks French with Carole and Miss Bao, and I listen. When they talk too fast, it is difficult for me to follow the thread of the conversation. I'll get over it and, as days go by, I will improve, I think to myself.

Suddenly, I am gripped by overpowering thoughts coming from an unknown source, maybe stemming from the unlocked house, my black suitcase, and the fear that I might be robbed even of my own identity. Why am I here? What is all this? What sense is there in all this? To write a book is the simple answer. To get to know the poor, who have been elevated to a more dignified life is an additional thought. To see Father Peter in his daily routine. To allow myself to stand in awe at the novelty is what stems the flow of my thoughts, while Peter hands me a piece of bread. For dessert we have bananas. We finish with a prayer and a song.

We leave the dining room, and Peter and I linger on, talking by the railing overlooking the patio below. A girl comes out to scrape the leftovers off my plate (I was the only one to leave anything) onto the stone floor for both animals to eat. The dog snarls at the cat and gets the best part. "Mankind behaves in this way when we forget God. It's the law of the jungle," Peter says.

A six-year-old girl grabs his waist. "Her parents are alcoholics and have abandoned her. She and her brothers have already run away to the city about four times. They go there to beg. The last time, we searched for days before we found her, but she has promised me that she will never listen to her brothers again." I notice the girl allows herself to be pampered.

He then tells me about the others. Three of them are sisters; their mother relinquished one of them as partial payment of a debt, but Akamasoa found out and brought her back. The mother of another girl is a prostitute and wants to take daughter away so that she too will practice the trade. Yet another girl's father is an alcoholic that used to beat her every night until she was brought here. One girl is ill. One was abandoned, and another is an orphan. Life stories—small, tremendous life stories of the outcast and excluded that Father Peter is trying to change.

I say good-bye; I am tired. "Veloma" ("See you later"). It has been too much for one day. Peter says good night with a hug. Tomorrow we will get together and begin talking more formally, with a tape recorder.

Some girls accompany me to my house. Close to the reception, by the school entrance, a group of two or three watchmen with long sticks stand guard over the food storehouses. The tap remains closed under the large jacaranda.

Olga explains that with the entrance key not working well (to lock up on the inside), it would be better for me to use the side door, the one that opens onto the vegetable patch. I lock the house and go up the stairs. The black suitcase is there, intact, the padlock on, waiting for me. I plunge into Father Peter's biography once again.

TEN

THE MISSIONARY

Peter continued at the seminary in San Miguel. It was a time of many changes in the Church, resulting from the process initiated by the Second Vatican Council. Peter dreamed of a Church that was more open to the world, a Church that would renew its preferential treatment of the poor. On Sundays, together with some of his fellow seminarians, Peter began visiting a shantytown, Saint Brigid, not far from the seminary. He wanted to be near the poor and help them.

He asked himself why the poor could not build decent homes on fiscal land (an idea he would later apply in Madagascar). "As I already wore a cassock, I went to the municipality and found out very easily the exact location of some fiscal land. A week later, we loaded a truck with timber and sheets of corrugated iron, and in one day, we built a house consisting of two large rooms."

"The narrow road consists of following Divine Providence step-by-step," said St. Vincent de Paul, and Peter began following that road. Providence intervened, and he surrendered to its designs. News arrived that the congregation needed volunteers to go to Africa, specifically to Madagascar. Since there were few volunteers available in France, they were looking for people from elsewhere. Peter raised his hand, and they took down his name as a future possibility. "I would like to go to a place that is poorer than Argentina," he told his friends. After finishing seminary, he traveled with some other seminarians and Father Víctor Morra to the northern part of the country to do some missionary work among the Mataco Indians. "Young people must continue doing missionary work in order to get to know other realities and become aware that injustice still prevails."

He visited Salta, Jujuy, and the Grand Chaco region along the Bolivian border. "In this way, I became acquainted with Argentinean folklore and the beauty of that area. But I couldn't understand how, only a few miles from such beautiful cities, there was so much misery." He saw the poverty the people lived in, a poverty that cried out for action to be taken. The heat, the lack of drinking water, and the insects (including the aggressive assassin bug) made the place far more inhospitable than what he had known in the south. "During the month we were there, a child died, and I built a wooden coffin. That was terrible, but I thought that the young Argentinean university students who were committed to social work would some day solve the problems of those people."

❧

On August 20, 1968, having finished his studies, he traveled to Europe for the first time, to continue his studies in the land of his ancestors. He said good-bye to his family, who understood that Peter was driven by his evangelical fervor and thought that perhaps destiny had reserved him for the poorest in this world. They accompanied him to the port, with tears and recommendations for the moment of his arrival in Slovenia, telling him he should see various relatives and not forget to visit his grandfather Anton. Peter embarked on the old steamship Augustus bound for the Old World where, according to what some people had told him, the supposed poverty no longer existed. He went with Rado, another seminarian and his great friend, also of Slovenian origin, with whom he had shared the same destiny since their schooldays together in Lanús. They stopped at the ports of Montevideo, Santos (where for the first time in his life he saw what black-skinned people look like. He exclaimed: "This is what my brothers in Africa will look like!"); Rio de Janeiro; Lisbon ("In that city, I discovered that there were also poor people and beggars in Europe"); Gibraltar ("When we crossed the strait, so near Africa, I was deeply moved again"); Barcelona; Cannes; Genoa; and Naples, where the voyage ended.

~❈~

"During the ten days we were at sea, crossing the Atlantic before arriving in Lisbon, Rado and I made friends with everybody. I can remember the great celebration we had when we crossed the equator, as well as the misfortune suffered by an elderly man from Spain. He was returning to his native country, having retired and sold everything he owned in Argentina. One day this man's wallet containing all his savings was stolen, leaving him in a desperate state; he even said he wanted to commit suicide. I told him it was stupid to think like that, having almost reached his home country. I asked the ship's chaplain to organize a collection during Mass. I talked to the passengers, and we collected enough money for the good man to change his mind.

"From Naples (which reminded me of Argentina because of the people's gesturing and shouting), we traveled to Rome by train. There we were put up by the Slovenian Vincentians, just as the congregation was holding its general assembly. I was deeply moved to meet members from all over the world. Later we visited the Vatican. I was so excited to enter St. Peter's Basilica and be able to visit the dome and the tomb of the apostle. We used to sit on the steps, watching people from all over the world going by and marveling at the universality of the Church. Afterwards, inside the basilica we attended the audience Pope Paul VI held every Wednesday. Rado and I were standing just next to the aisle. When the Pope went by, I shook hands with him. To have left Argentina, an ethnocentric and arrogant country, believing it was the best in the world in everything, and to be able to live all these experiences in such a short space of time was fascinating. I had such a longing to open up and get to know other peoples and nations—everything seemed such a novelty.

"Some time later, we set out for Slovenia. We reached the border by train. What a contrast! There the police—with red stars on their caps, in gray attire, cold and without any human warmth, with pale, sad faces—asked for our passports and our entry papers. They went through everything, turning our suitcases inside out. This was our first impression of Slovenia. Many people had to disembark, but we were fortunate enough to be allowed to continue. Soon we discovered the woods, the mountains, the valleys, the rivers, the towns, and the churches with their belfries. How beautiful Slovenia was! We had definitely entered another world, and I thought I was dreaming my parents' dream. We stopped in Ljubljana, the capital city. Everything was gray and silent—no one spoke in a loud voice, so different from the shouting in Argentina. We were told, 'Don't talk in a loud voice because you could be overheard.' You got on a bus and you encountered a deadly silence, with classical music broadcast from the only radio, belonging to the only political party."

Peter and Rado arrived in Slovenia shortly after the "Prague Spring," when the troops of the so-called Warsaw Treaty entered Czechoslovakia to subdue the popular uprising that was demanding more civil rights. They found the country under Tito's regime, where, even though it was different from Soviet communism, Peter still said, "The people were oppressed by fear to such an extent that nobody dared voice his or her opinion." He studied philosophy at the theological faculty of the University of Ljubljana for two years, part of a small group of eighty students in a country with over a million Catholics. He also took advantage of his stay to meet his relatives who had not managed to escape when the Second World War ended. A maternal uncle and his grandfather Anton lived about twenty miles from the capital, and Peter used to visit them almost every weekend.

❧

His mother, Marija, visited him in 1969. Anton was anxiously waiting for this reunion with his daughter after an absence of more than twenty years. When they were finally reunited, he only shook her hand. Marija ignored that Slovenian reserve, hugging and kissing him. Anton protected himself from the display of Argentinean affection, saying he was not a woman to go kissing everyone in that way.

"Unlike Latin Americans, perhaps Slavs do not show their feelings outwardly, but that doesn't mean they don't have any. Mother was already Argentinean in that sense. My father saying to his grandson today, 'I love you a lot,' from a Slovenian standpoint is revolutionary. Perhaps Argentineans are slightly colder nowadays. But the Argentina I left behind was very warm," Peter reminisces.

When he finished his studies, Peter traveled to France, stopping first at the shrine in Lourdes. "I went there because in Buenos Aires I used to visit the Sanctuary of Lourdes, near the General Paz highway. As a true Slovenian, I have a deep Marian devotion, which is why I was ordained at the Basilica of Luján. I don't try to look for too many explanations to justify this devotion. What I like about the Virgin is her humility and simplicity. Mary was surprised at the fact that she was the Chosen One, which is why I love her so much. I stayed in Lourdes for two or three days. It was overwhelming to see thousands of pilgrims and sick people, even though I didn't speak a word of French."

❧

The experiences in Rome and Lourdes were moments of great spiritual fervor for Peter. "They made me see more clearly why I was going to become a priest and for whom. I believed that a priest should be the face of God on earth, and I prayed to be worthy of showing God's loving face to others. I couldn't help noticing the fortitude of those pilgrims, a multitude of believers who were seeking God; it really made me think deeply about the responsibility of being a priest."

He then settled at the headquarters of the congregation in Paris, where he would wait for about three months before leaving for Madagascar as a volunteer. During the day he worked at the Saint Joseph Hospital, and at night he took French lessons at the Alliance Francaise. Whenever he could, he played soccer. "I've always associated soccer with life because I don't see it as simply a matter of running after a ball; I see it as creating something, making an effort, and being self-disciplined." Peter told his superiors he would pay for the trip himself by helping on the mission's building sites.

ELEVEN

THE LANDFILL SITE

I get up early, driven by the desire to explore the village of Andralanitra. When I get to the street, the first thing I notice is the people lining up to get water from the tap under the jacaranda tree. Women with their plastic buckets are waiting their turn in perfect order. And I have just had a hot shower—what a contrast! I haven't made any effort, while they have to haul those heavy buckets all the way home. One for the latrines, another one for their drinking water, a third to wash, and maybe a fourth or fifth one if it's someone's turn to have a bath.

The children are entering the school, which is next to the reception office. There are a few minutes left before the bell rings, and they all line up in front of the Malagasy flag which they hoist every Monday and lower every Friday. The flag has two squares on the left, one red and one green, and a white rectangle on the right. I learn later that red symbolizes virility and nobility, green celebrates the surrounding nature, and white refers to purity.

The kindergarten children rush towards me. Although I'm a foreigner, they are not afraid. With Father Peter's example, such fears no longer exist. I extend my arms, and they start greeting me. I can feel their hands once again, this time even tinier ones, clutching mine like claws. Small hands varying in hue from very dark to similar to mine—hands full of hope for a better future. These children will grow up one day to change the reality of this country, which, for the time being, seems like an adverse future in store for them. But here in Akamasoa, the seed is being sown, a small mustard seed that hopefully will grow into a flourishing tree. After fifteen years of education (two years in kindergarten, six years in elementary school, four in middle school and, perhaps, three in high school), they will be better prepared to face life.

I will never forget this experience of constantly receiving affection. The children's hands seem to replenish some of the vital energy I have lost through the years. I leave the school and go down into the dining room. I greet Olga, with a "manahoana" (good morning). On the table, there is some bread, condensed milk, sugar, butter, and marmalade. Olga serves me some coffee. I add a little condensed milk. I prepare two slices of bread with butter and marmalade (a small ritual I will repeat every morning).

Olga is a single mother who lives with her daughter Prisca in Miss Bao's house, together with eight other young girls. She says living in Akamasoa has changed her life. She always has a smile on her face and is happy to do anything I ask of her—whether it's washing or ironing my clothes, replacing my bottle of mineral water, or simply chatting.

Every so often Olga suffers a bout of malaria and has to stay in bed for a day or two. "The attacks are tremendous. First, your whole body aches, and then you begin to shiver and tremble with cold to such an extent that you cover yourself with blankets. Later, you begin sweating because of the fever; you end up exhausted, as if someone has beaten the daylights out of you," says Peter, who knows the disease well because he has had to fight it himself on many occasions.

As I have the morning all to myself, I go out for a walk. I go to the reception office and ask Honorine if someone can accompany me to the landfill site. Later, Peter will reproach me saying, "You shouldn't have started by going there," and I will agree. Now, however, my curiosity is strong because I have never been so near one. One of the men from Akamasoa, who works in the food storehouse, accompanies me. We climb the slope past the basketball court, the small market, the restaurant for tourists, the store where handicrafts made in the towns of Akamasoa are sold (high-quality linen, baskets, mats, belts, bags, and wood carvings), the school entrance, and the bathrooms for the students.

I spot the small road that stretches out along the landfill site and ends in a neighborhood of temporary housing. My companion opens a little bag and places some paraky on his lips, a kind of pressed tobacco, grayish in color, which is used as a mild stimulant in the same way that native Indians on the South American plateau use coca leaves. The first scene I come across is a group of about twenty-five women working on the oldest waste, which has turned into a mountain of rich soil. With small spades, they throw the soil through sieves that separate the nondegradable waste from the rest. The composted soil is later bagged up and sold. Even though the women have to put up with the smell, it is good work, the area is properly marked out, and on these old mounds (over twenty years old), with grass overgrowing their ridges, there aren't any rats and very few flies. I take a photograph, which they happily agree to, before continuing on my way.

Five blocks away, I come to a small group of temporary houses, called Antaninarenina (in Malagasy, "where the earth was leveled"). All the houses are built with the same building materials, 130 square feet in size, with tiny kitchens that jut out in an "L" shape and veg-etable gardens in the front adjacent to the dirt road. The layout of the village is neat, but it cannot help being what it is, with hens run-ning around, heaps of coal, a mess of reeds from which the matting is woven, a strong smell, and flies buzzing around. About 800 people live here, divided into 145 family groups who are all waiting for the state to hand over the land to Akamasoa so they can erect permanent housing or move to the hillside village of Manantenasoa, where they will join the wait to move into a solid brick house.

In all the Akamasoa villages, with a population of 16,000 people in 2004, some 426 family groups are still waiting with patience and hope for Akamasoa to obtain the resources to put an end to the tem-porary dwellings for good. "On that day we will have a great party," Peter tells me. He estimates that it should happen in two years, God willing. Resources and work already enabled other inhabitants to move into permanent housing, so the wait is worthwhile. It makes a deep impression on me because, despite some people being cleaner and neater than others, they all put up with the overcrowding pa-tiently—in some cases, there are up to nine people living together in these rooms.

A black couple, who seem very elderly but baffle me because of the age of their children, invite me into their home. The neatly made bed, where all of them sleep, takes up most of the space. Underneath it, the clothes are stored in suitcases; in front of it, there are two chairs and a little table, calendars hang from the wall next to a ran-dom photograph, and in the corner there is a small altar where Jesus Christ is worshipped.

I am describing everything in detail, the good and the pleasant as well as the not so agreeable, because since Peter has not hidden anything from me, I have no reason to conceal it from my readers. When I think of the state not wanting to cede these lands to the people or transfer the landfill site elsewhere, I am indignant—although that is another story, and in time I will explain the political history of the island. But in summary, it seems that there was a dictator here for two decades who did not like Akamasoa or Father Peter very much.

Two children come inside to greet me. They must be between ten and twelve years old. How old can their parents be? They might be around sixty, but they could be ten years younger. It is difficult to tell the age of the people here due to the lack of milk and consequently of calcium, which means people lose their teeth at a very young age and their faces wrinkle, as if sucked in by their mouths.

I say good-bye with a "veloma," and we continue on our way along the alleys that lead down the hill towards the marshes and rice paddies. Here there are pools for washing clothes; a very tidy house painted a red similar to that of the Malagasy flag; nearby a small room serves as a chapel, where those who feel like praying can gather in the afternoons. An elderly lady (this one is elderly without any doubt) lets me take a photograph of her for my souvenir album.

⁓❀⁓

We leave the hamlet behind, turn right, go through the ancient hills, and come face-to-face with the landfill site itself, still fresh, sending forth a thin mist and stinking of excrement that makes my eyes and nose itch and turns my stomach. Fifty trucks a day, each carrying eight tons of waste from the capital, amounting to four hundred tons each day, have been dumped here for years.

Is there any sense in describing a rubbish dump where men and women carrying pitchforks and baskets made of reeds rummage through the recently dumped rubbish barefoot, searching for something that might be useful to sell or to eat? All of us must have seen this some time, either in person or on television. It is enough to imagine the rats, the dogs prowling around, fighting with the human beings over a piece of rotting food, while thousands of flies swarm around spreading the putrefaction to other places.

Peter says, "In a poor country, rubbish is also poor," and this is very true. There are not many cans to be seen (I suppose they are set aside to be used as measuring cups in the markets), nor are there any plastic bottles. What is it people are looking for, then? Small chips of coal with which to heat their own braziers; pieces of cardboard, aluminum, iron, or glass to resell; an item of jewelry or a coin lost by someone richer who accidentally dropped it in the family rubbish; or maybe some rice, meat, or beans which, after having been washed, will be eaten by either the "tramp" himself or his or her children. Children, incidentally, are nowhere to be seen. And that is Akamasoa's greatest achievement, because all the children go to school, whether their parents belong to the Akamasoa villages (only a few of them come to scavenge here), or come from the neighboring villages (where the majority of the people who work on the rubbish dump come from).

I take some photographs—feeling embarrassed and afraid I might be noticed—and indeed someone does realize and looks at me with a smile. How is it possible to smile in a place like this? The only thing I feel like doing is crying, in hopes that my tears will wash the place, cleaning everything with a single stroke and taking away this smell and the dust that is sticking to my body. Descending into and becoming immersed in this world of poverty poses questions for me and fills me with doubts. A man approaches me, greets me with a brief "Bonjour," and tilts his straw hat with such dignity that all my doubts are dispelled.

On my return to Andralanitra, the contrast is obvious; a small village of great luxury in the midst of so much misery is like a great ray of hope. I think of Peter and his struggle for so many years, and I begin to comprehend how God prepared him for this.

TWELVE

PETER'S TRAVELS

Peter arrived in Madagascar on October 26, 1970, aged twenty-two, not yet having been ordained a priest. "I wanted to gain experience before entering the priesthood, to pave my way without rushing." He stayed for a few days in the house of the Vincentians in Antananarivo. He then set off for the southern part of the island, to the mission the congregation had in Vangaindrano, 500 miles from the capital. The Vincentians had reached that same southeastern region in 1648, sent by Vincent de Paul himself (they spread the gospel in the area of Fort Dauphin, where the French had settled, before having to abandon the island).

"We traveled by car with the regional superior who was French. When we reached the mission, we were received by Father France Buh, a Slovenian I knew from Argentina, who lived there with Father Norberto who was Malagasy." Peter found himself in an inhospitable region where most of the population is very dark, with African features, situated eleven miles from the Tropic of Capricorn—a humid and very hot climate where it rains almost every day, drinking water is scarce, and insects swarm around everywhere. "A poor but decent place" is how Peter described it.

Because he had promised to pay for his trip by doing work, he built a house for the mission there, to which a school was later added.

"The night before I began building the house, I had a nightmare that it would collapse. But at that time I had a lot of strength, spiritual and above all physical, so the house still stands after thirty years."

At midday, when he took a break from the heavy work, he would play soccer with the children of the mission. "When the young men of the city saw me play, they came to ask me if I wanted to join their team, and I said: 'Why not?'" So Peter began to train with them under the scorching sun until two o'clock every afternoon. "Those young lads were so happy that it was really worth it." Of course, having a white person running around with them, celebrating goals together with them, wasn't something that happened every day. Peter suddenly became known as "Frera" (Brother)—the term used to designate seminarians. At first, he played for the city team as goalkeeper because the one they had was very bad. "But when I saw they couldn't score any goals, I would run and play as a forward which was what I enjoyed the most." He ended up being center forward, and his fame spread all over the region—to such an extent that when they were going to play against another village, everyone asked if "Brother" Peter was coming because he was a top scorer.

"Man is a being that likes to play games and to express himself with his body. Everyone does so in his or her own way, but it is impossible to express yourself sitting down with your arms folded. Practicing sports is one of the best ways to express ourselves. By playing with the children, I broke my mold and entered the world of play—a world in which we are all alike and can show our abilities."

During those two years at the mission, which were "like being born again in a world completely different from mine," Peter slowly learned the native language and became immersed in the unique culture.

"I would ask myself: Will I ever understand this language? What made a deep impression on me was their cult of the dead." Practically none of the people in the area died of old age, but of hunger, diseases, or because they were poisoned. "There were many warlocks and sorcerers who were always up to their old tricks with the people who lived there. When someone died, they would carry the corpse on their shoulders, zigzagging along the roads, because they believed they had to disorient the body so the person wouldn't return."

Peter learned that the natives believed in a God who created all things called "Andrianjanahary," and who was also known as "Andria-manitra" ("He Who Is Above Everything" or "The Most Perfumed" because perfume is inherent to the condition of being human). "But that Creator was a distant God, who was only mentioned when blessings were being given or when the dead and the ancestors were being referred to. He wasn't close to them. So that was why whenever we spoke of Christ, we told them he had been sent to be amongst men."

Peter was so imbued with a desire to fulfill his mission that he did not miss his family, even though he loved them very much. "My desire to share my life with the people in the name of Christ was such that nothing whatsoever depressed me." Even so, it broke his heart when he saw a child die of hunger or as a result of diarrhea. Asked about how he adapted to the food, Peter admits, "My enthusiasm was so great that I pushed that into the background and attached no importance to the issue."

❦

In September 1972, he said good-bye to Madagascar and to his two-year experience there. Peter attached such importance to the priesthood that he wanted to reach his ordination only after prior intensive preparation. "It wasn't a matter of having a degree; I had to be fully prepared, and I still felt very young. Besides, when you have a vocation, you already feel like a priest." He traveled to Paris to complete his studies with three years of theology, during which he immersed himself in the world of books and knowledge.

On the way to Europe, he stopped in the Holy Land, just one week after the terrorist attacks against the athletes in Munich. "Traveling to Jerusalem, despite all the security measures that had been implemented, was another wonderful experience. I arrived with very little money, in sandals, wearing a beard and rather long hair." He stayed at the home of a Lazarist priest, who accompanied him while he toured Jerusalem. "I hitchhiked to the Dead Sea and to Galilee. What I liked most was Nazareth, Mount Tabor, the Mount of Beatitudes and Lake Tiberias. I was filled with Christ during those ten days."

From Israel he went on to Athens, where he saw the Parthenon and felt happy to be back in Europe. "I didn't want to return to study in Slovenia again because the communists didn't allow you to do anything. Catholics were treated as third-class citizens, without any rights. We couldn't even speak freely." Therefore, he decided to go to France. Once again, he stayed at the headquarters of his congregation, and he enrolled at the Institut Catholique in Paris. "My French wasn't very good yet, so I had to make a great effort to study theology in that language."

The memories of Madagascar accompanied him everywhere and with them the desire "not to betray the poor and to always bear them in mind." Apart from studying, Peter established links with Catholic youth groups who were interested in social issues, and he emphasized the need to help immigrant workers of Slavic and Latin origin, for which he acted as an interpreter. He was also in touch with the ecumenical community of Taizé. "Taizé brought people from all over the world together—especially young adults looking for spiritual renewal." It was a place for prayer and contemplation, a place where ideas could be shared. "Being in contact with young people during those years in Paris was a great help to me because at that time everything was questioned, even faith. And by answering these questions, I personalized and strengthened my own faith."

His other passion, soccer, appeared again in Paris. He began playing for the Sorbonne soccer team and then went on to play for Orgerus, an amateur Third Division club. It was there that he had the opportunity to play in the "French Cup" (an annual championship for all the teams registered in the federation, including those in the First Division). During the tournament, Orgerus beat several teams from the top division. On one occasion, Peter was mentioned in the French sports magazine *L'Equipe* for his outstanding performance as the top scorer. His fellow player on that team was Gilbert Mitterrand (whose father would later become the president of France).

During those three years of study, during which he had absolute freedom of movement, he took full advantage of this to travel widely and meet all kinds of people. "One day I would say to myself: 'I will go north,' and I traveled to Ireland. Another day, 'south,' and off I went to Algeria. Then, 'to the west,' and I left for the United States." When his superiors warned him of the dangers of worldly things, he would reply: "Prayer and sports keep me out of trouble."

So, dressed like a hippie, with his long beard and hair, "because you can be good and honest without being formal," Peter hung his backpack on his shoulders and set off to travel around the world, often as a hitchhiker. When he hitchhiked around France, to Marseilles, or Lyon, he used to sleep at the train stations, where he became friends with the vagrants. They realized immediately he was not one of them, and they would ask him: "Who are you?" He would reply he was going to be a priest, and they would laugh.

All those trips and encounters remain engraved in his memory. England and Ireland came first. "In Belfast, I learned what an armed conflict was like, and I realized the conflict was not about religion but about politics, because the English had kept part of Ireland's territory for centuries."

Then came Morocco and Algeria. "During my stay in Algeria, while I was hitchhiking on the highway, a Muslim, the son of the minister of the interior, gave me a lift. When I told him I was going to be a priest, he said 'You are a man of God' and explained that they respected men of God, so he invited me to his home. We arrived at a palace. The women were wearing their veils, we ate on cushions on the floor, and I stayed overnight. The following day, which was Sunday, they took me to church and paid for my bus ticket to Fez."

Later Peter visited Belgium, Denmark, and Sweden. "I observed the people, their behavior, their manner, their gazes; I wanted to get to know what people were like because I was going to be a priest and I had to understand them. I analyzed the differences and would ask myself if they were fundamental or superficial. I searched for man and his soul. I was eager to know my neighbor and to transmit Christ's message to him."

Next, he visited the Soviet Union, traveling with a group of sociology students from the Institut Catholique. "There were thirty of us. It was Easter, 1974. I realized then that it was impossible for communism to last. They had made a state religion, with Lenin as god. Despite the oppression, mothers continued transmitting their faith to their children. Not even twenty years passed, and sure enough, it all collapsed."

❧

Lastly, Peter went to the United States. He obtained an inexpensive student ticket and crossed the Atlantic. "I wanted to get to know the most developed country in the world. I stayed in New York, in Harlem, in the parish of some Vincentians." He tried selling shoes to pay for an English course in the Bronx. "I was a door-to-door salesman carrying the shoes on my shoulders in a Latin neighborhood, and I kept laughing because I couldn't lie to potential buyers—the shoes were terrible." He abandoned that job and instead did some odd jobs that did not pay very well.

"I managed with a quarter of a gallon of milk and a piece of bread a day because I didn't want to abuse the Vincentian hospitality." The great city of New York never ceased to amaze him. "I saw how rapidly sects had proliferated. One day, I was invited to watch a conference held by the Moonies at Madison Square Garden, which I attended out of curiosity. There were so many people there that I asked myself: How can a nation that is so studious and developed at the same time be so childish?" Before returning to Paris, he went to Washington, DC and Chicago. "I learned most of my English sitting on the buses, talking to the people traveling with me."

<hr />

Finally, Peter finished his theological studies, and on March19, 1975 (a Holy Year), he took his perpetual vows of poverty, obedience, and chastity during a Mass celebrated in the Church of Saint Vincent de Paul in Paris. "The church was full of friends from different parts of the world," he remembered. Later, Peter traveled to Slovenia to be ordained a deacon in Ljubljana. Returning to Argentina for his ordination as a priest, he stopped in Rio de Janeiro, where he visited the shantytowns and also the Maracaná soccer stadium.

THIRTEEN

MANANTENASOA

I return home overwhelmed and saddened by what I have seen at the landfill site. My head is spinning: the flies, the faces, the tiny temporary dwellings, the piles of rubbish, and the barefoot people. I go to the bathroom and wash my hands, trying to get rid of the pangs of guilt, convinced that poverty will continue to exist if more people like Peter, who move from compassion to action, do not appear.

Later I ask Peter what he would say to those who might criticize him because of the way people live in the temporary housing, and he replies: "I would tell them that we don't have any more resources, that we do what we can, and that we don't ask the people to come—they decide to come here. Whoever criticizes us, let him help us materially, let him take the people to a better place, or let him shut up. We give them hope that they will have access to a decent house in the future. Meanwhile, they have shelter, work, clothes, healthcare, education for their children, and even food rations. Besides, the state refuses to transfer the land to us to build something better on, so what else can we do? It's the same case with the landfill site. We have been waiting for ages for it to be moved elsewhere, and they still haven't done so."

I go out into the street and come across Miss Bao, who introduces me to Miss Theresa (whom I immediately call Mère Thérése). She is about to go up to Manantenasoa and asks me if I would like to join her. Without the slightest hesitation, I climb onto the small truck Marcial is driving. We climb the slope. I think of every stone, brick, roof, window, door, tree, vegetable patch, park, dispensary, sports field, school, chapel, or shop erected here with so much effort and dedication. I think of the four Akamasoa centers: Andralanitra, Manantenasoa, Mahatsara, and Antolojanahary.

I think of the 16,000 people who live (in 2004) in these villages, 3,500 of whom have been given jobs, the 8,500 children who attend the schools, the almost 200,000 people (1.2 percent of the total population of the country) who have stopped by the "Welcome Center" in the last fifteen years, and I find myself better able to understand Peter's response. It's a response that becomes more profound when one bears in mind Saint James' Epistle, which Peter never tires of mentioning and recommending: "What does it profit, my brethren, if a man says he has faith but has not works? ... Show me your faith apart from your works, and I by my works, will show you my faith."

Driving along the asphalt road, three miles separate us from Manantenasoa (which in Malagasy means: "A Place of Hope" or "Place Where One Expects Something Good"). Founded in 1990 by Akamasoa, on the hillside of Ambohimahitsy, it is the organization's largest settlement (about 9,000 people live there). We leave Andralanitra and the adjacent village of houses with red earthen walls and thatched roofs, and go up the Route Nationale 2. We turn off towards the hill on which the eight majestic neighborhoods that constitute this settlement stand. Later, I will know their names, although I will always find it difficult to pronounce them: Bemasoandro, Lovasoa I and II, Mahatazana I and II, Mangarivotra, Mahatsinjo, and Manantenasoa itself.

Every name has its own history, activities, prominent people, as-signments that have been completed, and ongoing projects as well as pending construction works. In Bemasoandro, there is a handicrafts workshop, a quarry, and a primary school run by Sister Isabelle (a Spanish nun of the congregation of St. Vincent de Paul). In Mahata-zana, there is a furniture factory managed by Patrick (the vice-presi-dent of Akamasoa). In Mangarivotra, there is the "Welcome Center" (run by Mrs. Vololoniaina) and another quarry. In Manantenasoa, there is another primary school, the sports hall (which serves as a church on Sundays), the dispensary, the maternity ward, the dental care center, and the site of the future hospital. The person in charge of all this is Miss Theresa, who also holds the position of Akamasoa secretary.

Before entering the village, we go through the market that rises up on both sides of the highway. As the neighborhoods have grown in size and the inhabitants have improved their standard of living, trade has increased and hundreds of stalls have been put up to sell all kinds of goods. Peter is not very happy that there are so many stalls along the way because he is afraid that through them vices will spread, but he cannot do anything about it, because the highway and whatever occurs on it is under municipal supervision and subject to political concessions.

The air is fresher here, and there is an extraordinary view of the valley. We stop in front of the dispensary. We inspect the first-aid and maternity wards where pregnant women wait for their weekly check-up. Then we visit the pharmacy, where the lady in charge explains that generic medicines are bought in the capital, while all specific medications come as donations from abroad. She talks to me about the most frequent diseases (diarrhea, cholera, malaria, hepatitis, and various infections). Listening to her sends shivers down my spine. My fears return. Of course, in this place, thanks to the work of doctors, paramedics, and social workers, the epidemics are kept reasonably under control. Last of all, we visit the dental surgery, where the problems arising from the lack of calcium in the diet are explained once again. "Their teeth fall out at a very early age."

We leave the dispensary, and Marcial takes me for a ride around the area in his pickup. The roofs of the houses are corrugated iron, not tiles like the roofs in Andralanitra. "It's because we are higher up and corrugated iron is more wind-resistant," he tells me. When the cyclones blow on the east coast, razing everything to the ground, uprooting trees, leveling houses, killing people and animals, they also hit the high plateau with considerable strength and intensity.

Cyclones are not at all unusual during the summer months, like the so-called "Gafilo" cyclone that devastated the northern part of the island a week before my arrival, leaving more than 150 people dead and many more missing—and nearly 200,000 homeless. On the walls of the square adjoining the sports hall, which also serves as a church, I read the same mottoes that have been painted in every Akamasoa village. "He who does not work should not eat" (in the words of Saint Paul). "If you do not work, who will feed you?" "Work makes man." These are mottoes that summarize some of the Akamasoa philosophy that Peter had explained when we met in Buenos Aires. Now I can see them, painted in red and black letters, written in Malagasy that Marcial translates for me and I immediately recognize them.

"Saint Paul was proud of not being a burden to others, of earning his own livelihood. I believe that whoever is able to work should work, even priests, either intellectually or manually. I am grateful to my father for having instilled this in me. When we started with

Akamasoa, I built the houses together with the people. Perhaps those were the most beautiful moments for me, when as a bricklayer I was able to chat with them. I would ask them how they had become so poor, and they would tell me their stories. They poured their hearts out to me; they told me their truths. Those were spontaneous and honest encounters where we spoke from the heart."

This is a philosophy that is not only preached but also practiced. "Work is what makes man. In Madagascar, they also say the spirit makes a person. It isn't money, fame, power, or wisdom. That is why, when one works, one also encounters one's soul." Everyone here works, either inside or outside Akamasoa. The project has the virtue of being open—not trying to become a state within a state but aiming to promote the process of social rehabilitation. Akamasoa (in 2004) provides jobs for 3,500 people, mainly in the quarries and on the building sites (almost 50 percent), in addition to those working in different workshops (metalworking, furniture manufacturing, and crafts), on the farms, and within the different social services (education, public health, public safety, village maintenance, and Akamasoa administration). However, this is not its main objective; on the contrary, during recent years the number has diminished because many have found employment elsewhere while continuing to live here.

As Peter tells me, "When one is strong, one must be self-sufficient and live off one's own work and effort. If others sweat on your behalf, you should be ashamed. Of course, a person who is out of work for some time requires assistance to avoid falling into other things, but the solution is to generate work. The solution should come from the ruling class. We see politicians begging to be elected, saying they will solve people's problems. They put up posters on the streets and announce their names on megaphones; they appear on radio and on television, asking people to choose them because they can find solutions to their problems. Well, let them abide by their promises. They must have more imagination and creativity—that's why they are elected."

Peter does not think the aim of Akamasoa is to transform its members into businessmen, but the organization has had to generate entrepreneurship in order to survive. In this sense, the two quarries have served as a balancing factor because they enable the organization to meet a whole set of objectives. In the first place, they provide employment for the people, with a lot of flexibility in the ability to absorb a labor force. Secondly, both the stones and the gravel are used in Akamasoa's construction work, building roads and foundations. Any surplus is sold in the market, and the profits pay the workmen's wages every Friday. That's why Peter says, "The quarries, with more or less people, will always be kept running."

However, the workshops meet other objectives. Both the metalworking workshop and the furniture factory are kept open to train students, enabling them to leave school having learned a trade (if they do not go to high school). They also cover internal needs and hope eventually to commercialize part of the production (as in the case of school desks).

Later I will study the cash flow of the organization, but the first thing I notice is that nothing is free; everything is paid for—both the work of the people (with goods or with money) and the services that are provided, even if the amounts are very small (as in the case of education, water, healthcare, or contributions for the houses). It is evident that Akamasoa is not a mere welfare program but one of social advancement. "I would prefer to be kicked out one day because I made them work rather than for them to say, 'Father was very good

because he gave us everything even though we didn't do anything,'"
Peter remarks.

❦

I abandon my financial thoughts when Marcial points at his watch, saying it is time to return to have lunch at Miss Bao's. We will gather together there every day of the week: Peter, Father Rok, Carole and Gregoire (for as long as they stay), Jean-Jacques, Maurice (another Akamasoa driver), Miss Bao, Miss Honorine, Miss Fideline, and Miss Pierrete. On the way, my thoughts turn to Father Peter returning to Argentina to be ordained a priest.

FOURTEEN

THE PRIEST

Peter returned to Argentina in July 1975. Seven years had passed since his departure, and he found many changes: his younger sisters had grown up, Luis and Marija are older, Mariana is about to get married, and the country is going through hard times due to terrorism.

"When we all met again at the Ezeiza airport, it was so exciting! It was all hugs and kisses. My younger sisters were so grown up I could hardly believe it. The time I spent at home before my ordination was like a great family feast. Friends and relatives came from all over to visit me. We looked back on the moments we had shared together in the past, and I told them about my experiences around the world."

On Sunday, September 28, 1975, Peter was ordained a priest in the Basilica of Luján. Friends and family from the Slovenian community congregated at the Virgin Mary's sanctuary to accompany their beloved son who would consecrate the rest of his life to God and the Church. The Mass was concelebrated by over thirty Vincentian priests. The ceremony began at seven o'clock in the evening and was presided over by Monsignor Tomé, Bishop of Mercedes. Students from the schools in Luján as well as some pilgrims were present. Peter chose an excerpt from the Bible (Mt 9:13), on which he comments: "From my point of view, this summarizes all of Christ's theology.

People want sacrifices and rituals, but God only wants mercy. They are two different things. Mercy is something from the inside, born of the heart; a ritual is something external. God wants our conversion, our love, not sacrifices like those made in the olden days with lambs or pigeons in the Temple. True liturgy is about mercy. Christ rose and is among us, promising eternal life. In this passage, I discovered the novelty of Christ's message for the world of those times: mercy. How to wash, dress, move one's hands, or talk are nothing but details. However, in the past they were considered the most important things because religion was only centered on rituals."

Peter remembers that ceremony as one of the happiest and most joyful moments of his life. Lying on the floor, with his arms stretched out in the shape of the cross (the position seminarians take before being ordained), Peter remembers his emotions. "I felt one with men, earth with earth, and I reflected on the fact, that despite my being so insignificant and poor, God had chosen me for a saintly and marvelous mission: to be a priest, to be a messenger of his love. At that moment, my whole life crossed my mind, along with the faces of all the people I cherished and all those that had guided me. I also thought of my weaknesses, and I asked the Lord to give me the necessary strength to fulfill his mission, without betraying him or any of the people who trusted me and prayed for me. After the ceremony, when I went over to embrace my parents, we cried together. These were joyful tears, celebrating the fact that God had chosen a messenger of his Gospel from the bosom of such a humble family—but a family which was very much united with him."

Immediately after his ordination, Peter wrote a reflection that was published in the Vincentian congregation's magazine that talked about the coherence of his religious life from today's perspective. "A priest is not someone who lives away from his people; he lives and acts in their midst. It is through his attitudes that he questions others. He is a man devoted to prayer, prayer that is contemplation and a struggle.... He is a man who identifies himself with the poor, the outcasts, and those rejected by the powerful in this world.... It isn't easy to follow Christ. We love comfort, convenience, the good things of life, and we reject suffering. To opt for Jesus Christ is to put yourself in the shoes of the poor, to share their fate and struggle together for a more fraternal, just, and better world," he wrote.

Further on, he added: "A priest is also a prophet.... Today, like yesterday, living a prophetic mission will not be welcomed but persecuted. The Spirit of God assists us, and those who listen to Him and live in Him are the freest people in this world. Today, like yesterday, we need priests who will be living images of God's love for mankind. They should be men of God in the midst of the lives of today's people who no longer believe in an afterlife and in a being who is completely Another. Today, like yesterday, Christ continues to call...."

The following Sunday, he celebrated his first Mass in the school of the Slovenian Lazarists of Lanús where he had studied. He posted a sign in the vestibule that read: "Every man is my neighbor." Peter later shares with me, "Today, that phrase is still valid from my point of view. Every man is my neighbor, even if he is a sinner. Of course, he must give up sin and repent; he must convert and do penance." His family gave him a cross made of wood brought from Slovenia (with the figure of the resurrected Christ, opening up his arms like the statue on the Sugarloaf Mountain in Rio de Janeiro), resting on a quebracho base in the shape of the island of Madagascar. Argentinean and Slovenian wood were united—a true symbol for Peter.

"I drew sustenance from the cheerful and spontaneous character of the Argentineans as well as the sense of responsibility, effort, and willpower of the Slovenians. I benefited from them both." In the afternoon, they had a party at the Slovenian community and then walked out into the street with the schoolchildren, holding hands and singing. "There was a lot of happiness in the midst of sobriety, because the Gospel is happiness."

Peter took the opportunity to return to the city center. He walked down 9th of July Avenue and Corrientes Avenue, reminiscing about the old days. "I felt as if I were flying among so many people, thinking that I was a priest for all of them. It was like entering a soccer stadium, but now the field belonged to God—a field where we were all God's children." He kept blessing all the people, as Saint Peter recommends in his first letter: "Bless, for to this you have been called, that you may obtain a blessing" (cf. 1 Pet 3:9).

In November, he officiated at his sister Mariana's wedding. "It was something I experienced with profound emotion, not only from the point of view of my family but also from a spiritual one. Marriage is a wonderful sacrament because the husband and wife exchange vows to remain united, for better or for worse, for the rest of their lives. Of course, today when spouses go through difficult moments, they break their vows very easily."

⊰❈⊱

On January 6, 1976, he departed for Madagascar for good. He traveled with three young Argentinean men, all of Slovenian origin, who wanted to have a lay missionary experience (they stayed and worked together with Peter for three years). The Bishop of Fianarantsoa named him parish priest of Vangaindrano, where he had worked four years before. "I remember the people's joy when they saw me again, no longer as a "frera" or seminarian but as a "mompera" or priest. At that moment, I said: "Now we are going to live the fruits of the Second Vatican Council; we are going to make this parish the central meeting place in this city. We are going to open the doors and windows to everybody, especially to the young people. This must be their home and they should feel they want to come here."

In this way, the parish youth groups were created (more than 500 young people participated) and they increased the number of commissions on the parish board, incorporating new members and giving different responsibilities to the laypeople so they would make a more serious commitment to the Church. "We looked for new initiatives, with the objective of renewing the parish which had come into existence seventy-two years earlier." Twenty-five thousand people lived in this town, and five thousand of them were Catholics. "But many Catholics were asleep."

Youth groups were formed, including a soccer team. "The young people were so happy to belong to these groups that if they didn't drop by at least once a week they felt bad." Those groups produced three priests, along with many of the people currently involved with Akamasoa, like Patrick, Mrs. Emma, Mrs. Lalao, and women such as Claudine, Monique, Hortense, Louisette, etc. About fifteen young people that joined those groups work with Peter here now. The fruits of that spiritual preparation can be seen today. "I always say that one must invest one's time in the young," Peter says.

Little by little, he mastered the language. "It took me about two years to give my homilies without reading them. This was a wonderful milestone, because it's different when words come directly from the heart." During the thirteen years he spent in the southern part of the island, Peter left visible traces of his vocation as a builder, putting up a new church, a meeting room for the youth, some rural schools, and barns to store the harvests. Not only that, but whenever there was a need he looked for donations to improve the standard of living in the city. Thus, in 1984, when Peter returned on a visit to Argentina, he stopped in France first to get together with his friend Gilbert Mitterrand (whose father was now the president), and while they were talking about the needs of Vangaindrano, Gilbert advised him to speak to his mother, Danielle, who directed the France-Liberté Foundation. Peter spoke to her and requested some aid for the hospital. The following year, when Danielle Mitterrand traveled to Madagascar (to celebrate the twenty-fifth anniversary of the island's independence), she reserved one day to visit the southern part of the island. She arrived with two planes full of equipment and medication for the hospital in Vangaindrano.

When it was time to work in the fields, Peter used to set an example. "I explained to the young people that the only way not to be hungry is by working." He would go into the rice fields, occasionally with the water up to his waist and his feet sinking in the mud, working alongside them, either sowing or harvesting. "When people are going through difficult times, they learn more from one's example than from words."

During that time of permanent contact with the people, either from the city or the countryside, Peter did not shy away from any inconvenience, often forgetting his own constitution and consequently neglecting his health, eating everything he was offered, and frequently drinking contaminated water. "I couldn't decline their invitations. You entered a house, and you were welcomed with such warmth with a Mompera this and a Mompera that, and of course you stayed for lunch or dinner." As a result, Peter caught all types of stomach diseases (due to parasites) and malaria (in spite of the medication he was taking).

"Those years were very hard, and I went through all kinds of trials, putting up with physical pain but also coping with the fact that my youthful illusions were shattered because people sometimes didn't respond as expected. For example, I would form a group of adolescents, and then one day I would discover that their parents had sold them or handed them over to get married. These were difficult times when I had to resort to my raw faith, but I counted on the help of some people who never stopped encouraging me."

In the beginning of 1988, all the Vincentians in Madagascar came together. Among the issues that were debated was the appointment of a new director of the seminary in Antananarivo. "I went to that meeting ready to ask for a sabbatical year. I was very tired. I planned to ask them for permission to go to a mission where English was spoken, in order to brush up on that language (either Ireland or the United States). However, they all suggested me for the position, saying that I got on well with young people and was qualified, on account of my studies, to do a very good job. I asked them to reconsider their decision, taking into account the state of my health. We met again after six months and they hadn't changed their minds. I had to accept the position. But they agreed that I would take a three-month holiday in Argentina."

At the end of 1988, he returned to Argentina and took advantage of the visit to recover from his poor health. "My trips back home were always a cause for family happiness and celebration, but the farewells were always painful." In April 1989, Peter was transferred to Antananarivo to take charge of the seminary. He arrived with the weight of his health problems on his shoulders (especially the frequent malaria attacks), but with his mind set on providing vocational training for fourteen young Malagasy who wished to follow in St. Vincent de Paul's footsteps. "I took it as a service to the congregation and accepted the position for four years, until 1992."

Paul's footsteps. "I took it as a service to the congregation and accepted the position for four years, until 1992."

PART TWO

ONE

THE BEGINNINGS OF AKAMASOA

I arrive for lunch at Miss Bao's home. Maurice helps me wash my hands in the basin they have left on the porch. I discover that I am the only privileged person that has water in my house, while everybody else must resort to the fountain. The connection to the water mains is extremely expensive, and who would take responsibility for its payment or consumption? Instead, the organization installs the electricity and the water mains (paying what is consumed by the street lights, dispensaries, and schools), and those who are able to do so can request and pay for the individual connections themselves. (I notice that many houses have electric lights.)

I take the bar of white soap, Maurice pours water over my hands with a plastic jug, and then hands me a towel. I do likewise with the next guest. Two cats—one black and one brown—that frequent the dining room at dinnertime follow us. I am not too keen on these felines, but I put up with this phobia for three weeks, watching them climb onto a bench or even the table itself, waiting to be given their share. Peter says grace, makes the sign of the cross, and we start eating our meal, which will be practically the same every day: rice, meat, pulse soup (mostly white beans), and some salad. But, as Peter says, "When there are more important things, food is only an insignificant sideline."

During lunch, we talk about the press conference Peter will give to-morrow to thank friends from Reunion Island for their donations for the victims who suffered the devastating consequences of cyclone "Gafilo" in the north section of the country. Peter traveled there last week and collected about 70,000 euros, which will be distributed among the needy by Akamasoa later on. When the time comes, I will listen to the phone ring with calls for help, and I will see trucks leave, loaded with food supplies, or parish priests and bishops thanking Akamasoa for its assistance because it has gone out of its way to ask for help on behalf of others.

At three o'clock, I meet Father Peter in the small dining room of his home, turn on the tape recorder, and listen to him tell the story of how all this began.

⤝✳⤞

"When I finally arrived in Antananarivo, I was surprised at the state in which I found the capital, which was worsened by the economic recession at the time. Thousands of people were living on the streets (next to the walls of the hospital) and in the waste areas of the suburbs. In the south there was poverty, but there was also dignity and respect. The capital, on the other hand, was like hell, a place where there was no respect for anyone; violence abounded and children fought with pigs for survival over a scrap of rubbish.

I found thousands of families who couldn't afford the rent for decent accommodations and found themselves on the street. Misery and social exclusion go hand-in-hand. The street causes harm, which generates violence and divests people of any kind of hope. Faced with this picture, I said to myself: This isn't possible; God cannot and does not permit this. Men can, but not God. I must do something."

Later something happened that would impact him greatly. "At the end of April, Pope John Paul II came to Madagascar on an official visit. A Youth Day was held at the Alarobia Municipal Stadium. While the Pope was sitting on the dais before the crowd, a ten-year-old girl, carrying her younger brother on her back, broke through the police cordon and went up to His Holiness. We watched it on television in the seminary. The Pope hugged that poor girl and closed his eyes, deeply moved. His hug was so full of affection and paternal love. It was a hug for the poor, the outcast, for those left out of the party. The picture traveled around the world, and it made me question myself. Some days later, one of the bishops who had been present told me that the Pope had asked a cardinal for money to give the little girl something because, faced with such misery, he could not give her a rosary."

That event and the sad spectacle of the waste areas impelled Peter to do something for the marginalized and the outcast. "From that moment on, I started going out into the streets every day while the young seminarians were at the university. I had to do something, but I still didn't know what. Today, when I look back and see what we have accomplished, not only in terms of material work but also in the human and spiritual reconstruction of the people, I cannot believe it."

What Peter defines as "the love story" or "God's adventure" of Akamasoa begins when he decides to visit the hills of Ambohimahitsy, talks to the people who live in houses made of cardboard boxes, and suggests a plan of action. "I remember the time and place, but I can't say that it was the decisive moment. It was only the beginning, because the important part of any project is how it withstands the passing of time. I was happy with my decision because it was certainly a good one, but I couldn't tell if we would make it, if we would be up to the challenges, or if the people would respond with enthusiasm. A poor man out on the street doesn't have a point of reference; he can say one thing today and something else tomorrow. That's when one must avail oneself of all one's talents and strengths, and transmit joy, peace, optimism, and enthusiasm to people so they will be able to persevere with their original wish.

"It was May 20, 1989. I knew the hills of Ambohimahitsy and was aware of what went on in that place because in 1985 somebody had taken me up there, saying: 'Come and see this.' And what I saw was hell. People lived in houses made of cardboard or plastic. I thought this might be a temporary situation, as the Municipality of Antananarivo had taken the people off the streets and moved them to that area promising them further help, but four years later the problem was even worse.

"During morning Mass, I prepared for that first meeting and meditated on what my plan of action would be. In those days, I read a lot of material on dealing with the poor, because I particularly like sharing the Gospel with them. Besides, there were fourteen young Malagasy men studying in the seminary who wished to be ordained priests. They came from a poor town, and I had to prepare them to go back to that environment. Consequently, I had to encourage them to promote social justice.

"The time had come to put God's word into practice in an even more radical way than in the southern part of the country. I left the seminary at ten in the morning, alone on a motorbike. When I arrived at the hill where the town of Manantenasoa stands today, a dark man approached me, asking, 'What do you want, white man?' 'I want to speak with you,' I replied. 'So speak,' he answered. 'But I'm not going to talk like this, in the middle of the street.' 'Okay, if you would like to come into my home, just do so,' he said, indicating a cardboard house less than four feet high. 'Why not? If you live here, why shouldn't I go in?' I said to him. I entered the house on all fours, together with a small group. Once inside, I introduced myself as a priest, and that made dialogue easier because they were familiar with some other religious people who used to bring them material help. I told them that I didn't have any money, but that if they were ready to work, I would get some land and tools for them."

While Peter talks, I think about what he is saying—the fact that I am recording everything allows me to do so. I think about the symbolism of his actions. Bending down, lowering himself, making himself equal to the other person in order to help him stand on his own two feet, in order to raise him up. Someone once summarized all of Saint Benedict's rules that refer to humility by saying: "We ascend by descending."

"At that moment, I thought that the best thing for them would be to return to the countryside, because in the suburbs they lived in the midst of promiscuity and violence, both physical and verbal. I knew it would be very difficult to change that reality without modifying things in a substantial way, and the proposal of working the land, in another environment, would be a way to start afresh. Therefore, I told them that whoever wanted to sign up for the project could do so.

"I still didn't have any land, but I felt confident that I would be able to obtain some based on my fifteen years' experience in the south. Whenever we had asked the farmers for some land, whether it was to build a school or a dispensary, they had always donated the lands. Besides, I knew that the state had fiscal lands available. But afterwards, unfortunately, I realized it wasn't easy to get something for these people because nobody wanted to have them nearby—everyone was afraid of them. Perhaps it was counterproductive for me to tell them the truth that these people had vices: alcohol, drugs, theft, gambling, or prostitution. They identified them with the so-called 'four Mi': Misotro for alcoholism (drinking toaka, a sort of rum, to excess); Mivaro for prostitution; Midoroka for drug addiction (including rongony, or marijuana); and Miloka for gambling (derived from loka, which is the name given to any gambling for money)—four elements which lead to violence.

"I was told there wasn't a single square foot available wherever I went, even if it wasn't true. On one occasion, when I was in the land office with some surveyors who were helping me, we identified almost 9,800 acres about fifty miles from the capital. But when we arrived at the municipality, the official told us there wasn't any land available. The surveyors started arguing with the official, but I told them that if they were going to treat us in that way, placing obstacles in our path, it was better to move on to another place.

"The rural population of Madagascar is very high (70 percent). Therefore, my proposal of returning to work the land made sense. Where they currently lived, they existed from begging or scavenging in the garbage dumps. Two hundred families signed up, only seventy of which would be able to go to the 340-acre property we were finally able to obtain near Route Nationale 4. The property is situated thirty-seven miles from the capital in a place we call Antolojanahary, which means: 'the Creator's gift.'

"We started training them with a group of Catholic youths, most of them university students, who offered themselves as volunteers to launch the project. These were young men between twenty and twenty-five years of age, members of the VTK (Vondron'ny Tanora Kristiani-na). Many were acquaintances of mine from the south that had come to study in the capital. With their assistance, a few months later, in January 1990, we founded Akamasoa."

I believe this was providential because when Peter was working in Vangaindrano, he would never have thought that several of his closest coworkers in Akamasoa would emerge from those parochial youth groups. I shared this with him.

"You're right—I could never have imagined it because I came to the capital to take charge of the seminary, not to deal with the social problems in that area. We began meeting once a week with the group of families, and we worked on the need for a change in mentality. We would tell them: 'We are going to do it together. You have to be ready to work at least eight hours a day. You will have rights and obligations. We will assume certain responsibilities towards you—we will provide you with land, tools, and materials to build the first dwellings, and with the necessary food until the land starts producing. Moreover, we will be responsible for your health and clothing.'

"I went eleven times to the fields which the state ceded to us to prepare the ground, to speak with the locals, to study the site, to look for water, etc. There were some squatters in that place who used to run away when they saw me, and I asked myself how a white man could inspire fear in a location only thirty-seven miles from the country's capital.

"After some time, I met an old man who lived there in a hut made of the red earth. When I explained what we were there for, he was happy that we were coming to work the land because they lived in constant fear of the cattle thieves who roamed the area. The elderly man thought that if more people moved into the area, fewer bandits would come.

Eventually, I ended up renting his shack so we could use it during the initial stages of the project.

"Later I had a meeting with the inhabitants of the town and the authorities of the region. After those eleven visits, we prepared for the arrival of the first twenty families, of the total of seventy we had selected for that project.

"We set off on November 24,1989, on the eve of Christ the King (this is why we called the first neighborhood 'Cristo Rey'). While we were crossing the highway, surrounded by some lakes that are found on the way to Antolojanahary, I imagined the crossing of the Red Sea by the Hebrew nation, because for these people, it was like entering the Promised Land. The families settled in the old man's shack, and we started putting up the first wooden houses that were ready the following day.

"We began distributing them in neighborhoods of fifteen or twenty families each, until we had covered all seventy, so that each family had its own plot of land on which to grow a vegetable patch, alongside the communal sowings. This is how we began organizing new lives for these people. It was a radical change for them, being used to noise and parties; here in the countryside, silence reigned. Only the sound of the wind could be heard, and there was work to be done. It was a complete change in lifestyle. We left one person in charge, and at the beginning, I would visit them every day, then every other day, and later once a week.

"Every time I traveled to the site, I was afraid of what I might find, because these people were violent; they were used to drinking, and when they got drunk, they would get into fistfights or beat each other with sticks. Many times they got into fights over their neighbors' wives. That was the reason we established some minimum rules for co-existence: work at least eight hours a day, no getting drunk, no stealing from one's neighbor (neither belongings nor women), and no swearing or criticizing others.

"During that period and throughout Akamasoa's first four years, we received health assistance from the organization Doctors without Borders and also from Noromalala, a Malagasy nun of the congregation of St. Joseph of Aosta who visited us twice a week. In two months, the seventy families began to sow rice, vegetables, and cassava."

The telephone rings. I turn off the tape recorder. Peter speaks in Malagasy. He hangs up, and asks me to accompany him to Manantenasoa. He says we will continue talking on our way. This way of talking and recording will repeat itself quite frequently, and I find that doing it this way it is like living the Gospel while on the move, giving a Christian answer to the situations that arise.

TWO

MOMPERA IN ACTION

When we pass through the gate and are about to set off, I witness firsthand what will be a common occurrence during the next three weeks: children greeting Mompera, or women approaching him, demanding all sorts of help. On this occasion, a young woman carrying a child in her arms and holding another one by the hand approaches us. She is rather short, barefoot, with her hair in a bun; she has slanted eyes and a thin mouth that whispers in desperation: "Mompera, this child is ill. My husband has abandoned me. He must be operated on immediately, Mompera." The mother cries, and her tears form a groove in the dirt that covers her face. "Look, Mompera, look at the way the gland in his throat is swollen." And she shows him the baby who, without question, has a ball in its neck. Her mouth trembles and her sobs make her voice crack. "I need help to get to the hospital, pay for medication, and take care of him."

Peter observes the young woman; he studies her look, gauges her sobs, asks a question, shakes his head, touches his long white beard, puts his hand in his pocket, and gives her a few thousand francs (today, one dollar is worth 8,000 francs). The woman takes the banknotes, kisses his hand, lowers her gaze, and dries her tears with one of her hands. "Misaotra, Mompera, misaotra" ("Thank you,

Father, thank you"), repeats the woman, stepping backwards, moving her head with such humility that shivers go down my spine and I am on the verge of tears. But I hold back my tears because Peter has said I must not cry. He explained that we are here to give encouragement, to support these people. "I feel like crying myself sometimes, but I bite my lip, especially when a child dies," he says.

Afterwards, Peter tells me that he knows perfectly well that simply giving money is not the remedy because the fundamental problems are not solved this way, but he also knew that the woman was not lying to him. "You could see it in her eyes." He could not look at her in the state she was in and not do anything, although the woman should have spoken to his assistants first, as he cannot be involved in everything. Dozens of people come here every day, and many do not even stop by the Welcome Center because they prefer to talk to Peter directly—perhaps because they know it breaks his heart to see people suffering.

In the pickup, when we are on our way again, he says, "Have you noticed? Every day, people arrive with their troubles. Who knows how many miles this woman walked to get here? But we are not the Ministry for Social Welfare. We cannot help everyone. The problem is that the state in this country is absent, and politicians don't deal with people's problems."

He starts the engine, takes out his anger on the steering wheel and, as we leave the village, I ask him if we can take up the thread of the previous conversation, which we were forced to drop at his house. He looks at me as if to say, "Look what you are asking of me," but he tries to remember and continues his story.

<figure>❦</figure>

"At that moment we were forced to succeed. It was almost a matter of life or death. The most difficult job was convincing the people to think ahead beyond their everyday life, because they didn't believe in the future. From their point of view, tomorrow was far away—all that mattered was being able to eat today. It was very difficult to keep up the pace, the will to work, and to overcome the past, because they were corrupted by their own misery. They said they would do it, but they didn't have enough strength to pull through, so the following day they said, 'I can't do it.' We had no choice but to persevere at all costs. We knew it was very difficult for the people, so we had to help them change their mentality and lifestyle. That is why we had to overlook many things at the outset. We had to bear in mind that they were not farmworkers, but they were willing to give this life a try, to see what would happen.

"I'm sure I was a major influence on them, due to my life experience and the fifteen years I spent in the south with the poor. When you see people that are so abandoned and marginalized, you cannot help feeling that you should give everything for them. They follow whoever has strength. If they followed me, it was because they accepted me. But their initial motivation must be sustained, and that is the most difficult challenge.

"It was a matter of saving human lives without thinking too much about the future. At that stage we didn't rack our brains, trying to imagine whether they would get to the point of being self-sufficient. First it was necessary for them to become conscious that they were people, that they had a duty towards their children, that they had responsibilities. If they didn't even realize that they were individuals with rights and responsibilities, there could be no progress in a project of this nature. I was convinced that the more time they spent in the countryside, the better it would be. Time was on our side. They would gradually get used to silence and to work."

Peter stops the car to greet some neighbors while I look at the smoking landfill site at the foot of the hill. Fortunately, today the wind is blowing away from Andralanitra.

"With the other families that remained on the hill, we did two things: we helped fifty families return to their native regions, and with the remaining eighty we began the Manantenasoa project. The hill didn't belong to anyone, so that is where we settled. We began by building the Welcome Center and the temporary wooden housing. The people did the work and we provided the materials. The place became more peaceful when we distributed the families this way: some went to the countryside, others to their native regions, and those who stayed behind settled down in a more decent way with our help. I used to tell those who stayed the same thing I told everyone else: 'If you are willing to work, to build your own homes, I will help you.' We never offered them help for free—we always asked them to put in an effort in exchange.

"Once we had finished the wooden houses, we began to make bricks with the red earth, drying them in the sun. Since we needed to generate income, we also began taking stone from the quarry where the Welcome Center stands today. In this way, new families could join the project. Many people were arriving, so we needed external help to handle all the difficulties that arose because many were in poor mental and physical health."

❧

Peter pulls up in front of one of the houses under construction. He gets out of the truck and goes over to the person who seems to be the foreman. While the foreman tells him that one of the future houses should be built somewhere else because it will be too near the other one, blocking its view or standing in a dangerous position on the slope of the hill, I reflect on what Peter told me in Buenos Aires regarding foreign aid.

In the beginning, Peter resorted to different sources. First he sought out fiscal lands, and then he went to the religious communities in Antananarivo in order to obtain funds to cover the initial expenses. To buy construction materials and tools, he turned to France-Liberté (President Danielle Mitterrand would visit the project on two occasions), to Manos Unidas from Spain (an international nongovernmental organization, or NGO, which has helped Akamasoa from the outset and continues to do so), and to MISERIOR from Germany. Finally, he asked the United Nations to donate food under the Food For Work program of the WFP. Obtaining all these funds was easier said than done.

So that was the plan: external resources on the one hand, and the effort of the people on the other; changing money into goods, and the latter into concrete and visible works. With this strategy, the temporary houses were followed by permanent houses, schools, dispensaries, streets, sports fields, workshops, and libraries. "There is more money than is needed in this world. It is just not used correctly. That's why the number of poor people is increasing. Despite economic development, poverty has not been reduced, and this is humanity's great failure. Something is not working, don't you agree?" is how Peter continuously questions the system. Every so often, he adds: "When the social resources are managed by the state, they don't reach the places they should reach and end up somewhere else, generally in the politicians' pockets. This is mainly the case in underdeveloped countries."

The Akamasoa humanitarian organization was founded by Peter on January 13, 1990, with some Vincentian priests and a group of young Catholics belonging to the VTK youth organization. "More than an organization, we considered it to be a movement, but we needed legal status." They got together that day at the nuns of Saint Joseph of Aosta's convent. The project, which was already up and running, needed a name. The name Akamasoa (pronounced akamashooa) cropped up—it means "the good friends." Akama is derived from the French word for "comrade" (camarade), and soa means "good." The motto of the new organization would be: "To serve, not to be served." Its two pillars are work and service, with the goal of helping the marginalized and dispossessed leave their culture of dependency behind.

THREE

THE WELCOME CENTER

Peter returns to the truck and tells me he would like to show me the Welcome Center. We climb the hill and walk past the square, the covered sports hall, and the school. We turn right and stop for a few minutes at the cemetery. They are about to install the gates that, like all the gates I have seen so far, are made of small iron bars, painted a light greenish blue, with the name of the town at the top. The cemetery gates, meanwhile, have the symbols alpha and omega, the beginning and the end. "When I die, I want to be buried here, together with the people of Manantenasoa," he tells me suddenly, pointing to the field full of white crosses which descends towards an imposing valley.

I ask him why he wants to be laid to rest here, as my gaze falls on a beautiful combination of different shades of green, looking as if they were sewn up with the red of the soil. Peter replies: "This is my place. I have put all my being here, surrounded by these people. Besides, I believe I can be something for them to refer to, because what is done with love, truth, and sacrifice never dies. When love is not a passing thing but the fruit of a profound communion, continually seeking the mystery in the other person, helping one another, that love cannot die." But he adds: "If they don't kick me out of Madagascar first!"

I am getting to know Peter. There are some things that he has thought long and hard about that he suddenly lets out from the deepest part of his being. I know what he is referring to. During the years of Ratsiraka's dictatorship, Peter put up with a lot of things and even had to go to France for a few months because his life was in danger.

We pull up in front of the Welcome Center. The name defines an attitude—welcoming someone, receiving him or her in a certain way, ready to talk and listen. On both sides there are huddles of temporary housing, some made of wood and others made from building materials like the ones I saw this morning next to the landfill site. Opposite, on one of the hillsides, permanent houses are being built. Further down, there is a small valley where the people wash their clothes and where the cisterns that gather spring water are to be found. There is much movement—people coming and going. Both men and women work in construction: Men erect the walls, while the women carry bricks, water, and cement. "A cobblestone street will be laid here, passing by every house," Peter comments.

We enter the offices of the Welcome Center. Mrs. Vololoniaina tells Father Peter the day's news. "So many people have arrived; we attended some who have left, and these others have remained." They talk to everybody, and then they investigate to see if what they have been told is true—to make sure they don't end up helping those who are not in need.

Peter explains that they recently made the decision not to receive anybody new, except extreme cases, because they aim to finish building all the remaining houses—in accordance with the target advertised on posters in every town: "To become self-sufficient by June 2006." In the past, the procedure was simple: Those who remained in Akamasoa went from the Welcome Center to the Arrivals Barracks for a period of fifteen days, where they received clothes and food and were examined to determine their health condition. At a later stage, if their admission was approved, they moved into a temporary house, the children were sent to school, and the parents began working.

I look closely at Mrs. Vololoniaina, who has black hair and a gold tooth that shines when she opens her mouth. She has been with Peter every day almost since the beginning, assisting the people who arrive sick, abandoned, hungry, and hurt. She fills in a form with the name of the family, the number of children, and whether they stay or leave. However, nobody leaves empty-handed because Akamasoa gives them a food ration, clothing, or the money they need to return to their native region once they have undergone a health checkup. By 2004, almost 200,000 people have passed through this place since the center opened in early 1990. It's a considerable number—appalling on the one hand but amply illustrating the scope of the project in a country of 17 million inhabitants. I analyze the statistical tables with annual figures that are hanging on the wall. I concentrate on 2003—fifty-four families settled here, a total of 174 people including adults and children. During that year, 8121 families received some kind of aid before leaving: a total of 22,200 people.

We walk towards the three large rooms where they provisionally put up those who stay behind: this is called the Quartier d'arrivage. Dozens of children come to greet Mompera. I notice the women carrying buckets of water and cooking rice on the patio. There are very few men. The statistics regarding this issue are horrifying: more than 60 percent of the families that come to Akamasoa consist of abandoned women with their children. Four, five, six, and even seven children are not uncommon. Since most couples live together without getting married, nothing can be done to force the fathers to help support the children. This is the case in many under-developed countries, and it's also true in Argentina. Couples live together, separate, the women have more children with other men, and stoically put up with the burden of caring for a family.

We enter one of the rooms in the Quartier d'arrivage. It is long and has many large windows, allowing as much light as possible to enter. There are ten double beds on either side, covered with green and white bedspreads, with small tables on either side where belongings and clothes are kept. Every family shares one bed. While they temporarily live in overcrowded conditions, it is better than living out in the open; and here they also are provided with shelter, food, and health assistance.

Peter approaches one of the beds where an elderly man is sleeping, covered with blankets and flies. "They found him unconscious on a city street two days ago, and they brought him here," he tells me. Peter nudges his shoulder and starts talking to him in Malagasy. The man opens his eyes, lifts his head, and tries to sit up in bed. He is black, with a thinning beard, and his head is sprinkled with white hair. He has thick lips and half his teeth are missing. He mumbles a reply while gazing out into space. He touches his ribs on the right side, indicating that it hurts a lot there. I can imagine that his heart must also be hurting due to the miserable conditions he finds himself in. Most probably, he fell on the street. Perhaps he was drunk, overwhelmed by so many problems, not knowing his place in the world. Peter calms him down with his words and asks if the doctor has already seen him. "Oui, Mompera," the elderly man replies in French.

We continue. Now we are in front of a woman who has three children (the last one was born prematurely, Peter explains). Two are on the bed with her. The young woman, around twenty years old, is not in her right mind. She has been here for weeks. She may be transferred to a hospital for treatment, and her children will be cared for by Akamasoa, but for the moment, considering her mental state, she cannot be allowed to leave. One of the children is eating rice. Twilight, soon to become sunset, gilds the young mother's face. "And the children's father?" I ask Peter. "He must be with another woman. They have so many problems that they lose their minds. When we determine that nothing can be done, we refer them to a psychiatric hospital because we also have other people to take care of."

When we are leaving the room, the elderly woman in the first bed asks him for money to buy "paraky," a kind of chewing tobacco that gives energy. Peter squeezes her hand gently and we leave, just as the elderly woman starts screaming. "Some people seek some type of insanity, like when one drinks or takes drugs. I sometimes ask myself why we must take charge of those who lose their minds through their own fault, when there are so many normal people who need help, but then I soften when faced with the situation and the suffering. We had already sent this elderly lady to the hospital; they told us that she had recovered, but look at the state in which she has returned. If only it were so easy to make people change..."

I ask him how he can sleep, with so many problems to deal with every day. "Fortunately, I sleep well. God has given me the grace to face pain and problems with love and patience. Problems solve themselves little by little. But the people themselves must struggle to overcome them. Of course, cases of insanity, like the young woman or that elderly lady in the corner, are very different."

How much pain! It's impossible to think of anything but how best to help the most needy, the abandoned, and the outcasts. Christ would have done the same: standing by their side, giving them back the hope which life has deprived them of, both through their own negligence and that of others. That is what Peter and Akamasoa are trying to do—light a real light, so the victims can say to themselves: "Tomorrow we will eat, and we will sleep under a roof, covered by a blanket, and someone will come and ask us how we feel so as to propose a solution and even offer us a job."

Before returning home, Peter stops the pickup in front of what will be the hospital. On the construction site, he is like a fish in water. He calls the foreman and starts giving him instructions. "This door is not right because it's too low. In that room over there, we have to put up curtain rails—look at how the sun shines in at this time in the afternoon. And you must fix the banister to this staircase here. We must hurry; we must finish before the end of May." To which the man replies: "Oui, Mompera."

Then he tells me: "Can you believe it? Soon, we will have our own hospital. Over there will be the offices and, on the other side, the laboratory." He imagines it all finished, with two beds per room and people being properly cared for. I foolishly ask if they will install fans on the ceilings, so that the sick feel better during the summer. Peter replies: "We have other priorities. Besides, it isn't so warm here. You should go to the south side of the island to see what real heat is."

On our way back, I am speechless; I can only tell him I am saddened by what I have seen in the Welcome Center. To which Peter replies: "Come on, cheer up. I've been here for almost fifteen years and have never lost hope." We arrive in Andranalitra, late for prayers, as the sun is already rolling over the horizon and the ducks in the marshes are returning home. I go to my house, enter through the door I am able to lock, drop off the tape recorder and the camera, wash, and come back outside.

❦

Peter is sitting on the white bench under the Chinese rose bush, talking with Carole (whom I have not seen since midday). I walk over and join them. Three girls sing and dance in front of us. They dance to traditional Malagasy music, which lacks a catchy African rhythm but possesses a gentle, oriental grace. They move their arms, fold their hands, take two steps, lift a leg and let it fall softly, followed by the other. They look like herons shaking off the dew in a lagoon, or walking in search of food.

We talk a bit about art, painting, and literature. When Peter studied theology in Paris, he was a tireless visitor of the great museums: the Louvre, the d'Orsay, the French History Museum, the Grévin. At that time, he used to read profusely—the great theologians, past and present, as well as good literature. He still remembers Antoine de Saint Exupéry's words: "I would have priests and poets governing the cities. They would open the hearts of men."

When he came to Madagascar as a priest, he slowly drifted away from these hobbies. The situation was completely different: "A new world." There was so much to do that he had no time for these things. Art was replaced by the natural scenery that surrounded him in the south. The heat, the rain, the wind, the rice fields, and the poverty of the people—each face became a new picture of life where there was no need for paintbrushes, oil paintings, or canvases. They were all there in front of him, the suffering faces of hunger, pain, and neglect. Peter began replacing museums and books with the harsh realities on the ground, which challenged him and demanded action on their behalf. He had to finish whatever had been started because, as his father used to tell him, "When you start something, you must finish it."

To imagine, to plan, to dream, to realize: Peter's dynamism is a special gift from God. To imagine a new neighborhood over there on the hill. To plan a street, the small vegetable patches, the roofs, the windows, the doors, and the people inside—living, cultivating, dreaming a dream that must become reality. Everything, finally, ends in action. One must start working; words and colors are not enough to satisfy people.

"A person must create something in life. It can be done with one's hands, one's mind, or one's heart. God has given each one of us a gift, and we must do something with it. God has created us in his own likeness and after his own image—he is the Creator. Therefore, he who does not create, who does not develop his gifts, is missing something and cannot be a whole person.

For example, somebody who builds his own house is already a creator, because effort and imagination are needed to build a house. You must stand in front of a plot of land and say: I'm going to build the kitchen here, the bedroom over there, and the dining room over here. It gradually becomes reality with work and sweat but also with joy on account of what is being done. Work shouldn't be considered an unpleasant burden—it is the means to personal fulfillment, to the development of one's gifts. It should not be thought of only as something to obtain income from but as the means by which you do something positive for yourself and for others."

Peter talks, makes gestures, becomes passionate, and again brings up the subject of housing. "That is the basis on which a family should constitute itself. As long as there are people in the world, there will be a need to build houses. A decent home is the basis for family life. Living in a house made of cardboard is unacceptable. A clean and pleasant place is necessary to enrich family life and relationships. When people are living on top of each other in overcrowded conditions, faced with promiscuity, there will always be anger, hatred, and violence. Roads must be built and electricity provided, because when people live on top of each other in darkness, a small gang of thugs begins to dominate and hinder the progress of the others. I ask myself why there are no housing policies in so many countries, or why, if they do exist, they are not implemented. It is every state's duty to ensure that its inhabitants enjoy this right. To construct new cities and habitations, respecting the environment throughout, is to construct a better world."

FOUR

MEMBERS OF AKAMASOA

Today I wake up when a nearby rooster crows. It must be half past five in the morning and it is still dark. I go down to my study and scribble some ideas in my notebook. How to overcome poverty? Several factors must come together at the same time: the interest and enthusiasm of those involved, a project, available resources, and someone to lead it. It sounds easy to explain in business terms, but something more profound is needed for a humanitarian project to survive in the long-term: faith, hope, and charity. It especially requires charity manifesting itself as great willpower, work, effort, and sacrifice, invested by all those involved.

I recall Peter's words: "There isn't a formula to overcome poverty. There aren't any strategies, only spirit and heart. There are no recipes for earning people's trust; there are only looks, gestures, and human warmth. One must relate to a poor person without overwhelming him, without wanting to convert him, and with patience; in this way, mutual respect develops and love will take root and grow. Suddenly, one day, people begin to respond."

It is a slow process, requiring patience, lasting years not days. It's like the growth of the pine trees that Peter planted next to the Holy Family grotto that now stand about twenty feet tall. At the same time, proof of progress must be shown to those providing financial support (so they don't lose interest) and to all those involved (so they don't lose hope). The combination of financial resources on the one hand and human resources on the other produce a special energy that generates mutual obligations.

When the project has taken root, the leader should step down, so the people involved can take charge. Peter spent four months in Argentina last year, and everything ran smoothly during his absence, although from what I have seen so far, I do not think his time has come to an end here yet. Perhaps if he extended his work to other countries in the world, he would accomplish two aims: diminish his involvement here in order to kick off hundreds of projects with the same principles in other places.

"A movement like this that is born from the heart could be transferred to any part of the world. The only necessity is people who are willing to give up everything for their neighbor: time, effort, and even their own lives. People who want to help the marginalized stand on their own feet, rescuing them from the conditions they live in, taking the path of self-sacrifice and service to others. Our motto is simple: Imitate Christ who felt compassion for his sheep without a shepherd," Peter explains.

At nine o'clock, we set off for the press conference that will take place in a hotel in the city. Today Gregoire, who has also come to write a biography of "Mompera," has arrived. He and Carole sit in the back of the pickup, and I climb into the front seat. The traffic is heavy, as usual, and it takes us almost an hour to reach the hotel, dodging potholes, carts pulled by oxen, and pedestrians walking along the highway (there are no sidewalks). I take the opportunity to ask Peter to describe the greatest difficulties he had to overcome in the early days of Akamasoa.

He tells me that when they had managed to put up the first houses made of wood and red earth on the hills of Manantenasoa, a fire broke out. "During one night in 1992, an elderly man lit a brazier in his house, the wind knocked it over, and everything caught fire." At the time, Peter was at the seminary, lying in bed, suffering a malaria attack.

The following day, they broke the news to him. All the houses that had been built with so much material and effort had burned to the ground—158 of them. He made an effort to get out of bed to go see what had happened. All the people were standing there, silently accepting their fate with resignation. "We were lucky there was no loss of life, but several of our people were injured." The moment he saw all the wood reduced to ashes, the cracked earthen walls, and burned thatched roofs, he felt like crying. He had to bite his lip to prevent himself from doing so. "The more painful something is, the more inner strength I find to cope with it." The people had lost everything: houses, clothes, and belongings. Peter gathered everyone together and said, "Are we going to continue feeling sorry for ourselves, or are we going to build new houses?"

They built the wooden houses all over again, some of which still exist today as temporary housing. The following year, there was a serious outbreak of bubonic plague that took many lives. Once again, they had to get to work and carry on. "When faced with difficulties, we must keep going. There is no point in feeling sorry for ourselves, although I will never get used to the deaths, especially those of children.... Five years ago, we had a terrible cholera epidemic; I think that was one of the most difficult tests because it was the children who were dying. We had eleven deaths and about three hundred cases of infection. Doctors without Borders helped us once again by teaching us how to prevent another epidemic."

Peter reflects for a moment and adds: "Yes, I think this was the most difficult test because when something burns down, it can be rebuilt; however, when a life is lost...."

I change the topic of conversation. I realize he has to give a press conference regarding another painful event. Cyclone Gafilo razed everything to the ground, including trees, houses, and piers, as well as sinking ships and taking lives. Living here seems like a continuous test for the people, where death is simply part of daily life and a step on the road to reunion with one's ancestors. Perhaps that is why there are tombs all over the place, at the side of the road or in the middle of the village. When the time of Famadihana (the feast celebrating the dead) comes, the surviving relatives open up the tombs and sing and dance around them, ending by changing the shrouds of the dead.

I ask Peter to tell me about the happy moments. "Our arrival in the countryside at the very beginning, the people's transformation, and every time we inaugurate a new building, whether it's a school, a street, or a dispensary—these are times of great happiness." He also mentions the Sunday Masses, important visitors, the unexpected donations, and the community feasts. "We always celebrate May Day with a lot of joy because we attach great importance to work."

We arrive downtown. As we pass the hospital, Peter points at it, saying: "Over there, next to the walls, thousands of people lived in tiny shacks made of cardboard and plastic, but—thanks to our work and that of others—there are no more people there today."

I can imagine it all because I have seen the old photographs, which also feature the hovels next to the railway tracks and the Ministry of the Interior. Hundreds of them, with rags hanging from the shacks, and plastic to protect them from the rain, pieces of wood supporting the cardboard, filth all around, the children playing among the puddles, the dogs sniffing around everywhere. I can even remember the photograph of a woman sitting in front of the dark hole that is her home, warming up her rice, with her gaze fixed on the mud as if accepting life with resignation.

⌘

Arriving at the hotel, Peter resolutely enters the room where the conference will be held. About thirty journalists are waiting for him. He walks up to the front, followed by his principal assistants. He takes a seat at a long table. I sit down next to Gregoire and Carole. Father Peter looks at his watch while the room begins to fill up and someone hands out flyers with information about Akamasoa to all those present. I take one. All the names, objectives, achievements, sites, existing human resources, figures and projects are mentioned, together with a list of the principal Akamasoa benefactors.

Founder: Father Pedro Pablo Opeka
President of the Organization: Marie Odette Ravaoarivo
Vice President: Patrice Ramanankohanina
Secretary: Marie Therese Razafimanandraisoa
Objectives: rehabilitation and social reintegration of the destitute, a return to dignity and self-respect, the responsible commitment of every person to his or her own personal development and that of the entire community
Scope of action: education and professional training, paid work, construction, agricultural development, health assistance, aid for those in need, active participation in the development of other communities

Human resources: 7 doctors, 1 dentist, 3 midwives, 189 teachers, 26 social workers, 15 technicians, and 7 persons employed in the management of the organization

Centers where Akamasoa operates in the suburbs of the capital: Andralanitra, Manantenasoa, and Mahatsara; in the province of Antananarivo: Antolojanahary (where the first center was built) and Ambatomitokana (also in the countryside where a forest reserve is owned); in the province of Fianarantsoa: Vangaindrano, Alakamisy and Safata.

There follow the figures that I have already mentioned, including the number of inhabitants, houses, children attending school and people who have been attended to by the Welcome Center. Peter begins speaking in Malagasy and, as I cannot understand a word he is saying, I finish reading the sheet.

Future projects: continue building houses, classrooms, libraries, and sports fields; improve the quality and productivity of income generating activities; support and encourage job hunting outside the organization; provide help for the province of Fianarantsoa; spiritual development.

Main organizations which currently contribute resources either in money or in kind to Akamasoa: Manos Unidas of Spain; APPO and Monaco Aide et Présence from the Principality of Monaco; Association Atlante, Les amis du père Pedro Opeka, Association Francaise des Volontaires du Progres, Energie sans Frontieres and Association Naitre a Safata of France; Regio Terzio Mondo from Italy; the International Rotary Club; the European Union; the embassies of France, Germany, and Japan; and Partage avec Madagascar, from the island of Reunion.

Peter continues speaking and gesticulating with his hands. Every so often, he makes the audience laugh for reasons I cannot understand. It is obvious that his gestures and the way he approaches people belong to his Argentinean legacy, but when he breathes and lets out profound phrases while closing his eyes, I am reminded of his Slavic origins. Now he touches his long white beard and sips some water. Then he continues to explain in French that the generosity of the inhabitants of Reunion should be made known in Madagascar. All the money that was raised came from church collections, contributions from ordinary people who care about their Malagasy brothers suffering nature's inclemency. Tomorrow we will read about this press conference in the main newspapers, with photographs of Peter talking, emphasizing his gratitude to the friends of the small island of Reunion (which belongs to France).

The press conference ends, and light refreshments are served while the journalists mill around Peter, microphones and tape recorders in hand. I converse with Gregoire.

On our way back, I travel in the back of the pickup with Jean-Jacques. I ask him about the history of Madagascar. This dark young man, who is thinking of studying archaeology when he finishes studying history, opens his big eyes, shows me one of his hands (representing the outline of the island), and starts explaining with the help of his other hand.

"The island detached itself from the African continent 250 million years ago, due to the movement of the tectonic plaques, when the supercontinent of Pangaea started splitting up." (I remember having studied something about this and the formation of Laurasia and Gondwana, but I cannot help being surprised at the extent of his knowledge).

"The first inhabitants of the island came from the lands that today are known as Indonesia and Malaysia. They covered almost five thousand miles in their canoes, taking advantage of the trade winds. Nobody knows exactly why they embarked on this voyage, but we can guess it took place during the first centuries of the Christian era—although, according to our Malagasy tradition, the first people to arrive were some white pigmies from Polynesia known here as the Vazimba. The Malayo-Indonesians brought rice and the techniques necessary for its cultivation. Because the eastern coast suffered from continuous cyclones, they started moving up to the plateau. Towards the 9th century AD, trade with the Arabs began. The latter settled in the northeast and the south, and they brought the first black slaves from Mozambique and what is known today as Somalia. They formed the eighteen principal ethnic groups which populate the island, with a major African influence in the coastal regions and a predominantly Asian influence on the central plateau."

Jean-Jacques pauses when the pickup bounces up and down, because the road is full of potholes and Peter does not slow down. He takes a ballpoint pen and draws circles on one of his hands. "Here are the Merina, the Betsileo, and the Tanala (the principal ethnic groups of the central high plateau, representing 35 percent of Madagascar's total population). Over here, on the west coast, are the Sakalava, and on the east coast the Betsimiraka, Antemoro, and Antesaka (which represent 30 percent)." I tell him that he will make a good teacher, and he replies with his usual smile, with a hint of pride but much more with sheer gratitude.

"The first European to arrive in Madagascar was the Portuguese explorer Diogo Dias in 1500. His boat drifted away from his brother Bartholomew's fleet (who had discovered Cape Hope beforehand), and he ended up on our shores. From the seventeenth century onwards, the Portuguese, the French, the Dutch, and the British all tried to settle in Madagascar without much success. The French built Fort Dauphin in the south but were unable to consolidate their position, so they were later forced to flee east to the islands of Sainte Marie and Reunion. It was the European pirates who every so often settled on the east coast in order to control the Indian Ocean.

"Meanwhile, in the island's interior, different kingdoms consolidated themselves. Towards the end of eighteenth century, the Merina kingdom began expanding and dominating the others. In 1817, Merina King Radama I achieved political unification of the island and established the capital of Antananarivo. The British governor of Mauritius, who supplied him with weapons and sent instructors, supported him. At that time, Protestants and Anglicans started arriving in the capital to evangelize the dynasty that held power until 1896. King Ranavalona II was even baptized and adopted Christianity. In 1885, the British allowed France to control and defend their protectorate in exchange for recognition of their authority in Zanzibar. The French entered Madagascar by force, defeated the Merina, dissolved the monarchy, and transformed our island into a colony."

FIVE

THE RULES OF AKAMASOA

I drop the conversation with Jean-Jacques when we arrive in Andralanitra for lunch. We proceed with the usual handwashing ritual before eating, then enter the dining room accompanied by the two cats, sit down, make the sign of the cross, pray, and start eating. Today we are surprised by some delicious spring rolls, to which I add soy sauce.

After his nap, Peter waits for me in his house. I get there at three o'clock, carrying my tape recorder; my mind is full of questions about the operation of the project. Above all, I would like him to talk to me about the rules of coexistence, or Dina, as they are called here.

"Dina is an agreement reached by the people. In the beginning, they established some basic rules. As the years went by, these were improved and eventually written down, with the consensus of all the inhabitants of the different towns. When a person joins Akamasoa, he or she agrees to abide by these rules or conventions. They are basic rules of behavior, which may seem very elementary at first, but one has to take into account what the people here are like, where they came from and what they brought with them: illiteracy, undernourishment, all kinds of diseases, vices, habits, and a mentality which is difficult to change."

Peter shows me the latest version of the rules, which was written in 2002. "Two girls from Akamasoa—Viviane and Nina—wrote the Introduction. One is already a teacher, and the other will soon graduate as a social worker. They both joined Akamasoa when they were little girls."

The two girls, now professionals, stress the importance of these rules, saying: "Akamasoa has given us many things, and we are aware of the importance of abiding by the rules of coexistence so that this effort and work may continue helping the young. It all depends on us and especially on the parents—whether they are willing to work for their family's progress and continue struggling against poverty and the problems that plague us. These rules help us live together and control our actions. They have not been established to make life more difficult but to enable us to enjoy more harmony within our community and to avoid conflicts."

Peter explains how over 140 people attended the 2002 general assembly: the Akamasoa representatives of each neighborhood and village, of each company, each school, and each dispensary. Every one of the conventions or rules was discussed and voted on. Nineteen different points were established. Some relate to people's behavior; others to community work and education; and some address internal relationships and dealings with the rest of society. Making a note of each point, while Peter translates them, one by one, from the Malagasy brochure, seems fundamental for a better understanding of the nature of this humanitarian project.

❊

1. The first rule refers to people that have been expelled from

Akamasoa. "They can never return, but if they have left any relatives behind, they can come and visit. Those who are expelled are not suddenly left out on the street; we always try to find a solution for their own good and that of the community, except when they commit serious crimes and are handed over to the authorities."

2. Concerning hosts and guests, "because we can't allow people to take up residence in a clandestine way; if we did, in a few months time, the population would double and we would run the risk of self destruction." Guests are allowed to stay only for a period of up to three days, unless they have specific permission to stay for a longer period.

3. Regarding the moral behavior of the people, sanctions, fines, and cases of expulsion are explained. Alcoholism, insults, obscene gestures, family abuse (above all, physical violence), prostitution, adultery, and polygamy are condemned. Fines are paid in cash, and the guilty party is warned to either improve his or her behavior or face expulsion. "However, if it's a rape case involving minors, they are expelled without notice and are handed over to the civil authorities."

4. It's recommended that young people marry only after they have reached twenty years of age. Husbands should have a job and a house. They should have a legal marriage and, if possible, undertake religious commitment. In accordance with Malagasy culture, the woman is the one who should follow the husband wherever he goes. "But these are only recommendations," Peter emphasizes, since the recommended age is often not complied with.

5. The clandestine sale of alcohol and drugs is forbidden in Akamasoa, and whoever is caught red-handed will be expelled from the community. This also applies to those who use sharp implements to injure others. "In both cases, they are handed over to the authorities."

6. Akamasoa children are forbidden to escape to the city streets. "Those who run away will be searched for until they are found." School is compulsory for all children. Parents are obliged to make sure that their children attend school under penalty of fines and sanctions. The neighborhood committee, the school heads, and even the teachers are also responsible.

7. Children are prohibited from playing violent games and climbing on the trucks that go to the quarries, in order to avoid accidents.

8. All gambling for money is forbidden under penalty of having to pay a fine. In addition, violent or pornographic films are prohibited because they damage the mind and spirit. The practice of sports must be fostered among young people and children.

9. "The ninth rule concerns housing and environmental care because we attach great importance to this here." Every person, upon moving into a new house, must sign a contract with Akamasoa. The first contract is established for a trial period of five years, during which small installments are paid; if at the end of the set period the residents have acted responsibly, the house is ceded to them for as long as they stay in Akamasoa. Adjoining constructions cannot be erected, nor can goods be sold on the sidewalks, because these are meant for the passersby. The cleanliness of the house, its surrounding area, and the village must be maintained; this is fundamental for a healthy coexistence and shows respect for the environment. Renting houses that have been given to a family is prohibited. If a family decides to leave, it loses all claims on the house. Every family must have a vegetable patch where fruit and vegetables are cultivated. Neither trees nor woods must be damaged.

10. Children are forbidden to go to the landfill site and eat from the rubbish.

11. All the sports facilities are at the disposal of Akamasoa's members. Those visiting from outside must ask for permission to use them. Violent individuals may not use these facilities. The heads of the neighborhood committees must make sure they are well-kept and respected. The organization's guards must note the movement of people entering and leaving the villages. Young men who do not respect girls will be sanctioned with fines and punishments. "We have to take care of our mind and spirit because it is the only way we can advance and progress. It is recommended that all young people take part in the different religious, sports, or choir groups."

12. This rule concerns the community work directed by commissions and committees. The only way to achieve unity is for villages and enterprises to appropriately share. Monthly meetings for the resolution of problems and project development are recommended.

13. Women who have arrived in the villages on their own or those that have been abandoned while they were in the village are forbidden to receive men in their houses at night. "If a woman loves a man, it is the latter that should make her his wife and take her with him."

14. It is compulsory for everyone to carry out community work at least once a week: cleaning the streets, schools, drains, etc. This is necessary so as to form a spirit of solidarity and union. The three cemeteries (Manantenasoa, Mahatsara, and Antolojanahary) must also be well kept.

15. Those who represent Akamasoa in the town councils must continually work for the dignity of Akamasoa's villages and must do everything within their means to defend the interests of those who chose them, above all when truth and justice are at stake. "The fact is that sometimes town councilors are chosen from our towns, and when they reach power, they forget who voted for them. We must

work shoulder-to-shoulder with the town councils, without jealousy or grudges, without blaming one another, bearing in mind that we are one people trying to achieve progress, development, and unity."

16. On sects: any person who joins a sect and looks for followers in the villages will be expelled. The people must always bear in mind that Akamasoa was the one who took them off the streets, gave them a house, provided an education for their children, as well as medicine, healthcare for the family, a school canteen, and jobs. Akamasoa is the one that helped them when they were ill and also the one that buries the dead.

17. Signs must be put up on the walls of every neighborhood announcing that by June 26, 2006, all the villages must become self-sufficient. This is the anniversary of Malagasy Independence, which is why it was chosen.

18. It is recommended that all parents encourage their children to pray, because it is through prayer that this miracle has come true. A Malagasy proverb says: "It is the spirit which makes the man." Peter says, "In a sense, we are not recommending anything new, because religious beliefs are inscribed in the spirit of the ancestors."

19. The young people representing other youth have the right and the responsibility to set an example for others in order to change their mentality and the way of life. They know what kind of mentality led them to extreme poverty in the past. They must remember that they are leading their young contemporaries and must not be afraid of taking on this responsibility. It is recommended that every month a new project for young people in every village be created at every level: cultural, spiritual, and sports.

The document ends with some words written by the Akamasoa president, Miss Bao: "These rules were written with the active participation of all the heads and representatives of the neighborhoods and were voted for and approved in the presence of the founding father (referring to Peter). They have been established so we can leave behind a way of life which led us to extreme poverty. It was with total freedom and of our own will that we took part in this assembly and voted for these rules, which are in complete accordance with our Malagasy mentality.

"We all know that the struggle against poverty begins in school with the education of our children; it continues with work, a decent house, and the possibility of being cured when we fall ill. It involves taking full responsibility for the community and society we live in. Akamasoa has made the education of children and the young a priority, forming them in every sense. We must also bear in mind that selfishness and discord, both in the family and within our neighborhoods, set a bad example and generate problems. Everything we have convened on here is in accordance with our ancestors' spirit and mentality. God has given us the freedom to choose between right and wrong.

"You, the young people of Akamasoa, bear an even greater responsibility because you came here as children and were not contaminated by extreme deprivation and vices. You have received help, and you must help others. If compassion has been shown you, then you, too, should be compassionate with others. Don't take the wrong road, because if you do, who will inspire hope? Don't ever forget that our main objective is to become self-sufficient by 2006, and these rules will—and must—help us meet that objective.

"I would like to finish by thanking Father Opeka for everything he has done for us to accomplish this new reality, which enables us to return to the wisdom of our ancestors. If we abide by these rules, they will help us respect each other, increase our love for one another, and become more human. This reciprocal help will help us to fulfill Christ's words: 'Love your neighbor as yourself.' Let us not forget it was a priest who began this struggle against our material, cultural, and spiritual poverty. That is why I beg you to increase your faith and devotion to prayer. Do not disregard the vessel which brought us from one shore to another. I wish you much happiness and may God bless you."

SIX

MADAGASCAR'S HISTORY

After the interview with Peter, I ask if someone can take me to a cybercafe. I have been out of touch with the world for several days, and I need to check my emails. I don't know if this is just a habit or whether there is a real need, but I do not want to be a nuisance by using Akamasoa's connection. Marcial and Jean-Jacques accompany me. I take this opportunity to finish the lesson in Malagasy history that was interrupted at midday.

❦

"The colonial period lasted from 1896 to 1960. During the First World War, our troops fought in France, Morocco, and Syria. During the Second World War, when the Germans invaded France and the Vichy government took office, the British occupied Madagascar to prevent the Japanese from doing so. When the war ended they withdrew, but the Malagasy began demanding independence from France. In 1947, the French put down a national uprising, with an estimated death toll of 80,000 people. Finally, in October 1958, France granted autonomy to Madagascar and on June 26, 1960, we gained independence."

We arrive at the cybercafé, but I am so anxious to learn about Madagascar's recent history that I ask Jean-Jacques to finish his account.

"In 1959, Tsiranana was elected the first president, with France's support—an SDP candidate who declared himself a fervent anticommunist and who governed until the coup d'état in 1972. After the coup, General Ramanantsoa seized power, tried to limit French influence, and broke off diplomatic relations with South Africa. In 1975, the foundations for a new constitution were laid (on socialist principles this time), and the island was renamed the Democratic Republic of Madagascar. That same year, due to discord in the higher ranks, another military man, Didier Ratsiraka, seized power. He would influence the destiny of the country to the present day.

"Ratsiraka began nationalizing the economy, imposing his Marxist ideas by means of political persecution and the implementation of his own cultural revolution with a so-called "red book." A single-party regime was created and Ratsiraka managed to be reelected successively in 1982 (with 80 percent of the vote) and in 1989 (with 63 percent). Years later, Madagascar would not be spared the changes the world and the former communist countries were experiencing. Consequently, in 1990 the dictator was forced to implement a process of political liberalization, which would be followed by popular uprisings in 1991, and he was compelled to call early elections, prior to a constitutional reform.

"In the 1992 elections, the opposition candidate Zafy defeated him in the second electoral round with 77 percent of the vote. Despite attempts to open up the economy and begin privatizing industry, Zafy's government had to struggle against the spokespersons of the former régime and ended up resigning in 1996. A new call for early elections marked Ratsiraka's return to power. He obtained 51 percent of the vote in the second round. The old dictator endeavored to adapt to the new principles of the international order, agreeing to the International Monetary Fund's proposed measures—which resulted in a rise in prices and social unrest.

"The 2001 elections gave rise to one of the most difficult moments in contemporary Malagasy history, almost ending in civil war. The opposition gathered round Antananarivo's mayor, Marc Ravalomanana, a successful businessman who was supported by the independent electorate. The unofficial results indicated his victory, but Ratsiraka declared himself the winner. Ravalomanana created a parallel government and denounced the fraud to the rest of the world. Ratsiraka took refuge in the port of Tamatave, cutting off all supplies to the capital and isolating it completely. (At that time Father Peter took sides with the true winner, Ravalomanana, and he traveled to Paris to denounce Ratsiraka's fraud and warn people about the danger of civil war if nobody did anything).

"Finally, both contenders agreed to a recount of the votes, supervised by foreign inspectors. The results confirmed what everyone already knew: Marc Ravolomanana had won with 51 percent of the vote. The old dictator fled the country and exiled himself in Paris. In December 2002, the elected president's allies won the legislative elections and secured their power in parliament. However, the Ratsiraka's supporters continued destabilizing the government."

⊱✦⊰

Two young girls who have been accused of prostituting themselves by their neighbors have come to talk to Father Peter tonight.

Peter tells me about it before dinner. He told them that they have acted wrongly and that they have let down the community that has done so much for them. "One of the girls blamed her mother, and the other remained silent," Peter tells me with great grief, and he adds, "Nothing is perfect. If anyone believes this is paradise, they are wrong."

We enter the dining room. The little girls give thanks as usual in the four languages, followed by the sign of the cross and prayers. Somebody fills my glass with mineral water. There we are, as we all will be during the coming evenings—Peter at the head of the table, Carole to his right, myself to his left, Gregoire next to me, then Father Rok (today is Thursday and it is his turn to dine with us), along with Tojo, Viviane, Felana, Olga, and Miss Bao.

Tojo had told me about her life on the landfill site that afternoon. "Yes, we, too, looked for food because my parents didn't have any money: meat, potatoes, carrots, beans, whatever came our way." I look at her and connect what she said with Peter's story of how he saw for the first time what was happening in the landfill site. "The children fought with the pigs over the food. Thank God, the pigs were killed off by a fever three years ago." Tojo—whose head hurts every day, but no one has been able to discover the reason for the pain—smiles at me; she realizes I am thinking about her. Indeed, I wonder if her persistent headaches may perhaps be due to a yet undiscovered infection, contracted several years ago when she was desperately trying to survive by scavenging piles of garbage.

After dinner, the girls at the neighboring table prepare a show for us. They start dancing to the beat of a Malagasy song. Nine adolescents line up in groups of threes. A step to the right, another one to the left; one forward, and another backwards. They are not embarrassed to be themselves.. Even young Tina moves and sings like the older ones. What happiness! God forbid they should return to the gutter of human existence, and may the values transmitted by Akamasoa triumph! However, that does not depend on the community—it is up to them. If that were not the case, there would be no freedom and they would become a sect, a closed circle.

What makes Akamasoa so attractive is its openness towards the rest of society and the freedom that exists within it, beyond the community rules that are necessary even within a family. For example, all are free to work wherever they want, outside or within the organization. Some go away, others return, and the quarry is always open to receive the unemployed. This is the reason why it is not mechanized —to be able to absorb labor with flexibility. If machines, like those of other companies, were installed, this would no longer be possible. This may seem to contradict the sense of progress which is instilled in the schools through the teaching of French, computer science, and pedagogical or sports competitions. However, using the quarry as an instrument for labor stabilization does not seem like a bad idea. I realize it is possible to devise strategies for a small community—even though this is a difficult task in a globalized world where scientific and technological progress does not stop and often fails to measure the consequences of unemployment.

Akamasoa is not a perfect community, as Peter says; it is a drop of living water which has spread among the marginalized and poverty-stricken, offering them an opportunity. "We are only a drop of water in the country but a strong one which must hurt when it lands on a politician's head!" Many residents will come out strengthened to face life with other resources and, of course, many will also scorn what they have received, but at least they will have had better food, education, housing, and healthcare. Later, they will be able to choose freely which path they decide to follow because nobody forces them to stay. Before there was only one path, that of living in houses made of cardboard or plastic, burrowing into the tunnels of the landfill sites in search of daily sustenance, or even worse, begging, prostituting themselves, and stealing.

It must be emphasized again: what is good, what is credible about Akamasoa is its openness and freedom. With regard to religion, people from different faiths are living together. Every afternoon, when it is time for prayer in the village, a peal of bells rings out from the nearby chapel. Whoever feels like it comes—mainly the children. Today we had Adoration of the Blessed Sacrament, which lasted for an hour and a quarter—after a long day of work and study, of carrying buckets of water, cleaning homes and schools, and doing homework.

Peter remained kneeling during the entire time, a true man of God, chosen to promote this project, chosen for his virtues that overshadow any shortcomings. He is full of energy, willpower, and the talent to encourage others, inviting them to become better, more honorable persons, better children of God. Leaders are necessary to promote certain projects. They can be trained but, beyond any doubt, the most successful ones are those who, like Father Peter, confront the world with total dedication to their chosen mission, with a messianic zeal, driven by love, which radiates from their whole being: their acts, their eyes, and their hearts.

SEVEN

WAKING UP IN ANDRALANITRA

Today, I wake up shaken by a nightmare. I wait patiently for dawn because, if I close my eyes, I do not know what lies in store for me in the semidarkness; my sleep, my conscience, my unconscious, the remote place where images, ideas, abstractions, fears, and desires merge into one. At dawn, I decide to get up and go out to see how this small village, which reclines on the landfill site, wakes up.

I go out into the street and down to the patio next to Peter's house. It is empty. The benches are waiting for someone to come and warm them up, while the flowers in the flowerbeds are opening to receive the multicolor gust of dawn transformed into dew. I hear a voice—it is Peter celebrating daily Mass in French at home. I do not want to interrupt, so I sit down and listen to his distinct voice echoing in the silence of the dawn. Every day, at half past five, he does the same thing, except on Sundays. Afterwards, he meditates. In the afternoon, he sets aside time for prayers. At midday, he makes a short visit to the chapel. Undoubtedly, he is a man of prayer, contemplation, and action, gaining nourishment from the Word in order to be able to confront the problems that crop up in Akamasoa every day.

I now contemplate the valley that is gradually waking up: the rice fields; the marshes that will soon become new rice fields; the stream that twists its way among the reeds and in which many wash their clothes on Saturdays; the hills beyond; the chill at sunrise; the tiny drops of dew falling on the roofs; a bird flapping its wings; the roses; the absence of any odor; Peter's voice; the sound of my own breathing.

I go out into the deserted street and start walking. I can just about make out two of the night watchmen who are disappearing into the distance in the direction of the landfill site at the top of the hill. I follow them. It is cold, and the chill penetrates my body from my bare sandaled feet upwards. I feel impelled to go back to the landfill site, though I do not know why. Now silence reigns. There are no trucks or people, and there are no flies swarming over the fresh waste from the city, dumped by the trucks from last night's round. The sight of the mountains of rubbish emitting low-lying smoke, like a ghostly fog, even seems picturesque.

The smell itself seems to be sleeping a deep sleep, without any visions or nightmares. But a gust of wind, the sunrise breeze, awakens it suddenly and brings it to my nose. It itches. It bothers me. It upsets me. I can imagine it a short time after, when the sun will be beaming down, warming the refuse, squeezing out its juices, while the "tramps" arrive one by one, thrust in their pitchforks and discover something that will end up in the wicker basket. The hands becoming dirtier and dirtier, the sweat drying on them and the people crouching, resigned to the same process day in, day out.

I retrace my steps; I no longer need visual contact with what is now engraved in my memory. I walk in the direction of the school in Andralanitra and go up to the Prince Albert High School (named in recognition of Prince Albert of Monaco, who donated the money for its construction). As I ascend, a couple of women who are descending to the landfill site cross my path. Peter cannot stop them from doing so, but at least they send their children to school. They greet me with a "Bonjour," tilting their heads. Moreover, they actually smile. What is nauseating for me is honorable for them. But what do I know about the implications of living at the lowest rung of society? I haven't the faintest idea. I have been blessed by God with a different start in life and an education. But if I were in the same situation, I think I would prefer to work in the quarry.

I go into the empty school courtyard; I take a peek at the school canteen where 2,500 children eat their ration of rice and beans every day. Next I walk through "Saint Peter's Stadium," which leads to the high school. A magnificent soccer stadium, with running tracks, stands, changing rooms, and everything that the Akamasoa team needs to make its début in the football federation's amateur championship in a few months time.

A young man is doing physical exercises in the solitude of the empty playing field, where the grass struggles against the dryness of the soil. What a contrast with the landfill site—only a few blocks away! It is half past six in the morning and the columns of smoke have already been straightened by the scorching sun, while from the top of the stands, I can see the people like small ants beginning their work—raking, rummaging, sorting, grabbing, smiling, complaining. The spectacle has something charming about it from where I stand. You have to actually be there, among the rats, fleas, and flies. It is a relief that there are no more pigs, but the dogs are there, waiting for their opportunity.

I go back to the road. What a different environment! I am now on a clean street with gutters on both sides, trees, vegetable patches, houses that are beginning to open their windows, people leaving their homes, some to get water, others going to school. Greetings. More greetings. Smiles. Open eyes. Self-respect.

I walk past the fountain and the jacaranda tree which reminds me so much of my beloved Buenos Aires. I observe the cars in front of the storehouse. The gate. The patio next to Peter's house. The empty benches. The Chinese roses. A step. Another. I go into the dining room and find Peter having breakfast with Tojo.

EIGHT

MAHATSARA

Peter is surprised to see me up at this time. He tells me he was talking to Tojo about what her life would have been like had she not been here. Perhaps she would have been sold for marriage in exchange for quite a few francs, and who knows how many children she would have had. They were also talking about how difficult it must be for a foreigner to grasp what is taking place in Akamasoa and to comprehend the full dimension of the effort involved, inolving every stone, every brick, every window, every human being, every life. I remain silent, sitting next to him. Tojo serves me coffee and leaves the room.

I tell Peter about my nightmare where a child, that could have been my own, died. I turn on the tape recorder that I always carry with me, together with my digital camera. Before we start, I ask Peter if he minds if I speak about death at sunrise. He smiles and looks me in the eye. He begins to answer the question that I hold responsible for my sleeplessness.

"When a child dies here... and hundreds have died... it's the most difficult thing to overcome. I will never get used to their deaths. But you must be strong in the face of a painful situation. You must use words that comfort the people. Child mortality is one of Madagascar's most serious problems, and Akamasoa is still part of this country. Many children die in the summer. Cholera, diarrhea...."

Peter speaks frankly. He does not need to don a mask when referring to death. "I cannot cry in front of everyone at a wake. I must be full of inner peace in order to teach them how to be brave, because I'm at the head of this project, and I must communicate strength and hope. Every time a child dies, I feel a great sense of impotence because often it is the result of the parents' lack of foresight and effort. They think they can cure the child just like that, or that it is the child's destiny to die. In this sense, they are profoundly fatalistic. We tell them they must take their child to the doctor; we stress the importance of giving them water, because many become dehydrated in the summer. Parents believe water isn't very important, but it is, even more so than food. I keep telling them this, but they still don't understand. However, when someone dies, I have to go and give my support to the family; it's my duty."

While listening to Peter, I imagine a child crying on the family's rickety old bed, the mother wrapping it up excessively and making it sweat profusely. The heat in the hut is unbearable, until the night comes and leaves it cold, hard as the marble of a gravestone.

"The funeral is a simple affair. During the wake, they carry out a rite, during which the situation is dramatized a little. Those who have lost the loved one, the family, and the people who come to give support are all there. One from each party speaks on behalf of the others. They express their feelings in a formal way. Those who go to offer their condolences give the representative an envelope with money for the family. Then the representative tells the deceased person's family: "Do not be overcome by grief." Everyone present repeats these words. The family expresses its gratitude for the words and the money, and the group of visitors goes outside so that others can come in.

"Wakes can last two or three days, although this depends on the region because in some tribes it can last much longer. The corpse is placed on a bed or on a table and wrapped in shrouds. Church hymns are sung all through the night. It is at this time that the family's popularity becomes evident. The more people come, the higher the family's status. The point is that here, to a certain extent, people live to die. They put the corpse in a coffin, a coffin that is passed on from one family to another because people are buried without it. The corpse is wrapped in different colored linen cloths. The color depends on the person's status. Also, the greater the quantity of cloth used, the more power the deceased had. I sometimes think this makes no sense because the deceased has lived his life barely able to cover himself yet, at the time of his death, he is covered by dozens of cloaks, and those who are still alive are freezing to death. But the people can't break with tradition."

While I am waiting for Miss Bao at the reception office in Andralanitra, the daily routine unfolds. People are arriving, burdened with their problems, looking for help and comfort. A seventy-seven-year-old lady arrives with her arm in a sling. Every time she moves it, it hurts. She fell on the city streets. A granddaughter, who is unable to describe her own problem in detail, accompanies her, carrying a scan in an envelope. Could it be cancer? Both of them would like to come to live in Akamasoa. Honorine receives them and calls the social worker. They refer the elderly lady to the Manantenasoa Welcome Center so they can put her arm in a splint, and they will see what they can do with her later. They advise the young girl to go to hospital because she has a serious infection and her life is at risk.

I go out and meet two bricklayers who have been working here for more than ten years. I ask them about Peter. "He is a great bricklayer," they reply. Then I tell them about the women I saw that morning, who still work on the landfill site, walking there from town, with their wicker baskets and pitchforks. "Well, they don't want to make the effort," is the brief reply I get. Effort—what a word! Some are willing to make an effort to overcome a certain situation, and others are not. Resignation and fatality push some people down into a world that follows the line of least resistance, the very opposite of "by the sweat of your forehead you will eat your bread." Fortunately, those who cling to hope and courage in order to leave behind the bottomless pit of illiteracy and deprivation outnumber those that don't.

"Fatalism and resignation go hand in hand; neither can provide solutions to problems. The poor generally believe that things cannot change, but things can and should change. I always tell the people coming here that there is no room for resignation; they must work, they must stand on their own feet and struggle. Together, we will all overcome our troubles. Many are honest and tell me they have given up in the face of so many problems: unemployment, lack of water, food, housing, and social security," Peter explains in the dining room.

We go up to the village of Mahatsara (which in Malagasy means "where it is good to be," or "a place that does you good") with Miss Bao. This town was founded by Akamasoa in 1993, and about a thousand people live there now. There is a metalworking shop, a primary school with a thousand children (from the town and its surrounding area), a dispensary, and even a church. The Swiss embassy provided generous support for the construction of the village, while the church was built with donations contributed by the Slovenian Missionary Center.

The organization's openness is noteworthy. Schools are open to the whole community, and so are the dispensaries. All the people living in the surrounding areas can send their children to school or visit a doctor here. The difference lies in the fact that Akamasoa members pay less than the others. The minimum charge helps sustain the work philosophy.

The two or three miles that separate us from Mahatsara are really beautiful. We take the highway, turn onto a secondary road, and cross a small bridge over a stream where I see scores of women washing clothes, and then we drive along a dirt track into the beautiful countryside up to the small hill where the village is situated. "The objective was to decentralize, to distribute the people in different areas," says Peter, and Miss Bao agrees. The village is a delight. I see the same two-story brick houses, but these are surrounded by more vegetation and are separated by privet hedges. It is true that they are a little farther from the highway and the buses only run every two or three hours, but the air here is different from Andralanitra.

First we visit the metal workshop, where almost forty young men are trained in the art of welding, which is how the gratings, windows, gates and legs for the school benches are manufactured. The foreman greets us, while a young man, wearing a protective mask, places the welding torch on the metal, causing a fountain of red sparks to shoot up. After stopping at the sign that bears the village's name, we visit the school with Miss Bao, surrounded by smiling children.

⌘

As we are about to visit the village church, which, like all the others, has a huge block of stone as an altar, a lady invites us into her home. In the large ground floor room, which is spotlessly clean, there is a bed with someone in it. Her name is Charline, though she introduces herself as Maria Estella. She is twenty-four years old but is less than four feet tall. She is the size of a six-year-old child and has been bedridden since she was born. She does not seem to have any legs and her arms are deformed: the right one is almost crippled, and the left one has a disproportionately large hand. She has light-colored skin, her hair is short, curly and black, and she has a twisted mouth. We greet each other. I look at her; she looks at me; she lowers her gaze. What can I say when faced with such a case? Bedridden forever, unable to do anything, to walk, run, jump, or relieve herself.

No, I am not going to cry. It is as if Peter were by my side, repeating his instructions. Encourage her, give her hope, boost her spirits. Raise the spirits of a soul that lives like this. However, she is charming when we hold a brief conversation in French. I summon up the courage to ask her if she can read. "Oui," she quickly responds. I ask her what she would like to read, and Maria Estella, as if she had been waiting for me, recites her wish list, while Miss Bao takes down what she says on a piece of paper. She mentions only four books, so I tell her she can ask for some more. It will be a pleasure to buy them for her, and I will send them to her somehow, or maybe I will bring them to her myself, if I can recover and be able to put myself in her shoes again.

Maria Estella continues with her list and Miss Bao writes down what she says. My eyes fill with tears and my nose starts itching; this time it is not because of the smells but due to feelings of the heart and soul for those of us who believe in something higher than ourselves. This situation and so many others I encounter every day in Akamasoa definitely go beyond what I can take—situations which, in my comfortable house in Buenos Aires, I could never have imagined and do not even want to think of. I am human, and humans tend to protect themselves from other people's suffering, though what we should do is go in search of our neighbor. That is why I get closer to her now, I touch her hands, kiss her forehead, stroke her hair which seems like barbed wire, because her suffering hurts me but tears will be of no use to her. Instead, I promise that I will return with her books.

※

On the way back, Miss Bao is as shaken as I am. We do not say much, but I study her now as she drives the car. This young woman, about thirty-five years old, the head of the organization, Peter's right hand, a certified accountant, is from the Betsileo tribe, with slanted eyes and a pensive expression. She is very short, very Asian-looking, with long hair worn in a bun. She met Peter more than fifteen years ago when her sister, Marie Bernadette, who is a nun belonging to the congregation of Saint Vincent de Paul, introduced him to her. She has followed him since then, managing the Akamasoa finances, yet this bureaucratic activity has in no way diminished her warm humanity. On the contrary: she lives in a house with nine young girls who were all abandoned to their own fate, and she has consecrated her material and spiritual life to this project. She is an exemplary laywoman, who does not need vows to offer up her life to the service of others.

"Mahatsara's principal problem is lack of water," she tells me. There is only one large cistern for gathering rainwater, so when the rainy season is over the people have to be resourceful and fill it up some other way. Peter later tells me: "The government has been promising that water will reach that place for years. However, nothing has been done. The state does not move a finger. Let's hope things will change with this government. If we build a large cistern in the highest part of Manantenasoa, we will be able to pump it to where it is needed."

PART THREE

ONE

FINDING PEACE

Dear reader, forgive me if I change my tone, but my encounter with Maria Estella has caused an inner revulsion and has temporarily influenced my style. Today is a Friday during Lent, and there were Stations of the Cross on the hill. Tomorrow is Saturday, but there is no point in my keeping track of the days, hours, minutes, and seconds.

At times, I do not know what I am doing here. Do I belong to this world? Is the world only one, or are there hundreds of dissimilar worlds only interconnected by trade, tourism, and a cyber-network? Tonight there is no water because it has been cut off. Not even a trickle of water comes out of the bathroom tap or from the nearby fountain. I am dirty, tired, and upset. I miss my family and my own world where comfort is something taken for granted, even though life in Akamasoa is of a much higher standard than in other parts of this country, higher than in the shanty towns that surround large cities, and higher than in the remote hamlets of the scrublands, mountains and jungles of Argentina.

Do you know this world? I am not an expert either, but sit by my side and let us contemplate together these bare feet: those of the grandmother with the broken arm, shriveled up like a raisin; the agile ones of the young man doing his morning exercises in the sports field; the smelly, dirty ones that walk on the rubbish; the tiny ones that hop around on the stones without getting hurt; or those of Maria Estella, which I did not see but can only imagine.

Walk every day on Mother Earth, which belongs to all of us. Perhaps these people know it much better than we do because it sticks to their toenails, their cracked soles and heels, weathered by the passing of time, whereas I wear leather sandals, double-soled, comfortable, aerodynamic, and soft and steady at the same time.

Which world are we talking about? None other than this one, where women walk barefoot and carry a child on their backs or balance a bucket of water on their heads. In this place today, they walk with their heads held high, whereas in the past they lacked any sense of dignity; indeed, like animals they fought over scraps of food. But someone took pity on them, gave them the opportunity to change, and encouraged them to join a project and begin to work with more dignity—a project that does not offer alms but a will to get ahead through effort and work. That someone is a leader that at times I can grasp and at other times is beyond me, because I cannot comprehend him. Particularly today, with no water and my bowels dry through having eaten so many beans, bananas, and rice, watching an enormous cockroach making its way under cover of darkness on this red cement floor, while the silent and empty fridge looks at me with indifference.

Peter is an innovative, charismatic leader, the kind described by progressive management specialists but with a great difference: He is motivated by a missionary spirit, ready to give up his whole life for others. In a half-globalized world, whose most developed nations shun any commitment or risk and are desperately looking for all kinds of security, there are fewer and fewer individuals willing to keep the torch of idealism and hope alive.

In Father Opeka's opinion, a fair amount of risk is a vital component of any mission. "This doesn't mean we must leap into space, because that would imply that we don't know what we want to achieve; it's more a matter of commitment in following Christ's example. A mission demands faithfulness, trust, courage, and bravery, but it also requires tenderness—because courage without tenderness doesn't get us anywhere."

I can see him now, talking with a bricklayer's simplicity but also with the wisdom of a person that has chosen to offer up his life for others, while temptations stalk me in the dark. To get out of here, hop on a plane, return home, eat with salt and pepper, cuddle up in bed, or say good-bye to my children when they leave for university. But a literary mission also exists, or at least that is what I have believed for some time. So I think I should stay and continue telling you about my experiences, relating Peter's words to you, so that we may rise to the challenge of imitating Christ on the narrow path as we discover God in our neighbor, seeing in what way our neighbor resembles God.

⁎

I get up this morning in a bad mood. I go to the bathroom and turn on the faucet. Nothing, only the echo of a void, the sound which is so characteristic of pipes that have dried out, like a seashell which, instead of reverberating like the sea, sounds like the desert. An inner voice snaps inside and weakens me. I can hear it coming from my conscience. If the water does not come back today, you must leave. You do not belong in this world. You cannot even brush your teeth. At least I have the bottle of mineral water on the little table in the bedroom. Yes, but you cannot wash; your body will start itching, you will scratch your head, the deodorant will be ineffective against the sweat in your armpits, and you will smell awful, like garbage. I continue my internal struggle. I will climb the hill with a bucket, and I will return with the precious liquid, even if I have to cover two, three, or four miles; if there are people who can do that here, why can't I do it? You are not like them. You do not belong here.

I change my clothes and go to the chapel; I want to pray. I need new things to emerge. Peter told me that peace is to be found in prayer. "When you enter a church or a chapel, you shouldn't leave until you feel at peace," he said. I go in and sit on the mat in front of the statue of Mary. Silence. Silence. I close my eyes. I see Peter kneeling down, motionless, for an hour or even more. I cannot do it. No, I cannot! I remain seated, but I begin to calm down.

The water. The people... here, people really do try hard. In Argentina, instead of helping the poor, politicians drive them down even further. They do not give them dignity; they enslave them. Every social program should be based on work, except in extreme cases. Work dignifies. Any social welfare project without a program for social inclusion ends up marginalizing people even further. Welfare beneficiaries are not the ones to blame. They are not aware of how harmful welfare is for them.

Silence. I am calming down. I pray. No more thinking. Prayer. No more words. A rosary. Peter is right, you come here to find peace, and I am beginning to feel it, on my palm like a breeze; in my chest, like a balm; in my soul, as joy.

When I go back outside, across the patio, and up to my house, I receive the good news: the water has returned! People crowd around the fountain, lining up with their buckets. Tojo's father is the one who collects the small fees that help Akamasoa pay for this vital service. They tell me the water supply was cut off to the whole region;

it happens now and then. I am happy; I go into the house, wash my face and hands, but I do not take a bath; it is no longer important, I am now on another wavelength following prayer.

I walk through the town. I stroll past the basketball court and the restaurant for tourists (although not many have come during these last few days). Up a flight of stairs, I reach the town's own bank. Tojo or Viviane run it on Saturdays, and it is meant for people to deposit their money so as not to keep it at home. They do so for two reasons: first, there is always the temptation to spend it on unnecessary things and remain penniless for the rest of the month and, second, even if it does not occur very often, there is always the danger of someone breaking in and stealing the money. Therefore, even though it is only two years since this idea was realized, three hundred people from this village already deposit their savings here. They can withdraw them whenever they wish. Peter is trying to teach the people the discipline of saving and of organizing their monthly expenses.

We go out onto the small terrace with Viviane. We talk, while watching the landfill site from above and the people rummaging through it. She tells me she lived in the cardboard hovels next to the waste area. Sometimes she and the others only ate what they found there. I ask her how they dared to eat dirty and smelly meat. She answered: "We would wash it, and then cook it." As simple as that!

Upon returning home, I meet Peter. He tells me that someone has died in Mahatsara and he must offer the prayer for the dead. I ask him if I can join him. "Of course, let's go." When we are already on our way, I tell him about my state of mind during the morning and how it changed after praying. It makes him happy. "You must realize that you are in another world; it's the only way for you to understand what goes on here." Afterwards, regarding my inner struggle, he quotes the French writer Arthur Rimbaud: "The spiritual battle is as brutal as any battle among men. O dark night! My face reeks with blood!" To give it a more general and personal meaning, he then adds: "Being Christian doesn't mean that we don't have problems, doubts, and temptations, or that the spiritual battle is easy. It's very hard, and we must continuously fight the evil that wants to drain our strength away, deflate us, and harm us so we stop struggling in the interests of justice and truth."

When we arrive at the village, a group of people is waiting for Peter. After they exchange greetings, we walk together to the deceased man's home. We go onto the patio, where someone has prepared the humble coffin made of wood. Peter steps into the house; I prefer to remain outside as a sign of respect, but I can see everything through the window they have left open to allow air to come into the room.

The man, who was seventy-seven years old, the father of one of the schoolteachers, had come for a visit and suffered a sudden heart attack. He is lying on the bed, covered by a white cloth that has been pinned to the wall like a veil. On the chair, next to the bed, there is a vase and a burning candle. Peter recites the prayer for the deceased in Malagasy, says some words to the family, and then they all pray together the Our Father, Hail Mary, and Glory Be (by now, I am able to recognize the prayers after hearing them so many times in the chapel). Somebody hands Peter a glass of water and a sprig for the blessing. Peter dips the sprig into the water and sprinkles the corpse of the deceased and all those present. They end by singing a song. How simple!

It is midday, with the sun at its zenith, its light bathing the room and the face that I can distinguish through the veil. It looks like it was made of wax, with the eyes and mouth shut. The man's hands are on his chest, as they would be anywhere else in the world—a world that seems united in death, regardless of whether the departed is rich, poor, or middle class. The deceased man's son thanks Peter for his presence, and Peter replies with a few words of encouragement. The ceremony is over. Afterwards, Peter tells me that all the neighbors held the wake last night and that today one of the sons who was missing will arrive. Tomorrow, they will take the deceased man in the coffin to his region of origin and he will be buried, but his memory will live on according to the cult of ancestor worship.

❦

During lunchtime, I ask Peter: "Why does God reveal himself more easily to the humble?" Peter answers, "Because they have nothing; their hearts are more open to receive whatever crosses their path. He who has much is busy keeping hold of what he has and replacing what he consumes. He searches for security and closes his heart, so he cannot listen to God. The truth is simple; for this reason, Christ talked with simplicity. If a great intellect was needed to comprehend it, God would have failed in the way he communicated with man, and this would have been unjust. Great things are very simple. That is why Christ said: 'I praise you, Father, Lord of heaven and earth, because you have hidden these things from the wise and learned, and revealed them to little children.'"

I pluck up the courage to ask who Christ is for him. "Who is Christ for me? The humblest man on earth, a man who was close to his friends, someone who forgives me seventy-seven times, someone who is full of love, compassion, and mercy, someone who raises me above all evil, filling me with joy and peace. He is the one who is always walking around the villages, knocking on our doors, and never tiring of doing so. He gives us the strength and the courage not to be afraid of anything or anybody. He is not afraid of being considered ridiculous or of dying on the cross for me and for you. He is the one who gave us the Holy Spirit and sent us out all over the world. He makes us live for God's kingdom."

TWO

PLAYING SOCCER

The afternoon is reserved for playing soccer. I go up to Manantenasoa with Marcial. The red earth field is on the top of a hill in the Bemasoandro neighborhood. The match is played in the sun, with the slope descending towards the beautiful valley. Beyond, one of the lakes can be seen, and behind it, the capital. Marcial and I agree that the two best players on the red team are numbers six (a centerfield) and seven (the right forward). The ball climbs high into the air, reminding me that we are at about 4,200 feet in altitude.

The boys play very fast, passing the ball without looking. The ball seems to move without any direction or purpose. Marcial agrees that neither team is very good. On our side, the raised ground serves as a grandstand, where the spectators laugh, chat, and, once in a while, shout, but without raising their voices much. It is amazing: the players do not complain about the opponents or about the referee. Moreover, there are no dirty fouls—very different from the Argentinean style of playing I'm accustomed to.

The children on the stand observe me because I am a vazaha, a foreigner. Since they know I am with Father Peter, I'm fortunate enough to be called vahiny, which means guest. A girl walks in my direction carrying her little brother in her arms. The baby looks at me in fright and starts crying. When I try to touch him, he screams as if I were from another planet. It makes sense: he does not know many white people, and what is different often inspires fear. When the girl walks away, the baby calms down, and I ask myself if the same thing would happen in my country with a dark-skinned man.

Sitting on the red, parched soil, I follow the game attentively. Clearly, they are not playing well, but how they run! Soccer is good for all young people, whichever world they belong to. It does not matter how they play, because the important thing is to compete, have fun, and make friends.

After a while, the organizer of this tournament, in which twenty-two teams of young people from Akamasoa are taking part, walks towards us. I give him my opinion of the game and he answers intelligently: "We are concentrating on teaching the younger ones; it's difficult to change the game with these lads now." And he is absolutely right—it is important to learn as children whatever it is we want them to learn. Peter knows that well, which is why he believes that the new generation of more than 8,000 children attending the Akamasoa schools, regardless of the example their parents may have given them, will have better opportunities in life. Nevertheless, Peter still emphasizes that family example is vital. Schools, however, fulfill an important role: when these children finish school, not only will they have learned to read and add and subtract, they hopefully will take with them the values instilled in them by Akamasoa. These include responsibility, discipline, and work, which will be useful for them when the time comes to think about the future.

The game ends with the Reds beating the Blues three goals to one. I approach number five of the Yellow team, which is about to play against a White team. I can't resist giving him a few instructions. I tell him they should play more slowly, stop the ball, raise their heads, and look for a fellow team member who is free to receive the ball. The youngest player thanks me, saying he has understood, although when he passes on my advice to the other team members, it seems as if what he really is saying is more like: "Who does this fat so-and-so think he is—Maradona?"

The new match begins, and the same mistakes are repeated. The only players that stand out are number five from the Yellow team and number fourteen on the White team. The latter skillfully volleys the ball, missing the goal by a narrow margin. Ten minutes later, the head of one of the quarries comes over to greet us. His name is Guy, and I met him during one of the press conferences. I try to make my point about the ball again. He answers: "You're right, but we sponsor this sport primarily so they have good clean fun, and it keeps them out of mischief." He laughs, and I swallow the simple answer that sends me off the field, as if the referee had expelled me for not seeing the forest for the trees. It's just that I see everything through different eyes; I can't seem to stop making mistakes. They have other kinds of problems: alcohol, prostitution, drugs, and gambling. Anyway, Guy tells me that they are forming a team made up of the best players from the twenty-two teams, and they are going to register it in the Federation of Amateur Clubs.

Peter has certainly found this game useful, not only as a source of fun but also as a subject of conversation with other people and as a means of making friends. That is what happened in Paris, with Gilbert Mitterrand who would later help Peter when Akamasoa was being set up; and in the south of Madagascar, where it enabled him to overcome cultural barriers and learn the first words of the Malagasy language. It is the same today—every time he gets together with the children in the stadium, his spiritual parenthood shines in a warm embrace of celebration or consolation.

When the first half is over, we return to Andralanitra. At prayer time, we pray a Rosary. A candle is lit in front of the statue of the Virgin Mary. Peter prays on his knees, as he did before the Blessed Sacrament the other day. Praying the entire rosary on his knees— what courage and what an example! He continues to inspire awe and respect.

I spend the time sitting on the mat, caressing a two-year-old black girl's hand. She does not mind affection. Her hand is dirty with dust, but that is not a barrier. Do dirty or clean hands have any particular significance? Pontius Pilate washed his hands and look what happened. Every now and then I stop caressing her hand so that she does not feel obliged to hold out her hand, waiting to see if she wants me to keep doing so. She leaves her little hand extended on my palm, as if giving her consent. There is no need for words to understand her feelings. I feel her warmth and her need for affection. There are no frontiers when affection prevails in a relationship; neither race nor class matter. Bridges of dialogue and love must be built, like the one Peter erected between the landfill site and this village.

⁕

Akamasoa is not only a humanitarian organization that helps the marginalized and the outcast; it is a mighty bridge connecting misery and dignity. A bridge leading to the hope of being able to raise one's head and contemplate life's marvels, like the stars I can now see through the window.

THREE

MY FIRST SUNDAY MASS

I get up early, thanks to the people who come to the fountain for water and act as an alarm clock, but I am quite rested. Today is Sunday, the day of the sun and of God. It will be the first time I attend a Sunday Mass at Akamasoa. I take a shower and go upstairs to get dressed, when I hear Peter's voice calling me: "Hurry up and come down—we're walking to Manantenasoa." As usual, he is surrounded by children. I explain that I have not had breakfast yet, and he replies: "Okay, we'll wait for you." I run to the kitchen, dressed in my Sunday clothes, the best I have brought with me. The village people too are all well-groomed, wearing clean clothes and even shoes. Olga serves me some coffee; I add condensed milk, eat some bread with marmalade, and off we go.

We climb the hill. We go on foot up to Manantenasoa, along the road which forks right after crossing the highway. It is supposed to be less than two miles, but it is an effort for me, not so much because of the altitude but rather due to my excess weight and smoking. Peter climbs it as if he were twenty years old. The weather is mild, and there is not a cloud in the sky. It is a quarter past eight in the morning, and Mass will begin at nine. However, when we arrive at Manantenasoa, the sports hall that serves as the church is already quite full. According to what Peter tells me, it can hold between six and seven thousand people.

Peter greets everyone he meets on his way to the vestry. I stay behind with Tojo and Viviane, my two young friends, with whom I can practice my French without feeling self-conscious. Tojo has lived in Akamasoa for thirteen years, and Viviane, eleven. Tojo had lived very near the dump in a tiny house, while Viviane lived next to the landfill site, in a house made of cardboard boxes. Both girls finished their studies in the Akamasoa schools. Today, they are teachers and they also teach the children catechism. Tojo, besides speaking French and Malagasy, can say a few words in Spanish and dreams of traveling to Argentina some day (she has been corresponding with one of Peter's nieces for years); Viviane also gets by quite well in English. They are the living example of what a project of this nature can do for young people. Despite a past spent in abject poverty, with adequate tools, their talents have come to light and it is possible to imagine a future lived in dignity and with better opportunities. For Tojo, Peter represents "love and faith," and Viviane states simply: "Thanks to him, we have been able to get out of the situation we earlier had been in."

The sports hall slowly becomes crowded. Elderly people stand on the right; there is a young group wearing soccer T-shirts (they will bring the offertory gifts to the altar today); at the back, entire families; around the corner, young school girls mingle with more families; on the ground, children on mats sit on by themselves or with their mothers; behind the altar are the choir and scores of tourists who have come to take part in the celebration; in front, the band and those who will lead the Mass are standing. It smells like Africa, and the tangible joy reflects this continent as well. So many different colors! There must be about 5,000 people. The crowd conveys happiness and hope, which are contagious as I sit elbow-to-elbow with Tojo and Viviane in the middle of one of the stands.

This is a great feast, like Peter said it would be while we were climbing the hill; he compared it to a soccer stadium. It's a great, multicolor feast

167

that begins with songs accompanied by an accordion, a mandolin, and drums. Peter makes his entrance from the back of the hall, preceded by about twenty altar boys dressed in white tunics and purple cloaks matching the color of Peter's stole. The people begin clapping to the rhythm.

Today, the Gospel reading is the parable of the prodigal son. An enormous image of Jesus of the Divine Mercy has been placed next to the altar. I look at those red and white rays coming from his heart —blood and water pouring from his side, pierced by the spear on Calvary. Peter goes up to the altar, a handful of foreigners take photographs, and the people show him their affection by singing louder —all in an atmosphere of order and respect worthy of admiration.

I imagine that Peter, at the altar, must feel like he is in heaven, since it is his favorite place next to the streets of the villages where he is in touch with the humble and the needy. There is the priest, the consecrated, and the missionary, but also the bricklayer, the builder, the soccer player, the top scorer, and the man. Peter raises his hands to give the initial blessing. His hands are large, open, white, firm, and sincere. Hands shaped by the hard work of construction: carrying buckets, stirring cement, handling the stripping knife, holding the square, or laying rows of bricks. Hands weathered by the sun, the cold and rain, while he put up the walls of his house in Ramos Mejía, in Junín de los Andes, in San Miguel, in Vangaindrano, or here in Manantenasoa. Callused hands that have been softened by the sweetness of absolution, the tenderness of a caress, the strength of a hug, the firmness of a handshake, and the gentleness of forgiveness.

Peter raises his hands and I cannot stop looking at them, while he says in Malagasy: "In the name of the Father, the Son, and the Holy Spirit," to which we all reply, "Amen." That amen, that "so be it," knows no borders and allows us to penetrate the mystery of Catholicism, the universality of the Church.

What can I say about this Mass, which respects the liturgy but at the same time reflects this special culture? It is not enough to describe the different moments with words. The silences, which seem the same as those in other places of worship, sound different, as if the soft voice of poverty has turned into a breath of hope. In this place, prayer is the murmuring of the voices of the poor who are becoming richer. The voices transform themselves into a prayer of thanksgiving for having recovered their dignity. The songs gradually transform past marginality into a torrent of inclusion, which becomes harmonious. No, words are not enough. You have to live, feel, and immerse yourself in this Mass among the thousands of people who enjoy it as a celebration of their encounter with God and their brothers.

When Peter finishes reading the Gospel, he descends from the altar, carrying the book in his raised hands, as if it were the tablets of the law. He walks down the sports hall, to the rhythm of the drums, the mandolin, the accordion, the songs, and the clapping of hands. He laughs with joy, swinging his body slowly, raising the Bible in his hands, extolling the Good News the Lord came to bring to the simple of heart, to whoever wants to drink living water, know Christ's truth, and give meaning to his or her life.

When he returns to the altar, Peter says the homily in Malagasy, but he does not forget about us foreigners and adds something in French. The words he uses may be in two different languages, but both are based on God's mercy. He speaks to the people of Akamasoa about forgiveness and the love of the Father. He asks them: "Which of the two brothers do we resemble?" Then he goes on to say: "We must also be merciful with those that suffer, with the lonely, the outcast, and the excluded. Let's remember where we came from." To us, on the other hand, he talks about the "new man" that St. Paul mentions in his epistle. "We are all called to be ambassadors of God and his kingdom, which is the kingdom of the Father who embraces his sinful children."

After the young men in soccer T-shirts have presented the offertory gifts at the altar and before the consecration, it is time for the collection. Two chairs are placed in front of the altar, each with a basket on top. People who are waiting to leave their contribution form two lines along the center. I join them, descending from the stand towards the center. It is incredible to see so many children, mothers, fathers, and elderly people—so many who have so little, transforming that small amount into something much greater because they are sharing what has been hard to earn. That spirit of solidarity leaves me speechless once again. This may not be paradise, but it could be a preview of what a more just and generous world could look like, a world made visible during this Mass that lasts two and a half hours.

Peter continues with the consecration, the white host larger than usual, so that everyone can catch a glimpse of it from every corner of the sports hall. He invites us to pray the Lord's Prayer together. We raise our hands and sing the Our Father. Then we go forward to receive Communion. I smile at the people, stroke the children's hands or heads, let an elderly lady go ahead, or step ahead because someone else has given up his place to me. Peter is there in front, in the midst of the crowd, distributing the Eucharist. When I stand in front of him, he says in Spanish: "El Cuerpo de Cristo" (the Body of Christ). "Amen," I reply.

"Love one another as I have loved you," said Jesus to his disciples. How difficult this is! So many wars and conflicts, so much injustice, so many people left aside, marginalized, excluded—whether in the developed world, in developing countries, and, of course, in this world of underdevelopment where unbelievable things like this celebration can take place.

After Holy Communion, the choir behind the altar sings for us, followed by a song prepared by a family in the congregation, and we finish with some folk songs, sung in tune by everyone. Next a group of elderly women, dressed in their best clothes, walk towards the center of the sports hall where they perform some traditional dances. When they move their hands, they are like birds in the air, their shawls hanging down like wings. The steps are slow, rhythmic, and very oriental. One of them dressed in blue passes close by me as I sit on the ground with the children—her wrinkled skin, her gaze lost in the brightness of the music, her hands clinging to the air like the branches of a tree, and her feet like naked roots kissing the earth.

❦

Peter ends the Mass with the final blessing and then tells everybody about Carole, Gregoire, and me. He tells them in French that I have come from Argentina, his homeland, to write a book on Akamasoa. Then he says a prayer in Spanish, which is meant for me: "May the Lord bless your hands and give you the strength of spirit to write it." It is too much, at least for me; I do not know where to look because tears sting my eyes. Just being here, in the midst of so many people that are watching me, while Peter adds in French pointing at me, "He is here, sitting in the middle of our town," and the people applauding—I am still on the verge of tears that cannot be stopped because they are tears of joy, not sorrow.

FOUR

PROVIDENCE

In the morning we go to the center of Antananarivo with Jean-Jacques and Marcial. I asked them to take me to a bookstore in order to fulfill Maria Estella's wish. The traffic is heavy as usual, despite the fact that trucks are not allowed to enter the capital at this time. Everything seems slightly cleaner than on the day of my arrival, perhaps because habit has changed the way I looked at things. Jean-Jacques suggests going to the Saint Paul bookstore on Independence Avenue. There is nothing special about the capital, except for its charming location, spread out over the hills, and some architectural vestiges of the colonial period.

As soon as we get out of the car, we are assailed by a swarm of peddlers selling cigarettes, handicrafts, CDs, shoes, dresses, etc. Itinerant commercial activity is the major symbol of underdevelopment all over the world. The best way to avoid these vendors is not to catch their eye and to continue on your way; if you stop, there is no getting away and you will be forced to buy something from them. Next we are confronted by beggars, a completely different group of people. Our conscience troubles us and we do not know whether to give them something or whether to doubt their need.

At lunch, Father Rok tells me that he suffers from migraines and

I notice that Miss Bao is eating only vegetables because the doctor told her she has to take care of her stomach. Peter talks about local politics while flicking through the daily newspapers (which are always delivered at lunchtime). The civil servants of the old régime are continuing to conspire against the new government. A short time ago, Peter was approached by another newspaper in the hope that he would criticize the current administration, but he sent them away as rapidly as we had dealt with the peddlers.

Afterwards, he listens to his assistant's update. Miss Pierrette tells him that they are running out of rice for the schools, and they do not know when the new shipment with food aid from the European Union will arrive. The following day they will load the trucks with food for the victims in the northern part of the country, and Teresa will deliver it. They must decide how the sale of the newly arrived bicycles should proceed. They go through this procedure every day because things are dynamic and always changing in Akamasoa like in any other village or town.

After a refreshing nap, recommended by Peter because I was feeling rather dizzy (perhaps due to the altitude), I walk over to his house. He invites me into his small study. I turn on the tape recorder and ask him if we could talk about Providence.

<hr />

"You cannot describe Providence; you simply live it and believe in it. It is something we do not think about or even expect, but as we have faith and believe that things will work out, it appears. God knows when we are in need of it. We cannot demand it as a right. He knows what we need before we ask for anything. Man cannot give orders to God or ring a bell for him to come to his rescue whenever a trivial problem arises. Help arrives because we trust in him. Christ said that if we had faith, even the size of a mustard seed, we would be able to move mountains.

"What we did here was to have faith, to trust in God and in the poor. And God, who understands us, has been at our side. I will never ask him to do such and such a thing, because I know he is present here in everything we do. It is difficult to put into words, but you can feel it and see it in a very concrete way. Every time we have been in trouble, an envelope with a check, completely unexpected, has arrived from people we sometimes didn't even know. That is Providence. Maybe I wasn't even asking God for a hand, or asking him where he was or why he wasn't helping us. In other words, we continue working while putting all our trust in God, leaving everything in his hands, without begging him for what we need in our daily lives. That is how Providence works—we must live as if everything depends on us but know that everything depends on God."

Peter pauses and offers me some tea. I meditate on his last words, which remind me of Saint Ignatius of Loyola. "Akamasoa is the result of the work of Providence. First, through all the people who surround me, without whose help the project could never have become a success. I did not find these people by chance; it was God who sent them to me. Many of them are professionals who could be working somewhere else, yet they choose to be here. That is the work of Providence. Second, I think about the way God has made this project known abroad, above all in Europe, either by word of mouth, books, documentaries, or interviews. I have never asked a writer or a journalist to come here; it was always they who wanted to come. That is why I say they are God-sent. They come here and they leave, happy to have been able to see this project for themselves. Like the famous French television journalist [Patrick Poivre d'Arvor who conducts the eight o'clock news on TF1], who was here for about a month and wrote several articles.

"Third, the financial aid we have received all these years has also been the work of Providence. When we were suffering food shortages, the European Union appeared and offered its aid. On so many occasions, we were short of money to continue with the construction work, and Manos Unidas of Spain (which has helped us right from the start) gave us a hand or anonymous donations turned up. Once, a man donated a check for $155,000, telling me: 'Use it for whatever you think fit,' and we built the church and funded many other projects with that money. This man's case was special, because at first his check was for $55,000, and then he changed his mind and wrote a new one, adding a "1" at the front. That is Providence."

Peter pauses to drink some tea. I think about the important people that have visited this place: Danielle Mitterrand, Albert of Monaco, and Captain Jacques Cousteau himself, who came to visit in 1995 and said: "You are the man I have always wanted to find," and Abbé Pierre (founder of the Emmaus Community) aged ninety, who came in 2001 and did the Way of the Cross with Peter on Good Friday.

"People are continually blocking the work of Providence. If this wasn't the case, the world would be more honest, fair, and fraternal. The world is in its present predicament because man is not interested in Providence and does not allow it to work. If you do not allow for its intervention, it is difficult for it to work. There are no given recipes, but there are roads that are only opened and paved by the power of God. In my opinion, the key is to work on a daily basis as if everything depended on us, to the best of our ability, with the knowledge that when something is missing, God will provide. It is not a commercial transaction, although many people think of it that way. They say to God: 'If you give me this, I will give you that.' The work of Providence is revealed in God's own good time; this means that we must carry on in the knowledge that Providence will appear at some point. It is not like plunging into an abyss in the certainty that God will help because that would be putting him to the test."

I watch him while he speaks, stroking his beard with his right hand. I think that the founder of a project like Akamasoa must have complete trust in Providence. I remember Mother Teresa and how she began her work in Calcutta. She never imagined what God had in store for her or that her work would spread all over the world.

"You can't simply leap into the abyss because Christ didn't do this either. You shouldn't tempt God as the devil did in the desert. You only have to believe in him. However, the fact that we believe in God doesn't mean that he has to solve all our problems. My faith at this moment implies putting all my trust in God, believing he is the one who guides history. God calls many people, but only a few respond, and those few must convey hope and transmit their absolute certainty that God is the maker of history, despite everything that man does and the evil he generates."

The phone rings, but Peter does not answer; he wants to finish sharing some ideas. "A missionary's life involves placing his trust in Providence. When you leave everything behind—family, friends, possessions, and even your own culture—to work as a missionary in a completely different world, you are diving into water (not leaping into an abyss where you have no idea what you want or where you are going to end up), and all you have to do is swim.

"It took an enormous effort for me to adapt to missionary work.

The important thing was not to bring theories or great amounts of knowledge, but rather to come as a brother bringing a message of love, and to make it clear that I am not the exclusive owner of this message, even though it might seem like it is mine. I am simply the one who brought it in God's name. It was very difficult to learn Malagasy, starting from scratch like a child. It was also difficult to leave my study of philosophy and theology and exchange them for a different kind of progress, creating connections between one heart and another, between one human being and another. To some people, this wouldn't be a big deal, but it means a lot to me. The problem is that in the eyes of the world, only wealth is considered valuable and only that which empowers is considered to be great.

"From a certain perspective, you could say I haven't made any progress by coming here, but I didn't come here to acquire more knowledge or to obtain more wisdom; I came to bring a message which has brought meaning to my life. I came to tell people that they are loved by God, that they are children of God, and that they have as much dignity as everyone else. Telling them this is what gives meaning to my life—saying this without a weapon or a shield, even to the point of being helpless, because I was helpless in the face of the heat, the rains, and the insects. I came to Madagascar eager to live something special with the people, in a forgotten place in the middle of the jungle, and I was helpless in the face of everything.

"My fellow missionaries and I could be considered crazy because the climate in the south is so extreme that it really affects your body and we had been warned about the risks. But our faith, our enthusiasm, our trust in God, and our will to make it work were much stronger than all the dangers. When you are young and you commit yourself fully to a mission, you are perfectly aware of what is at stake."

It is difficult for me to interrupt Peter to ask a question, because when he talks about missionary work, he is completely transformed; he seems possessed by his motivation and devotion to others. "I couldn't have set up Akamasoa if I hadn't lived those fifteen years in the south end of the island. This project only appeared at a later stage—not when I wished it to appear but when God thought fit. I didn't want to take charge of the seminary here in Antananarivo; I wanted to take a sabbatical year in one of our congregation's homes in order to improve my English. I felt strong when I first arrived in Madagascar, but it wasn't when I felt strong that Providence drove me to do something important. On the contrary, it was when I was weak and ill.

"I set up Akamasoa when God knew the time was right, after fifteen years of 'novitiate' in the south, learning the language, the customs and the culture of this nation. It didn't happen when I wanted it to, because I didn't have any money or means, but it was Providence that drove me to take action. Later, the climate here in the capital enabled me to recover my strength and sleep well at night—down south it was impossible to get a good night's sleep due to the heat. Also, the time I spent in Madagascar moderated my impulses, although it is good to be impulsive at times because it stirs you to do things."

Peter looks at his watch; he has to do something outside. His world is not one of words, although when he speaks to me, he gets so enthusiastic I find it difficult to stop him. We get into the pickup and continue our conversation on the way to the next place he is needed to solve problems, give instructions, or simply listen to the people.

"Human beings must discover their mission in life. This is not an easy task. It isn't automatic; it depends on people's upbringing and the environment they grew up in. Our mission is like a plot of land:

very few things can be sown in arid soil, but if you fertilize and improve it, many things can be accomplished. That's why you must try to improve the place you live in. Those who have a clear mission, as in my case, can find it difficult to accept. Sometimes we rebel against our own mission because we don't want to abandon certain things. I had to give up many things to come here. You also have to struggle and work to allow your mission and vocation to develop. You have to water your call continuously as if it were a small plant. I don't have any formulas on how to do it; for me, more than anything else, it means observing people's lives, finding God in my neighbor, and discovering how God acts, in what way he is present. But you must also try to see him in the world. I put a lot of energy into trying to find God in today's world.

"For example, we can find God in our neighbor through soccer. I believe that God is present in the players, even though they may not realize that they are instruments of God. It's a pity, because if they were aware of this, they could do so much for their own good and for the good of their fans by setting an example. Every person has something of God that can be discovered. When I was in France, I let my hair and my beard grow and I went to different parts of that country and the world, seeking to learn about people and discover how God was present in them. I slept on the streets with the people or wherever they invited me without any fear; I lived with the strength that Christ and his Gospel gave me. I went everywhere alone; I was a great adventurer, but my strength came from Christ because I was convinced of the power of his Word and I believed that his kingdom was real."

Peter speaks with so much charisma and spontaneity, moving his hands as if even the air were listening to him, that you are left without any questions. "The motivating force is Christ's courage, his bravery in the face of difficulties, and also his love. He was both courageous and loving, and we too should have both qualities. Courage means believing in the other person, and if that person sees that you respect them, love is possible. Courage without tenderness is dangerous. I always say one must have one's feet on the ground and one's heart in heaven.

"One of the passages in the Gospel which most inspires me is when Christ calls his disciples and they leave everything to follow him. Moreover, watching Christ speak the truth without feeling afraid—living without fear and traveling around—has always filled me with courage. We must offer everything up to Christ, not just a part of our lives. This is why I am very happy when I see seminarians that are fully devoted. Christ is everything. Let everything you do today be for Christ's sake, to transmit his message, and to enlarge his kingdom.

"Society has a tendency to turn everything into recreation, but the purpose of life is not only to have fun. Having a good time is fine, but if everything in your life is amusement, you are absent and you cannot discover your mission. Fun taken to an extreme makes you lose consciousness; you forget about your mission and you lose your inner peace, joy, courage, and loving nature. I too am assailed by that kind of society and I must defend myself, even though it is very difficult. However, I have my own life as a reference point, with the certainty that it is possible to live in this way, fully devoted to God and to others."

At this point, it seems that Peter is almost finished. "Nowadays, risks are kept to a minimum, virtually being confined to films. No one wants to run any risks in their lives. Nothing is done unless there is an assurance that there is no risk. But I can assure you that there is no such thing as a mission without risk. I can't say that if we take a risk for God, there won't be any suffering involved, because it is man who is the cause of our suffering. God left the world in our hands. He doesn't have any hands, feet, or mouth, so it is our own hands, feet, and mouths which have to take us to God.

"It has never occurred to me to blame God for my illness because I came to Madagascar in 1970 with no assurances. I knew it was a difficult place, but the mission was a happy one because I took the risk. I never blamed God because the problem lies among men. I didn't take care of myself; I entered people's homes because I wanted to be with them, and I ate anything they served me in order to share their lives and become one of them. I never worried about drinking coffee or tea made with contaminated water, nor did I refrain from eating anything they offered me. The risks you run may well have repercussions for your life."

Peter makes a final pause and closes the subject. "A mission without any risk is not a mission. Our mission is a challenge that must be accepted on an ongoing basis. This is also true for laypeople. Christ accepted the challenge of becoming a man. He knew they were going to crucify him, but he still accepted the challenge. I know that one day I could be kicked out of Madagascar, but I am sure that all I have done here has been done with love and faith. If the people think otherwise, it could be because we haven't been sufficiently attentive to the evil one infiltrating our work and generating problems, and we weren't wise enough to stop him on time. If that were the case, I wouldn't be able to do anything, but I wouldn't complain against God if that happened because he is love. Everything bad that might happen to me is the natural consequence of human imperfection, of nature, of the evil side of man's heart—not of God. Men can suc-

181

cumb to the temptations of evil, pride, and selfishness, and a time can come when we are no longer human because we lose track of truth, becoming beasts that do not hesitate to undermine the innocent or entire nations just to safeguard our pride or our power."

⚜

At ten o'clock in the evening, I go outside to get some fresh air. I have been writing since half past eight when we finished dinner. Listening to the recordings of my conversations with Peter and transcribing them into my copybook, I did not feel the need to add many words. The dogs are sleeping on a deserted street. The village is silent. All I can hear is the orchestra of crickets and, farther up, the noise of some trucks dumping waste. The night watchmen chat in the reception office. A white sheet sways in the wind on the balcony of Miss Bao's house. I sit next to the flowerbed, near the leafy jacaranda guarding the water tap that is now in a profound sleep, not letting even a trickle out. I watch a rose quivering in the middle of the flowerbed with its mouth open. In the distance, some lights are shining on the hill. I go to sleep with Father Peter's last phrase on my mind: "I am like this: I always tell the truth, directly. Nevertheless, with the passing of time, I have improved the way in which I say things because love and truth should go hand in hand, like love and courage."

FIVE

SOCIAL JUSTICE

Waking up in a good mood is a real blessing. That is how I got up today, hearing the children yelling and the high-school students nearby. It is a cloudy day; it looks like rain, which I have not seen since my arrival, despite it being the rainy time of year. I meet Olga in the dining room and greet her; she says good morning, serves me coffee, and goes outside. Her daughter's father ran away with another woman, never to be seen again. It is a typical story here because women are not protected by the law if they are abandoned. Men take them and leave them as if they were objects, as if the cultural heritage of polygamy was still common practice. They can do nothing because, in Peter's words, "some men sell their daughters in exchange for alcohol or a handful of money."

There is no doubt that the Malagasy woman is the one who carries the greatest burden in life. I see them carrying buckets and children, cleaning vegetable patches, building fires, breast-feeding, delousing their children, weaving mats, plowing the fields, shouldering sacks, washing clothes, and quarrying for stone. Peter tells me: "A Malagasy woman is worth ten men."

Later in the day, we go up to Manantenasoa with Viviane and Tojo. There is to be a feast in the sports hall. Monsignor Bruno Mussaro, the papal nuncio, has come to say good-bye to Akamasoa. After a four-year posting to Madagascar, he is being transferred to Guatemala. The hall is crowded with children and youth from the schools of Mahatsara, Andralanitra, and all the neighborhoods of Manantenasoa. Peter prepares the ceremony, encouraging the young to sing, and every village competes to see which one sings better. Afterwards, the nuncio will address them: "Continue studying and working hard, never give up, and I am sure that one day someone who was brought up in Akamasoa will govern this country." During the reception, Monsignor Mussaro hands Peter a check, and Peter says to me: "See, it's Providence."

In the afternoon, I meet Father Peter again, this time in his office, which is situated on the upper floor of the school, next to Miss Bao's. It is three o'clock in the afternoon and the Malagasy flag is flying in the playground; the sky is clear and not a drop of rain has fallen. Peter's office is modest, as everything here is, but nothing is missing. Two little sofas, a desk with a pile of papers on it, the telephone, a closet in which all the folders are neatly archived, another closet containing soccer trophies; on the walls there are two pictures painted by the locals: one showing the school kitchen and the other depicting a rural scene.

We talk about social justice. I turn the tape recorder on. Peter thinks for a moment before speaking.

❧

"Love must work to promote justice. It is so easy to say: 'This is not my responsibility, I'm not a politician, nobody chose me to work for justice, I have another mission.' It's a real pity that so many people find excuses so easily! Adam in Paradise did the same, blaming Eve for his misfortune. You hear so many excuses every day. People must work for justice in order to find personal fulfillment, no matter what their chosen field of work is. Love and justice go hand in hand. One cannot exist without the other. Both must be worked on day by day; they are not permanent acquisitions. You must always be in search of love, which increases with justice.

"Simply searching for those who are guilty of causing injustice is not enough. You must have better ideas, be able to imagine new roads and new possibilities. If you make a breakthrough and blaze a trail of love and justice, others will follow suit. However, you can expect it to be an uphill struggle at first because, in general, it is a very lonely path."

From justice, Peter jumps—as if crossing a bridge that seems novel and invisible—to the revolutionary man who brings about changes and breaks fresh ground. "All religious communities have sprung up from a revolutionary idea, with the desire to modify a certain situation. If at a later stage the original energy is lost, there is always the danger of becoming too structured, of erecting walls, and becoming overprotective. The problem is that man is afraid of inventing things, afraid of taking risks, and afraid of the future. However, we are obliged to go forward and act, because the essence of man lies in action. This does not mean that we must put aside contemplation. On the contrary, contemplation must drive our action; contemplation is what directs you, points you in the right direction, and if necessary, gets you back on the right track.

"There has practically never been a true revolutionary. Even the word sounds horrible because it hasn't been used seriously, just as the word charity hasn't. When words are used in the wrong context and taken lightheartedly, we empty them of meaning. Nowadays, a revolutionary is someone who shouts in the name of justice and then fills his pockets with other people's money. Words have gradually become devoid of meaning. It's the same with the people who talk about justice but use violence. They say, 'I'm a revolutionary,' but a true revolutionary is someone who would never take up arms. A revolutionary person is someone who does what he says, who perseveres in the attainment of the objectives he has set for himself, and who gives up his life for his mission.

"Christ was a revolutionary because he wanted to transform people by changing their hearts. The Beatitudes are very clear about this, and the Magnificat explains it. Christ was a revolutionary because he loved so much that he even surrendered his life. We may never be able to change the world, but we can change the existence of some people if we manage to convince them with our example and testimony. Actions speak louder than words."

So many people say one thing and do another. If I analyze my own acts, I do not think I am an exception. Peter continues by saying: "It's a matter of changing at least some part of reality. In my case, it was a garbage dump. It's about changing people's lives, contributing something positive to their lives. Love and a thirst for justice should be the motivating factors. Gestures speak for themselves. When you extend a hand to a child, you know it is a gesture of love, of affection, even though not a single word is spoken.

"That's how we started this project. I didn't do any more than that—I only bent down, placed myself in their shoes, spoke with the adults and the children, and made gestures so they would be able to understand me. When you see a woman who lives a forgotten, marginalized life, with several children on her back, you can continue on your way… or you can say, 'She needs someone to help her.' There are millions of people like this all over the world; that is why the Church frequently says the poor suffer more than other people and chooses especially to help them. Anyone can suffer physically or psychologically, but these people are even worse off: they have no food, housing, education, or work. Faced with this situation, the Church is not mistaken in trying to help them first. This doesn't mean the wealthy are excluded; it's just a question of priorities."

Peter has some rice water at hand; he takes a sip and continues. "Man is fearful by nature. He tends to secure his future and doesn't believe much in Providence. He accumulates money because he needs security. But more than half of the people on our planet don't have a secure future. They lack social protection. It's a contradiction: While some people have enough for themselves and their descendants, others don't have anything for today and even less for tomorrow. This is where injustices arise.

"This even happens with the religious, who at some point stop generating change, preferring security instead. They don't realize that by this they are putting an end to their mission; they stop imagining, inventing, and creating. As a result, they end up isolating themselves. It is easy to lose track of that first love, that initial spurt of energy in any job. I always say that the day I stop listening to a poor person will be the beginning of my bourgeois ways. Revolutionaries have always been very close to God, ready to surrender their lives to him; that's why there have only been a few. We have all been chosen for this mission but not all have the same commitment. We have all been called to live some of that divine madness which goes beyond the ordinary —or rather, that people consider out of the ordinary."

At this moment, I imagine St. Francis of Assisi, relinquishing even his clothes, speaking in the town square, ready to lose everything for the Gospel. It is almost too much for me to take in.

"You never really overcome fear. Fear is part of our human nature. We carry it in our genes; it's also our original sin. We must keep combating it. Christ said this to his disciples several times. Pope John Paul II keeps repeating it: 'Don't be afraid.' Of course, if it were easy to fight against, there would be less injustice. If you are close to God, and accept him as your first love, you can never be the cause of injustice. But you naturally run the risk of losing that initial blaze, and as time goes by, fear increases while the will to change your life and the lives of others decreases, and so you struggle less against injustice.

"Social justice is so simple that a six-year-old child could understand it. It's eating enough, enjoying freedom, having a decent house, a job, having access to education, being able to be yourself. It starts right there. When you see someone on the streets begging for food, it's because there is no justice, and you must act accordingly to make things improve. It's not a question of using beautiful words or giving trite speeches that don't come from the heart and are only made for convenience's sake. Working for justice is something concrete; it is action, not theory. Methods may vary, but the first thing you should say is, 'We are going to do something about it.' Anything is better than nothing. The problem is that those who take on the responsibility of governing, be it a country or an international organization, generally do so out of arrogance and vainglory, not to combat the injustices of the system. They take over through sheer pride and the search for prestige, lacking the willingness and moral courage necessary to put what they preach into practice. Power should serve the interests of the people, but it is very hard to be at somebody else's service."

A new pause allows me to turn over the cassette, press a button, and begin recording again. "In a world which is supposed to be making progress, just seeing injustice and inhumanity should make us rebel inside. We should say to ourselves, 'I'm going to do something.' Poverty and inequality will always exist, but we must fight them continuously, although we know we will never all be equal. I think a poor person only wants to be treated with dignity, to be respected. It's not a question of being equal, it's a matter of allowing for growth, of finding oneself, of becoming a person every day, of not running away from oneself, of finding peace in one's heart, and sharing it with others. This is the direction in which a person should be moving.

"A person cannot be forced to submit to the laws and criteria invented by a social class because that will only end in exploitation. This has never worked because there was no search for truth, ideas were imposed by force, and attempts were made to reach a false equality. It's the same with consumerism, where a small group of people monopolizes freedom, truth, and people's idea of utopia. And when dialogue disappears, society crumbles because justice cannot prevail."

"And how can justice be achieved?" I ask.

"Justice is the fruit of sacrifice. It is attained by fighting for the truth with sincerity and courage and by not suppressing others. It cannot be a utopia because perfect justice is an attribute only found in God, but we can get closer to it and make it more accessible to everyone with as little discrimination as is humanly possible. When we analyze our attitude, we realize that we aren't perfect either. This is where God can intervene, leading us along the right path because he knows us well; he knows our thoughts and what we carry in our hearts. We will never have heaven on earth, but we can anticipate it a little. We can start enjoying it, although it can only be a foretaste of that great future happiness which could never last here because we are limited, imperfect, selfish, and we don't know how to share.

"At one time, Latin America thought that social justice could be achieved through violence. It was very tempting and deceptive, especially for young people. I was also tempted, but I never succumbed to violence. Life doesn't have to be violent; violence shouldn't be used to impose anything. We can resort to courage, determination, and words, but we should never kill in the name of justice. Many believed that violence was the shortest and most effective road, but they only ended up destroying themselves. Man shouldn't rebel against God either, blaming him for poverty and injustice, because the root of the problem lies in men and not in God.

"To conclude, if anyone has any sensibility, he or she should be moved to pity in the face of poverty and injustice, because it isn't normal for human beings to live in such conditions. If people don't react when faced with these circumstances, there is something wrong with them."

❖

Our conversation is interrupted when Miss Bao enters the office, the look on her face suggesting she has bad news. "What's wrong?" Peter asks.

"I have just been informed that the European Union has withdrawn its food aid for Madagascar for budgetary reasons. The measure applies to three countries: Madagascar, Eritrea, and a third one which I can't remember," says Miss Bao.

"It cannot be true!" Peter exclaims, while he grabs the phone and starts dialing a number. I ponder the seriousness of the news. The three million euros that the European Union annually allocates to

Madagascar is distributed among different aid agencies, and almost 5 percent goes to Akamasoa. The aid arrives in the form of food: rice, beans, condensed milk, sugar, etc. This food makes up the daily rations for the schoolchildren, as well as for the elderly and those who arrive at the Welcome Centers.

"What are we going to do?" Miss Bao asks with deep sorrow and despair. "How are we going to feed them?"

In the meantime, Peter waits patiently to be put through to a government official, who can only confirm the news. "Since when?" is the question he asks.

"As of today, March 22," the man at the other end answers.

"But they can't do something like that without even letting us know, allowing no time at all for us to adjust to the new state of affairs!" He hangs up, dials again, this time calling the EU representative. He doesn't reach her, but he leaves a message explaining the reason for his call. Then he looks at me and says: "Can you believe it? Eritrea and Madagascar! It's incredible—the officials take measures without even worrying about the implications."

I think of the ships that transport the containers, the trucks that bring them from the port of Tamatave, the men that unload the food and store it in the warehouses, Pierrete who opens the padlocks every day so the food can be distributed among all the villages, the women who light the fires in the school kitchens, the steam from the large pots where the rice is cooked with a little milk and the pulses and potatoes, the thousands of children and young people lining up with their plastic dishes and spoons, the people in charge of the soup kitchen who serve them, the children leaving to look for some shade or going up to their homes to eat what they have been given, their stomachs enjoying that succulent helping which is a source of energy and protein to keep going, studying, attending classes, doing homework, playing, smiling, and waiting for a new day.

Here we have just been discussing justice, while someone in Brussels tapped a key on his computer, deleting the consignment for three countries as if it had no implications. Only the sound of a key modifying an Excel spreadsheet, not batting an eyelash, not even asking where these countries are situated, or how the people there live, or what is done with the money, or which mouths are fed, because he only takes orders from somebody above him, who takes orders from someone even higher up, and the latter from a whole legion of officials who, perhaps for political reasons, or who knows why, reached that decision, while drinking coffee with acquaintances, because spring in Europe is blooming after a winter that has not been too cold. Then those officials will go home or eat out in one of the nice restaurants in the market square, drinking good wine and perhaps indulging in some oysters, going home to have a good night's sleep afterwards, swallowing the unperceived or ignored injustice for the sake of falling asleep—and they might even feel that they have done their duty.

We go out, leaving our conversation for another time. The blow has been too hard. We fetch Carole and Gregoire, and together we go towards the landfill site.

SIX

ANOTHER VISIT TO THE LANDFILL

I am writing this immediately after returning home. My feet are still dirty after walking on the landfill site, my nose is itching, I can feel the stinging sensation of the filth on my body, I smell, and my throat is burning due to the air I have been breathing. But I must write—the need to put on paper what I have just experienced is stronger than anything else because I risk forgetting what I have seen and heard. Never in my life have I descended to such a lowly place, to emerge in such an elevated state. From the village of transitory housing (Antaninarenina), which I saw on the day of my arrival, I went with Peter to the village located behind the landfill, which is part of the Andralanitra center. It is called Ambaniala (which means "below the woods" in Malagasy, although it is actually situated above the garbage). About 1,200 people live there. The village already existed, in that same place, when Akamasoa began its work. Of course, the housing was extremely poor, not like the two-story houses that exist today.

You might wonder why the village was built right there, its sole access route leading through the landfill site, but that is not the issue. Peter's arguments are convincing: the people did not want to leave the place, these were fiscal lands and they always thought the government would move the landfill site to another place, and besides, many of its inhabitants work on the site. Akamasoa's prime concern was that they should live with more dignity, that the children should go to school (they now do so every day, attending schools in Andralanitra), that they should have access to medical care, and that the people should slowly obtain proper jobs. It is too easy for people like myself, who are only passing by, to criticize, using terms such as the "viability" or "sustainability" of a project. We should have been there when this rapid solution was opted for, with the aim of improving the quality of people's lives.

When we arrive, we walk for a few miles through the landfill site. The children follow us, many barefoot. I am afraid I might step on some excrement, or see a rat, or be sick from the nauseating smell. My head itches and my eyes sting as we arrive at Ambaniala. Gregoire and I take pictures. Carole does her best to avoid the juicy puddles that have oozed out from the garbage. Peter is in front, answering our questions. He says that the smell is not so bad in the village because the wind always blows from the east, and that is why it is more offensive in Andralanitra.

We can already distinguish the typical arched gateway in wrought iron with the name of the village. Waste has been dumped at the very entrance to the village. Peter is indignant when he sees it, remarking: "It just can't be true! It's incredible! If we don't do something soon, they will dump the garbage inside!" And he is absolutely right. We look in astonishment at the garbage piled up against the walls of the village. "Something must be done," is the first thing Father Opeka thinks, this man of action as well as contemplation. There is no time for words, or for finding out who is ultimately responsible for such a decision. Immediate, urgent solutions are required.

The person in charge of the village comes out to meet us, and Peter asks him why nothing has been done. The man stammers an answer but knows it will not be acceptable. "We told them, Mompera. We've been telling the truck drivers, but they don't pay attention to us." Peter is still indignant; perhaps his anger is heightened by the more serious problem—the news that the European Union has withdrawn its food aid to Madagascar. He asks the man to gather all the people from the village at the entrance, while we start our rounds.

We pass through the entrance gate. On the right-hand side, there is a small kiosk selling food and candy, in front of which children are playing billiards and table soccer. The scene reminds me of my childhood when I used to play table football in one of the best schools in Buenos Aires; here they are doing so next to a landfill site. But the children live their poverty with dignity; they smile in the same way that I did when they score a goal.

We walk through the village with its brick houses and cobblestone sidewalks, vegetable patches in front and trees on the side. The water tap has very little pressure here, so the buckets are lined up, waiting for their turn. The green one is mine, the red one belongs to so-and-so, the blue one belongs to the grandfather on the corner, and the white one to somebody's uncle.

We enter the house belonging to the oldest man in the village and the first of its inhabitants. He is eighty-four years old and is a relic of the place, not only because of his age (which is very rare) but also because of what he stands for. I bang my head against the beam of the doorway leading onto the vegetable patch, and all the children laugh. I have made the same mistake twice, and I think to myself, These things always come in threes; it will happen again somewhere else. The problem is that I do not watch where I am going because everything I see catches my eye due to its novelty.

We go into the elderly man's home. It contains a double bed, a wardrobe, three chairs, and a coffee table. We talk in darkness because they have not yet managed to bring electricity to the village (in the streets, light comes from battery-powered street lamps). The man talks with Peter, who says with deep emotion: "He is one of the first ones, an institution within Akamasoa."

The elderly man smiles and lets Peter hold his hand. He offers us some tea, and Peter tells him about the garbage. "They have dumped it on the village doorstep, and we cannot allow it."

"No, of course not, Mompera," replies the man. "Something must be done, Mompera."

When we go out, we find the men gathered at the village entrance. Peter speaks to them in Malagasy, and I imagine he is saying something like: "If we don't do anything, tomorrow they will dump the garbage inside the village, as if we too were garbage. We must stop them. It's a question of dignity. Everything we have achieved so far will be lost if we don't do anything. We must go and talk to those in charge of the dumping. Let's all go together so they realize how indignant we are."

"No, we cannot let this carry on," they all reply. The charismatic figure of Father Peter can easily be distinguished in the semidarkness, which indicates that night is about to fall. "Let's go right now."

What I do not know because I do not understand what they are saying is that Peter tells them that only two of them must do the talking and that they must not behave violently because violence generates more violence.

We set off. Practically every man from the village marches behind Peter. It is already nighttime. I can barely see the path we are following or what we are treading on. I feel that my sandaled feet are at an even greater loss than I am. They are trying to figure out what they are stepping on: this is paper, this plastic, that is a piece of cloth, those are pieces of iron over there, this wet substance must be food, as well as the mud, a wooden stick, some glass, the trail of a rat, a page from a newspaper. The whole village is marching, and the landfill site is angry. It is not right that the garbage-truck driver, a poor man himself, is dumping refuse directly under the noses of other poor people. Surely he cannot have forgotten his human condition this way, no matter whose orders he was obeying. It is an offence against the dignity of the people living here. Maybe it is an act of aggression, intended to make the people leave once and for all.

Some bonfires light our path, while the gray smoke remains imprinted in our photographs as if it were the ghostly shape of misery. The children are sent back home. I too become bolder, without knowing what they are about to do, and I tell myself, whatever the outcome, I will remain at their side. They have no right to do something like this, as though the people living here were animals, as if they were the pigs the fever killed some years ago, or the dogs that continue prowling at night, or the owls which swoop down on the garbage and fill me with dread, their eyes like the living conscience of an atrocious world in which there is no longer any respect for anything.

Carole and Gregoire walk by my side. "We were supposed to have a meeting at seven o'clock in Antananarivo, but we can't miss this," they tell me. Peter marches on in front, a few feet ahead of us. I ask him in a loud voice: "Why didn't they do this before, of their own accord? Why did they need your words of encouragement?" He answers, raising his voice above the hooting of the owls and the crackling of the fires: "They are just too fatalistic." I don't say anything. What can

I say? Instead, I concentrate on where I place my feet, avoiding the dogs, and I listen to the village people encouraging each other.

Suddenly the lights of two trucks appear, coming towards us. What will happen? They look like war tanks ready to do battle with the enemy. I imagine that the people will all sit down, or that they will remain standing where they are so as not to let them drive past. The trucks, with their eight-ton cargoes, are getting nearer and making a racket. The headlights in the night are like the eyes of monsters that want to devour us with their arrogance. The smoke puts up a fight against these lights, creating a dismal atmosphere. Peter is still in front. I imagine he will say any moment now: "We won't let you pass." I am already preparing my shout in agreement with him, when an owl screeches on the side and flies away, shaking a scrap of meat in its beak. But I am mistaken.

Peter is not someone who calls himself a revolutionary and uses violence. No, of course not. He is the torchbearer of love, of love for the poor and the outcast. I see how they all step aside, letting the trucks pass. The tanks advance. I too step aside, even though I am stunned. I cover my nose when they drive past, dripping with juices like the slime of indignity. Off they go to unload their trash, which for those living in the world of poverty is not really trash. At least it provides work for those who have no alternative, for those who have no decent way of earning a living. I think about the cardboard scavengers in Buenos Aires, rummaging through the rubbish every night. Yes, they disrupt my orderly life, but at least they do not go out to steal, nor do they resort to violence.

My thoughts return to reality. We have arrived at the offices that manage the loading and unloading of the trucks. This is not fiction, although it could very well be a Fellini film. The men begin to gather in groups. I imagine the moment of the real protest has arrived. Perhaps we will grab sticks and destroy, or cover our faces with pieces of cloth and block the roads, burn tires and destroy store windows, becoming "piqueteros" (people who block roads in Argentina). But that is not the case; again I am mistaken, or maybe the violence inside me is confusing me. Despite having listened to Father Opeka all afternoon, I have very quickly forgotten what he said. Peter calls Carole, Gregoire, and me; he moves us toward the road that turns left to return to Andralanitra, saying: "We can't go any further. They must solve the problem themselves, in a peaceful way yet fighting for their rights."

A few feet ahead, I meet Claudine and take her warm adolescent hand (she is fourteen years old). She stays by my side so I do not get lost. I let her lead the way. I have risen proudly from the lowliest of places because I was able to accompany these people in their march for dignity, on their way to fight for their rights, on their road to hope.

❦

That evening, at dinnertime, I look at Miss Bao and say, "Cheer up! Courage; have faith; everything will sort itself out." She understands that I am referring to the European Union and replies: "Don't worry. I have a heart of stone." We then begin to play a game. I ask Peter, "What's Viviane's heart like?" and he answers, "Like rice," to which I add a reflection: "It's very important because it can feed other hearts."

And we continue playing, going around the table.

"And Tojo's?"

"Like a sponge," she answers herself.

"It's very important because it can retain water and offer it to other people," I say.

Claudine's? "It's made of chocolate," said Peter.

"It's very important because it can sweeten other hearts," I answer once again.

And Prisca's? "It's made of coal," she answered.

"It's very important because it can light a fire in other hearts."

"What can you tell me about the one made of stone?" Miss Bao asks, looking at me.

"It's very important because it serves as the foundation of the house where other hearts live..." I answer.

✦

And so the game ends, and the night flies by. Tomorrow we are going to the countryside to visit the first village built by Akamasoa. This humanitarian project makes me live a whole life in one day, with moments of anger, sorrow, joy, happiness, and bitterness. However, I must confess that, in spite of everything, I always go to sleep with a little happiness in my heart. Why? Simply because the children in the dining room say good night to me with the hope of rising in a better world.

SEVEN

THE COUNTRYSIDE

Olga was absent from the dining room this morning. While we were having breakfast, Father Peter remarked: "She's had an attack of malaria. It can last two or three days, depending on how strong it is." He reminded me again of his years in the south and what he had to go through: first the cold, then the fever, the body sweating then shivering, the feeling of being nothing, the helplessness. "I had a lot of energy in the south until I got sick. When your body is sick, it's very difficult for the spirit to fly. There is a struggle between your body and your spirit—you don't feel well; you feel heavy, weary, and you must resort to your faith, continue praying, receiving people with respect and joy," he added.

"The things I experienced in the south have been of great use for my work here. Before my departure, I had to intervene in defense of a young man who had been condemned to death by one of the tribes. In that place, the dina (the law) has no loopholes. They beat them to death."

"With sticks?" I ask.

"Yes, it's like being stoned to death. I went to talk with the chief of the tribe and managed to stop them from killing him, but after I was transferred to Antananarivo, I heard that they eventually beat him to death anyway."

After breakfast, we set off in the direction of the village of Antolojanahary. We travel in Miss Bao's car—Peter at the wheel, myself as copilot, Carole and Gregoire in the back. Thirty seven miles seems like three times that distance because we have to drive through the capital in order to reach Route Nationale 4, which leads up to Ankazobe. Later, the road follows a sinuous course with many bends, making driving difficult. The scenery is gorgeous, however, and reminds me of some parts of Brazil.

During the journey, we talk about the serious problems that cropped up the day before: the garbage dumped at the entrance to Ambaniala and the cutting off of food aid. Peter is much more worried about this last issue, even if he does not admit it. "I have to go to Europe at the end of April, and only time will tell what solution we will find. If we don't find one, we can always resort to other friends."

But as befits a man of action, he has already taken certain measures. Regarding the first problem, Miss Bao tells me that a solution is already in sight, even if the person responsible for the dumping began by shouting at them: "It's your fault for building that village in the middle of the landfill site!" How cynical! He knows that 1,200 people live there. He gradually calmed down, promising that they would not dump any more garbage at the entrance to the village, and that as soon as they were able to repair the bulldozer (in about two days' time), they would remove the filth.

After leaving the capital, the highway follows an endless range of desert-like hills interrupted by sporadic small valleys where rice is the main crop. The houses in the countryside are made of red earth, and the roofs are thatched. There are almost no trees, so the wind and rain erode the fertile topsoil from the hill slopes, depositing the scant amount in the tiny valleys. These are the only areas that can be cultivated, and in this part of the high plateau, pulses and fruits like pineapple and banana are grown alongside rice. Every now and then, we see some cattle, similar to zebu (domestic oxen developed in India). "Are there any horses?" I ask.

"There are no horses in this part of the country, and there are very few in Madagascar."

"Why?" Carole asks.

"Because of the climate and the pests."

This is all part of Madagascar's cruel reality. Even so, the scenery is beautiful, and I can imagine the Indian Ocean coast must be even more so, but I have not come all this way to swim in the sea.

"First, we managed to obtain 140 hectares, and we bought the rest later," Peter explains. "Today we have 430 hectares, of which only 20 or 30 percent are able to be cultivated for the above reasons. Who knows what would happen if 'green gold,' the soybean, were introduced? I believe it could be the agricultural revolution that is needed to balance the country's accounts. But for the time being, foreigners can buy no more than five hectares, for fear history should repeat itself and what took place during the colonial period should occur again. The largest plots of land are tribally owned, divided into small holdings, making it difficult to think of leading-edge farms unless large cooperative organizations were formed."

There is no point in pursuing these thoughts. One must try to understand this island for what it is. The same applies to Akamasoa. Its foremost objective was to rescue the people from the miserable state they were in, and it has certainly achieved that. Health and education were the next objectives on the list, above all for the younger generation. These objectives will be fully met when the hospital is finished and, God willing, a college is opened. Akamasoa also provides subsidized work, but it prefers people to get jobs outside the organization. This is why nothing is free, even though it is usually very cheap: housing, education, medication, water, and electricity. Costing little, but enough to enforce a philosophy based on work, solidarity, respect, discipline, and effort.

⚜

This is what I find yet again, as soon as we enter the village and its largest neighborhood, called "Cristo Rey" (Christ the King in Spanish), in honor of the eve of the day when the first twenty families arrived. You can sense the industrious atmosphere permeating the place. Peter's profound feelings and pride for this enterprise provide the setting for our arrival. "We have planted more trees here than actually exist in the whole region. Eucalyptuses, monkey puzzle trees, acacias. Just wait—today it's the high-school atudents' turn to go out and plant trees."

However, the many fallen trees along the entrance boulevard are a witness to the devastating damage caused by Cyclone Gafilo. Peter points to each one, as if he had lost a child. After having invested so much effort, taking advantage of the summer humidity, digging up the hardened soil, weeding the young trees, transforming the poor people from the hellish suburbs of the capital into rural workers, it's quite a loss.

We enter the village, whose two-story houses are made of brick as in the other towns, with windows and balconies painted green, tiled roofs, vegetable patches on the side, thirteen- or fourteen-year-old trees, the shed where the locally produced rice is threshed, the grocery, the dispensary, the school, the basketball court where the wind destroyed the hoops and the backboards, a dirt square, the chickens, the small grocery store, a road that continues on its way, the children weeding, the soccer field, two or three brick houses (the first ones built), the countryside, the grass.

The people in charge of the village and the school come out to welcome us. As usual, more than one person approaches Peter with some sort of request.

"Mompera, I have no news of my twenty-year-old son who was taken to the hospital by Father Rok on Sunday."

"Mompera, we have run out of cement for the classrooms we are building."

"Mompera, we are running out of rice and there are still two months to go until the new harvest."

I walk away along the road, mingling with the kindergarten children, taking photographs of them, greeting them, making them laugh, showing them affection. Then I approach the small grocery store where a group of women are cooking. One of them is in a wheelchair. They offer kind greetings: "Manahoana"; "Salama tsara." I observe the dark room, blackened by the smoke of the fires, the missing teeth, the long skirts, and the feet, worn and weary from endless walking.

Next to them is a young man with a guitar, very black but with slanted eyes and teeth that look like a corncob because they are so yellow. I ask him to sing. He strums the guitar and begins to play a Malagasy folk tune. The women start clapping in time; they smile, swinging their bodies. The one in the wheelchair follows the rhythm with her arms, and another one starts singing. It sounds beautiful, mingling with the breeze that is still blowing quite hard. Peter calls me from a distance; I pat the guitarist's shoulder, saying, "Très bien."

"Misaotra," he responds, which means "thank you very much" and we say good-bye. In my heart, I say to him, Thank you for making me feel so welcome, for making my morning a happy one, for being what you are today, for wanting to advance in life, for making an effort, and for having recovered your dignity.

We enter the church with Peter. Behind the stone altar and on the wall, also of gray stone, there is a painting of the Sacred Heart of Jesus. It's a unique painting—Christ opens his arms, but instead of pointing to his luminous heart, he extends his arms towards the Earth. At the bottom, people are shown working in the fields, with the children going to school. This is an icon which reflects the spirit of Akamasoa: education and work. It reminds me of the three mottos engraved on the walls of the towns:

"He who does not work should not eat."

"If you don't work, who will feed you?"

"Work makes you human."

However, opportunities have to be generated, and that is the greatest challenge for mankind, which to this day continues to limp between abundance and want, inclusion and exclusion. Social help is not enough; man must be promoted as a whole, and that is attained through the combination of "education and work."

"We mustn't provide assistance because, in doing so, we would be demeaning the people; we would be forcing them to become dependent, almost like slaves. God didn't come into the world to turn us into slaves but to set us free, to make us stand on our own two feet. Obviously, when we are sick or unemployed, it is only right that we should receive assistance, but that should only be a temporary solution. We must work. We must combat this social welfare mentality, even within families. If we don't, we are not allowing our children to grow up. Children get used to receiving everything from their parents, and then their parents grow old. It's the same with the poor. This even happens within religious congregations. In our congregation of Saint Vincent de Paul, every region has to be self-sufficient. We are obliged to create our own means of subsistence. Laziness is one of man's weaknesses; it's a defect. Laziness hinders any kind of creativity. Who will serve a lazy person? Society? No.

"Both society and an individual's own family have a right to demand that he or she should work. The problem in many countries, including Argentina, is that the politicians lead the lazy to believe that the state will solve all their problems. No wonder politics finds itself in its current predicament. It creates false expectations for society, and when a house has poor foundations, it ends up crumbling. You can't build on illusions, on lies, on promises that are not kept."

What about education? "Without education, you cannot make any progress in life," Peter always repeats. "Education is the best inheritance parents can leave their children." Here, in this village, 1,100 children go to school, not only from the Akamasoa neighborhoods but also from the surrounding rural areas. Twelve years of education are offered, which can be followed by a further three years in Andralanitra to finish high school, if they wish to do so.

"The main problem we have is absenteeism, especially with pupils who live far away," the headmistress remarks at lunchtime. She says this with a tinge of sadness, but I tell her that this also happens in rural Argentina, as well as in the suburbs of the great cities where there is much poverty nowadays.

We then get into the car, and Peter takes us along another road where men and women are clearing the underbrush using small spades with long handles and hoes. They all greet him: "Manahoana, Mompera."

Peter knows everyone's personal history, their names, their problems, and their sorrows. "That man over there was such a challenge. In the beginning, he complained about everything: the soil not being good, the work being very hard, the wind blowing continuously, and the sun cracking the earth. But see for yourselves, today he no longer complains."

Afterwards, we walk to the place where the teenagers are planting trees. "In twenty years' time, all this will be extensive woodland, and the people will say: 'It was the work of the children and young people of Akamasoa; it was thanks to their effort.'" There they are, with their light-blue pinafores, barefoot, dark, Asian-looking, observing us while some dig holes.

I approach a little girl, take her spade, and try to dig. The earth is hard, thirsty, as red as brick, and I find it hard to dig. Peter laughs and shows me how it is done. Then he talks to the young children about the importance of weeding and removing the lower branches of the newly grown trees.

I look at the horizon. How beautiful! How much hope! The children are like light-blue buds scattered around the slope of the hill. "They are the ones we are most worried about; they shouldn't have to live through what their parents did or repeat their cursed childhood with their own children. This is our main objective. Just look at them, working in this peaceful atmosphere!"

We have French fries, breaded meat, and the compulsory rice for lunch. We have brought mineral water with us from Andralanitra, but Peter prefers to drink the rice water he is used to. I think about the children that I have just seen next to the school at lunchtime. They are so respectful of others that they wait until everybody is served before they start eating, even though the rice is getting cold and the flies begin fluttering around the beans.

After lunch, we depart. We leave behind this "Gift of the Creator," this little village of hope set in the middle of the countryside. Just as in other countries, many people do not want to return to a rural environment once they have moved to a city. It was difficult to convince them to come back, but of the seventy families that settled here originally, most are still here. And they have advanced, not only in their personal and social lives, but also in the use of farming techniques. Currently, a couple of French agricultural experts are living with them, and they are exchanging ideas, experiences and methods.

Returning to Antananarivo, we pass through a large town without running water or electricity. The lines in front of the taps are similar to the ones in the Akamasoa villages, with the difference that in Akamasoa, the housing and urban order, are far superior. You cannot analyze a project without taking into account its context, and from this point of view, there is no doubt that Akamasoa stands out above the rest of the country.

EIGHT

CHARITY

Today I woke up feeling well. When I go down to the bathroom, I am surprised to find that the water has been cut off once again. I will not say anything because, if the others do not have any either, how can I complain? Besides, to whom could I complain? Akamasoa is not responsible for what is going on. This is the state's responsibility, despite the fact that Akamasoa is sometimes forced to build its own roads, or lay and connect its own electricity cables. A private project cannot be expected to have to invest its money in basic infrastructure.

After breakfast, I go to a cybercafe with Marcial and read my week-old email, discarding hundreds of items of junk mail—another type of rubbish which contains nothing valuable that can be saved. To make matters worse, it comes loaded with viruses, and the rubbish in the landfill site must also have some since bacteria and microbes abound there as well.

Afterwards, we return to the village near Mahatsara in order to take the books to Charline. I come to the village with the happiness of being able to fulfill a promise, breathe the healthy air of the hills and, without meaning to, once again bang my head against the entrance gate to the house. I knew it; bad things come in threes, but the third one is the last! Charline was delighted to see me, and it was not difficult to look at her this time. Her minute hands danced on the pages, and her eyes strayed with eagerness to discover the hidden secrets that lay inside them.

After lunch, I go to Peter's house and we begin another conversation. I ask him to talk about charity.

⁘

"Charity is another word that has lost its real meaning over the last fifty years. The term has become part of everyday speech. It was used often, but it was not put into practice. It was gradually emptied of meaning to the point of making it a word that represents promises not transferred to daily life. It became more of an excuse than a commitment to the needy. 'We will give you something so that you don't die, so that you can survive,' the politicians and leaders started saying. Charity means so much more than that, though. It comes from the Latin word caritas which means sharing; to give something that belongs to us; to treat our neighbor as our equal; to love another person without expecting anything in return. It is depriving oneself of something for love. It is an act done with love and respect. It involves parting with our possessions so that someone else can have something. Today it almost means the contrary. Charity that doesn't look for social justice isn't really charity."

As usual, his words are simple but profound. "In my opinion, to talk about charity today is to talk about solidarity and development. I would use those words because they sound stronger. Solidarity is understood as sharing. Sharing is giving of our own free will what we have to those who don't have. That's all. It isn't so difficult. It's clear and simple. Whoever searches for another explanation for the word does so because he or she doesn't want to share or hasn't understood. You shouldn't expect anything in return from the other person when you share, although surely something will come back to you. If it weren't like this, it would turn into commerce. 'I will give you something if you give me something in exchange.' This is bartering, not sharing.

"Development, meanwhile, is a matter of progress and not necessarily one of consumption. However, there is an irrational consumption of goods and services taking place. Real development of the human being has nothing to do with that. We are destroying our own world with this mentality because our raw materials are not infinite. A consumer society is mankind's new virus, even more so than AIDS. Those who consider themselves to be developed are showing us precisely what not to do. The heart of development should be man—not money, profit, or earnings."

Peter looks at me and says something even more radical. "Despite all this talk about progress, the world seems to be moving backwards. In poor countries, the political class is corrupt, while in wealthy countries, politicians promise what society cannot attain and what it doesn't even need simply to attract votes. They are creating a society that is not real, although on the outside they do have a better standard of living. The end seems to be the same—self-destruction. In one part of the world there seems to be no future due to lack of means; and in another, there are more than enough means, but they are not being put to good use; they are being used selfishly. Wealth should be shared. In order to be happy, man must live a balanced life; he should avoid extremes. At one extreme we have laziness, while at the other there is unlimited ambition, wallowing in the pleasure of its possessions. The resulting situation is that the whole world is suffering. The poor suffer in resignation, while the supposedly developed world suffers emptiness and fear."

I allow myself to be carried away by the novelty of his idea: solidarity and development as a summary of the significance of charity.

"Christ set the best example of charity for us through his generosity. Nothing belonged to him, and whatever he had was for others. That is the attitude we should have. We should say: 'Whatever I have, however much or however little it may be, is there to serve others.' It should also be enjoyed in moderation. I think we are all meant to live in moderation, because when you live that way, your life becomes healthy. You are healthy in body and in spirit because you are not attached, and you know that what you have will not enslave you. If we depend too much on comfort, everything starts getting complicated and doubts and fears arise. It is easy to say all this but much harder to live it, but we must work on this because the riches of the world are meant for everybody. Nobody who sees a child starving to death can be indifferent. It is our duty to save human lives, to pay heed to the feeling of compassion coming from our souls.

"Wealth must constantly be produced to take care of the increasing population. Jobs have to be generated so that everyone can live with dignity. Unfortunately, what we see in today's world is millions of people living below the poverty level. This is a challenge, a challenge for all of us who try to think and live like Christ. We Christians should be the first to stand up for people's rights. Not with clubs and drums, but with concrete action and with our modest contribution in each neighborhood and parish.

"Even though public authorities and governments may try, they will never solve the problem of poverty on their own. There will always be poor people in society, but what can be changed is the way in which they are poor. They should have housing, education, and food. I believe this is possible, but there is still a long way to go. Our generation may not see it, but in the future inflatable or plastic homes might be built. Each generation should look out for its poor, and the poor should always be the friends of Christ's followers. We cannot wait until sociologists or economists tell us who the poor are. We should see them for ourselves in our daily lives and apply our own imagination on the spot."

A short pause; a sip of water. Peter places his hand on his cheek because one of his teeth is throbbing with pain. He looks at his watch. He has to go to the dentist, but he wants to finish what he is saying. "None of this is easy, but I always tell those who want to listen to me and are concerned about social issues: 'Continue praying, place all your trust in God, listen to and show respect to God, and one day you will see things clearly in your heart. He will show you what you have to do to help others. Without prayer, you don't get far.'

"Prayer must always be present to help inspire our imagination and love. St. Vincent de Paul used to say that love is creative. Consequently, when you love, you are always creating something. It is a very good thing that so many nongovernmental organizations (NGOs) have appeared, although not all of them have the same objectives. For example, in South Africa, many have been closed down because they were opened only for the benefit of their leaders. But as long as the NGOs exist to serve others, they should be welcomed, and let's hope many people are helped by them."

❧

We set off for the Adventist clinic. Peter must have an X-ray done, to see if he needs a root canal performed on the tooth that is hurting him so much, or if the tooth will have to be pulled due to the lack of calcium everybody suffers from on this island. On our way, we continue talking about development.

"We are far from the sophisticated development of the First World, but education is a priority here. All we have done so far is to save people's lives and offer children a better future. In this way, they will be the yeast. We are not interested in competing with businessmen. A little development is necessary, but we are not going to make our small enterprises so sophisticated that we lose track of our main objective. We can't take that risk. We are well prepared for that temptation.

"Many of these things are only understood when you actually live here. That's why, when European specialists come to audit our accounts, I sometimes get angry when they question a project that is already working well, one that has been implemented for a long time and has obtained national and international recognition. I cannot accept experts coming and philosophizing with us, when things are already up and running and we are standing on our own feet. We occasionally reject potential aid for this very reason. While our need is so urgent, there is so much paperwork to fill out that I prefer to tell them to keep their money. It is the same case when members of the local government, whose help we have requested, turn up. Everything is so slow and bureaucratic, but the poor can't wait."

On the road we meet a bricklayer who worked in Akamasoa for some time. Peter stops the car on the hard shoulder, and the man greets him with affection. When we continue on our way, Peter explains: "I liked his father very much; he used to work with me in the southern part of the island. I even carried his coffin when he died. He worked for me for fifteen years. When his son came to the capital, I hired him, but he thought that because I liked his father, he could do whatever he wanted and I would always defend him, no matter what. He stole from us—he took part of the workmen's wages for himself. When we discovered what he was doing, I fired him immediately because we must above all be loyal to those who help us materially. But you have seen how he greeted me, and I don't hold any grudges against him. I am not fooled by insincerity, even if many people may think I am unaware of it."

Later in the afternoon, we attend a farewell reception at the nuncio's residence with Carole and Gregoire. Monsignor Mussaro has invited us and we accompany Peter. Incredibly, there is not much traffic, and we get there in twenty minutes. The cardinal, at least ten bishops, as well nuns, monks, priests, brothers, and lay people from different parts of the world who live in Madagascar have come to say good-bye. The house is white and the garden immense, with ancient trees and a huge pine tree, beneath which an orchestra is playing.

Peter introduces us to all those who say hello to him. There are priests dressed like laymen in suits, as well as in cassocks or habits. All kinds of people are in attendance from different countries, and practically all of them know Peter and his work. Peter introduces me to two Argentinean nuns and then moves away to talk with someone else. The nun's names are Ana and Josefina, and they are dressed in cream-colored habits. Both belong to the order founded by the venerable Camila Rolón, originally from San Isidoro (in Argentina), and whose case for beatification is under review. They work in the countryside near Antananarivo, helping people, mainly the sick, in different ways. Josefina has been in Madagascar for eight years, while Ana has been here for just under two years.

"Life here is hard, but it is our apostolate and mission. Our order has several houses outside Argentina, and a small community has just opened in Rumania." The two young Argentineans are many people's favorites due to their warmth and charm. I cannot help wondering: Why do we Argentineans stand out abroad and yet are a complete failure at home? It is a strange case, deserving profound analysis. But the truth is that, even in Madagascar, I have found Argentineans: Peter, the two nuns, and the doctor we found in the Adventist clinic who works in South Africa for the AIDS program.

There is such an interesting variety of religious people from different parts of the world, and I try to speak to all of them—Portuguese, Italians, French, Spaniards. Monsignor Mussaro arrives, and everybody greets him. Shortly after, the nuncio remarks that he thought it would be a good idea to say good-bye with a concert. He presents the first piece, "Christus vincit," in honor of the Holy Father, and he invites us all to sing, encouraging us by moving his arms and hands to the rhythm, as if he were an orchestra director. A Portuguese priest, a native of Madeira, says: "See, despite all the problems, the Church is still alive after two thousand years." And he is right. It is marvelous —unity within diversity. Koinonia, or Christian fellowship, enables people to remain united in the same Spirit.

The cardinal is sitting at the place of honor, dressed in cream-colored vestments, with a red sash and skullcap, wearing the ring and the great cross which symbolize his investiture, bearing his years well and gracefully in spite of his white hair and advanced years.

"Christus vincit" is followed by other pieces, culminating with "Salve Regina" in honor of the Virgin Mary, which fills my heart, reminding me of a monastery. When the music stops, the food arrives, and it is time for more encounters. Everyone talks about what they do, and those of us who are here for the first time take advantage of the opportunity to learn more about this country.

On our return home, we are all happy. Peter says, "These meetings are a nice change from our daily routine and provide an opportunity to meet old friends and discover new faces." It takes us an hour to get back home because there has been a power outage in a large part of the city, and traffic is moving at a snail's pace. When we arrive, our "good friends" in Akamasoa are waiting for us.

NINE

THE QUARRY

I spend the morning talking to Jean-Jacques about the geography and climate of the island. "Madagascar can be divided longitudinally into three great geographical regions. The eastern region is very narrow and falls steeply from the high plateau onto an almost straight coastline, with short rivers that flow torrentially into the Indian Ocean, plains covered by tropical jungles, and a hot and humid climate. It is usually the east coast that is lashed by the cyclones. The central plateau is of volcanic origin, with an average height of almost 3,400 feet. It is highest in the north, around the Tsaratanana massif, whose Maromokotro peak rises to 9,840 feet. This high plateau covers 60 percent of the island and is home to the majority of the population, who enjoy a mild and benign climate, thanks to the altitude. The western region, which descends slowly from the high plateau towards the Mozambique Channel, has a dry, tropical climate and longer and calmer rivers. The most serious problems are soil erosion, deforestation, and a lack of drinking water."

⋯❖⋯

In the afternoon, we go with Father Rok to the neighborhood of Lovasoa. Leaving his Renault parked in the shade of a large tree, we climb the hill towards Bemasoandro on foot. The view is incredible, and clusters of wildflowers decorate the slope in violet, white, and yellow, rocking softly as if a hand were stroking them as we walk past them. In the distance, there is the typical scenery: the valley, a lake, the capital, the houses, the people.

Today, the altitude is not making me feel so tired. It is as though I have become used to it; the world of poverty has given me a new kind of air to breathe. Father Rok climbs with the burden of his sixty years on his back, wearing that permanent smile that gives him a special, peaceful appearance. He is another Vincentian missionary who has devoted his life to the most needy, putting up with migraines and who knows how many other illnesses after thirty-four years on this island.

Arriving at the quarry, we see the men and women who work there every day, earning their daily bread to feed their children. Guy, the man in charge of the quarries, whom I already know from the press conference and the soccer match, comes over to greet us. His small glasses and permanently colorful clothes give him an exotic look.

At present (in 2004), 300 people work in each quarry, although in the beginning there were more than 1,500. "The work is seasonal; during the summer the rains and the heat mean that the demand for stone decreases because the rate of construction slows down," he explains. People have also gradually been able to get other jobs, either in commerce, Akamasoa's own services, construction, or in other quarries nearer to their homes. I remember Peter's words: "If we had a choice, we would concentrate only on health and education, but job opportunities should also be made available. That is why the quarry will always remain open. On the other hand, construction work will diminish as we finish the last houses that are needed. At that point, we will have trained many in the trade, and they will be able to find work elsewhere. We cannot assume responsibility forever; it's the country's economy that should grow and provide more opportunities for the people."

Every blow of a hammer on rock echoes in the heart of the quarry, and the echo becomes a voice with which the Earth responds to man. The enormous pit dug into the slope is like a bite taken from a cake. In its center, there is a great heap of gravel, about thirty-two feet high, on which women unload their bags of pebbles. Three products are obtained here: stone blocks for the foundations of houses or for cobblestone streets, gravel which is produced by chipping the stone, and the stone dust which remains. Every blow reverberates like the tolling of bells during Lent. The rock splits along the line on which man sets his eyes, all the while listening to the stone's words. For the stone has a voice, as does the wind that blows on this open pit in the hill. As Guy says, referring to a man who is chiseling a large piece of stone: "The stone accepts him," and I add: "And he accepts the stone." He knows it, caresses it, and loves it; he can get angry with it and even hate it, especially when it breaks into unexpected pieces, but he knows his daily bread depends on it.

Two hundred Malagasy francs are paid for each almost square block of stone, used to build foundations or cobblestone streets. So many francs are paid for each cubic meter of gravel produced by women, and much less for the stone dust that will be added to cement. The hardest job, giving blows with the hammer, is reserved for men while the chipping is for women.

"I'm going to have a try," I tell Guy and Father Rok.

"It's very hard," Father Rok warns me.

"I will try anyway; I want to give it a go." I want to feel the flexible handle, the weight of the hammer, the shattering blow on the rock, see the fissure, listen to its voice, and understand the language of these stones. One, two, three, four blows, and all I get are splinters from this small block. The dark-skinned man who owns the tool laughs at me. Of course, I do not know the trade or the hidden secrets of the rock. All the people in the quarry watch me and smile at the foreigner, the vahiny, who doesn't know a thing about stones or quarries, or what it is like to bake in the summer sun, or how one's hands freeze at dawn in winter; who has not experienced what chipping stones in the rain is like, has not run for cover when the whistle announces a dynamite blast, or found shelter in the shed above the pit when a cyclone hits the coasts of Madagascar.

Guy asks the man how many blows are needed to split the rock in two, and he replies that four are enough. Now it is my turn to laugh, and I invite him to take up the challenge. He walks towards me and I give him the hammer; he stands in front of the rock, his arms tensed like a bow. He raises the hammer, lowers his left hand, and lets the hammer fall right on the face of the rock. One, two, three, four… the rock plays a trick on him as if to say: "Remember, man, that I also put in my own effort, and if I let myself be opened, revealing my heart to you, it's only because I want to." Five, six… "…lest you should think you can dominate me at your whim, but don't worry, I won't cause you embarrassment, nor shall I hurt your pride to such an extent that you will never return." On the seventh blow, the rock splits open like a ripe fig. The man smiles at me, even though it took him three more blows than he had claimed it would take. I remind him of this, using my fingers, and everybody laughs.

I walk with Guy along the perimeter of the quarry, the heap of gravel always in the center. He tells me the amount of euros the workers can earn in a week. Of course, it sounds like very little, but here in Madagascar it is a decent amount. We approach a group of women that have just filled a bag with gravel. Guy lifts it off the ground and says to me, "It must weigh thirty-three pounds!" I do likewise, with a show of much effort, and say: "It must weigh forty-four pounds." I like challenging them, even though I do not have a clue. It allows me to get closer to them so we can have fun together. Guy, after so many years in this trade, must have weighing scales in his arms by now.

A tiny woman, no taller than five feet, with a circle of rags on her head and appearing quite young, comes closer, saying to the others: "I will take it." It seems like an impossible feat for her, but the others help to mount it on her head. After securing it and straightening her back, she walks the hundred feet or so to the heap, and then, incredibly, she climbs all the way up to the top!

We continue our rounds. At various points, there are men working on the blocks. "They all respect each other and know their own place and their own tools. It wasn't like this at the beginning. There were arguments because they stole from each other, but relationships have improved with the passing of time." Peter is always telling me that time is the best ally for this kind of project because the process of social reintegration of marginalized people is very slow. Father Rok explains that achieving objectives isn't the most difficult challenge; it's being able to sustain the effort through time.

I now realize that everything here is like an art or a science. For example, I watch a man who wants to split a big block of stone in two. He does not want it to split just any old way. He thinks of the francs he will earn if the piece is the right shape and size, and so he works very carefully. He drills two little holes in the middle, working with three different types of chisels and some water. Next, he places two iron pins, shaped like arrowheads, in the small holes and bangs the hammer down on them. He pounds on one until he hears something like a click—it seems as if the stone would like to escape. Then he hammers on the other one until he hears a clack, and an almost straight line appears, splitting the great square in two. There are tricks to this trade, and learning them demands certain talents. "It's knowing how to look at a rock, being able to listen to it, knowing precisely where to hit it, and knowing what to expect of it," Guy explains, and then adds: "It's hard work, and you must be in good physical condition. Above all, you must have strong arms and a steady back."

I say good-bye, congratulate the worker, and continue walking towards the exit where a group of women are resting in the shade of a gray wall. On our way back, Father Rok repeats: "This is a slow process. There are steps forwards and steps backwards, but the important thing is the final objective, and I think we are getting close."

When we arrive in Andralanitra, Claudine, Viviane, and Tojo come to fetch me, because the Way of the Cross is about to begin in the village, as it does every Friday during Lent. I join them, arriving just in time for the Twelfth Station: Jesus Dies on the Cross. We all kneel down on the stone road. Claudine, Viviane, and Tojo pray in Malagasy.

I cannot understand anything, but I imagine what is going on. Christ dies in the same poverty he was born into. They have removed his cloak and sandals. Some even say that he was crucified naked. As a man, he was left with nothing. He is shedding blood from all over his body; it is gushing from his forehead due to the wounds caused by the crown of thorns and from his back which has endured the scourging; it is pouring from his wrists which were nailed through and from his feet torn open by lack of understanding. Yes, Christ who was born poor in a manger in Bethlehem because there was no room for him in the inn is now dying on the summit of Golgotha, but nobody can take his dignity or his divine nature away.

The walk down the street to the chapel is a real gift, with the waning moon like a silver horn in the sky. The evening star is already lit, and the clouds are turning red in the darkness. The hills sparkle with the shining lights of the houses, and we can see the swamp down below in the silence of the sunset. It is a real blessing to be here, surrounded by children, young people, and adults, sharing songs, kneeling on stones which came from the quarry. We reach the station where Christ is taken down from the Cross. This descent means climbing down to the world of humbleness and simplicity, in order to be able to ascend along the way of the Cross, towards the mystery of the night and creation—a mystery that the simple people of Akamasoa reveal to me with their love and hope.

⚜

Peter returns from the city. We sit down at the table, and he tells us that he has just been to a meeting with representatives from other religious orders, the Prime Minister of Madagascar, the ambassador of the European Union, and the representative of the World Bank. They met to discuss the issue that is worrying everybody—the canceling of food aid. Peter has put forward his arguments for the case. Just listening to him, I can imagine him standing in front of the group, moving his arms like the sails of a windmill, touching his beard, closing his eyes, showing them how they are wrong, slowly releasing all his energy, explaining the disastrous consequences of their proposed measure, and questioning them with a gruff voice, the voice of those who do not have anything. I hear him asking the ambassador to review the decision, looking at him with eyes as clear as the Indian Ocean, inviting them to reconsider, while the Prime Minister applauds and the ambassador does not know where to look.

Peter fights for those who have no say, and he does so while living like them and living with them. I do not think they can stop him; he is in full control and draws from his experience to find a way to say things firmly and tactfully.

Later, when we are sitting on the white bench under the Chinese rosebush, we receive the news of Viviane's grandfather's death, so our conversation is interrupted. Miss Bao and some children come bearing the news. Peter stands up instantly and starts telling them what should be done: "Marcial should drive Viviane and her mother to the town where her grandfather lived."

When Viviane turns up, looking very sad, he expresses his sympathy and hugs her tenderly. The young girl lets out her grief by sobbing on Father Opeka's shoulder.

PART FOUR

ONE

PLAYING "TANTARA"

At six o'clock in the morning, I am awakened by a symphony, led by the pealing of the church bells from the other side of the valley, the rooster's crowing (I imagine it has overslept today), and the voices of the people at the fountain. A long weekend is ahead, as March 29th is a public holiday marking Independence Day. It will be a long weekend, during which I will experience a variety of things, all accompanied by a phrase constantly present in my head: "These types of projects are slow, very slow."

Obviously, politicians cannot wait. They need to show something immediately in order to win votes. Therefore, long-term or medium-term projects are of no use to them. They mistakenly believe that nobody will remember them for such projects, especially if it means pulling people out of extreme poverty with education and work. They come to power, and it corrupts them. "Love based on the external aspect of things, on our own interests, or with an aim to obtain recognition, is ephemeral and dissipates fast. Love acting in self-denial, on the basis of our surrender, discreetly and even invisibly fills man with an unfathomable energy to help his brothers and sisters in need," Peter wrote in his book of reflections, as if to answer my own thoughts.

I walk through the village, in the area where the old earthen houses mingle with the new brick ones. The people living in the earthen houses did not want to join Akamasoa's project and tried to sell their plots of land to the organization for astronomical prices. Many of these people still work on the landfill site. Regarding prices, something remarkable has happened. As the area has become more peaceful (due to the strategy of spreading the people around and helping them overcome marginalization), the price of land has increased dramatically, and many rich people have built houses on the surrounding hills. Peter believes they will manage to get the landfill site moved elsewhere (due to the pollution it causes) and make water accessible to all. This is a typical case of injustice, where rules are adjusted according to who is affected.

I see Marcial and Theresa go by in the pickup, heading in the direction of the Welcome Center in Manantenasoa. Today is the day that rations for the temporary inhabitants are delivered, and I ask for permission to accompany them. I climb into the back of the pickup and enjoy the scenery, despite being jolted by the bumpy road. A teenage girl, about thirteen or fourteen years old, accompanies me (it is customary for everyone to ride in the pickup in order to save themselves from going on foot).

I discover that the girl's name is Jacqueline, she lives in Manantenasoa, and she has five brothers and sisters. She lives with her mother because her father left. Her mother works in the quarry, and Jacqueline studies at the school in Andralanitra. When I ask her what she thinks of Akamasoa, she says, "We live well here." She's not sure if she will attend university later, but if she does continue studying, she would like to be a social worker so she could help other people just as her family has been helped.

When we arrive at the Welcome Center, people are lining up,

bags are being opened, cans are being used as measuring cups—a cup of rice, a cup of white beans, half a cup of sugar, a little salt. A lady greets me, and I ask her how long she has been there.

"Ten days," she replies.

"Why did you come?"

"I was thrown out onto the street."

"Are you well taken care of?"

"See for yourself—I have something to eat, a bed, a blanket, and some hope.

❦

In the afternoon, it is time for an outing. Together with Marcial, Gregoire, Carole, Tojo, and fifteen young girls and teenagers from the dining room, we set off in the minibus to see the fortress of the first Merina king to unite the island politically. This is a sacred place where sacrifices of oxen, roosters, and pigeons were made to honor the ancestors. The young girls are so happy to be going for a drive, even though it is only a simple outing. It is difficult to put their happiness into words. Seeing them laugh out loud and listening to them sing without stopping until we reach our destination is wonderful.

At the entrance to the park, something happens which I only learn about later. I do not know how I would have reacted if I had found out before. The woman selling entrance tickets gave me less change than she should have, and Marcial complains. She argues with Marcial and tries to cover up her deceit by treating the Akamasoa girls disparagingly, simply because they belong to Father Peter's poor. These things too make up Madagascar's harsh reality.

The king's ancient cabin is of noteworthy simplicity; located on a hill and well fortified. The king slept upstairs, climbing a ladder to the bed in order to protect himself from traitors and the enemy. His wives slept below (the guide tells us he had twelve), and they took turns spending the night with the king upstairs. Years later, his granddaughter introduced European culture to the place, building a palace that she decorated with Murano glass, chairs brought from France, and tables from Toledo, with Chinese and Japanese ornaments decorating the dining room.

Later, we climb the king's watchtower, where an immense block of stone gives us the best view I have seen since arriving on the island. Majestic! The surrounding fields offer a panoramic view that seems to encompass the entire island. The girls pose as models and I take a photograph of each one, but Balita (the only boy in the group) has to be forced to sit down because he is too embarrassed.

Knowing their life stories makes you realize how Akamasoa has changed their lives. Watching them laughing and dancing with a group of Boy Scouts on the way out of the palace or singing during the return journey are the best testimony. Some are orphans, others have been abandoned, or have parents that are mentally unstable (be it through alcohol, prostitution, or drugs). Balita used to run away to beg in the streets of Antananarivo, in front of the French Embassy. "That is why we are proud of what we do. Here they have found a decent life."

Afterwards, Balita, Carole, Gregoire, and I go to the city. We walk through the old part of Antananarivo that—apart from the presidential palace, the residence of the former prime minister, the royal castle, and the two cathedrals—does not have many other attractions, with the exception of the alleys that go up and down the picturesque hills. Bringing Balita with us, buying him clothes, inviting him to have something to eat and drink, or simply walking with him in the street (full of pride at being able to join us), is enough to justify our outing.

Among the games I have seen here, two in particular have drawn my attention. One consists of pushing old car tires, with two sticks as axles, as far as possible without letting them fall. It is mainly boys that play it, and I observe them going up and down the neighboring street with admirable dexterity. The other one, played more by the girls, is called "tantara." It is a game that represents their everyday reality, either within their families or in school. They take four or five stones, which they proceed to throw against the ground. At each strike, a character speaks. They can spend hours staging their small world of reality. I imagine they are trying to rectify what they do not like about their daily life.

❦

Seeing them at play, after returning from the city I decide it would be a good idea to invent my own written tantara, using Father Opeka's reflections. I grab the first stone and knock it against the ground:

"No man, who puts his hand to the plow and then looks back, is fit for the kingdom of God. Christ's words are very clear. We must face our problems and not live with nostalgia for past times. It is a matter of looking to the future of our lives, of our faith, of our Church, aware that we do not know anything, that nothing is absolute. However, each of us must find a way of searching, inventing, creating new roads, new tracks, and new routes for our future generations."

This is fascinating. I take a second stone. I feel it in my hand and let it drop:

233

"The children of every continent are the world's heritage. Young people today are being robbed of their greatest wealth—their souls and spirits—in such a subtle way that they do not even realize their lives are being emptied of any meaning. Often young people themselves participate in this process, without realizing that they are destroying themselves. Are we capable of stopping this moral and human deterioration?"

I grab a third one. Again I bang it against the cobblestones:

"We are the salt and the light. We must know that a little salt seasons food, even though it cannot be seen and we cannot tell where it is. The essential thing is that the food has taste. It is the same with light. A flicker of light in the darkness is enough to shed light all around and can be seen by everybody. Are we capable of seasoning people's lives or giving happiness to people? Are we able to fill with hope the lives of all the people we meet?"

And the voice of the fourth stone:

"There is no time to lose. Today, at the beginning of the third millennium, mankind and the Church are in need of many holy vocations, of prophets, of men and women with courage, who are not afraid of commitment. Jesus needs you and asks you to surrender completely to the service of the new evangelization. What will we do? How will we respond to this challenge to our faith and our vocation as Christians?"

I take a fifth stone, because it also has something to say:

"How can we adapt to today's world? How can we understand and love it? How can we show God's love and mercy, which have no boundaries? How can we do this with the poor, with young people, with those who are far from God? We must have imagination, courage, bravery, and, above all, perseverance. We must not be afraid of anything or anybody. We must always receive the poor and give them a warm welcome because they too are Christ's image. We should be fighting to help them. When will we do so?"

There is a sixth stone:

"Will we be able to transmit values to young people who are living an easy life of comfort, immersed in pleasure? What is the purpose of our life? Why are we in this world? We should not get tired of thinking and meditating on new ways of living Christ's Gospel. Who dares to say that young people today are not interested in God's love? Perhaps we are afraid of being ridiculed for continuing to believe in Christ. Nonetheless, he is God's love made man."

I take hold of the last stone, the seventh—the number of perfection.

"Lord, give me the strength of spirit to go out to the sea and look for other horizons where you wish to lead me. Give me the strength to live the charism you have bestowed upon me, together with my friends, brothers, sisters, and fellow workers. Give me the strength to go out to sea, to know how to take risks and have the courage to live and preach the Gospel wherever I happen to live."

⚜

The night passes and Sunday arrives quickly, with another of those Masses that stir the soul, this time in the presence of the Malagasy Bishop of Ambanja, who has come to express his gratitude for the aid received by his diocese, which had been badly affected by the recent cyclone. I meet Peter for breakfast, while the girls cook what Olga is preparing for lunch (it smells like meat and onions, perhaps for stuffed green peppers or to prepare dumplings).

Peter, looking at one of the girls, says: "She seems free like a bird and is always smiling. I always tell her she must think about her two little brothers; it is for them that she must study so she can help them have a different life."

I ask him about today's Gospel, the story of the woman they wanted to stone to death for adultery. Incredibly, last Sunday's story of the Prodigal Son is followed by this one, so strong and self-examining. They all accuse her, while Jesus writes something on the ground. "What could he have written?" I ask Peter.

"Well, I don't know, but when he told them that whoever among them was sinless should be the first to cast a stone, they all left," he replies.

I know that Peter is not a moralist, nor does he want to go too far regarding sin, "because this word has also been used too much and has been applied to all sorts of things." But I ask him anyway if we are not heading toward the other extreme, abandoning any awareness of evil.

"Man is like that, going from one extreme to another; it's difficult for us to achieve equilibrium, but God has a lot of patience with us." He then adds: "At half past seven, we are going up to Manantenasoa because I like to hear confessions before Mass."

Climbing the slope with Claudine and Rina (I call this twelve-year-old girl "Princess" because of her Asian good looks), the conversation with Peter continues.

"Seventy percent of the people who come to Mass are women, but this is the case all over the world."

"Could it be because man has more doubts and is afraid of making mistakes?" I ask him.

"That would be the case if men were searching for the truth. However, men tend to focus more on the present and expect immediate satisfaction. Women are more receptive and think about the afterlife. If men were afraid of making mistakes in their search for truth, it would be wonderful because they would be looking for God, and as Saint Augustine says, 'If you desire to know God, you already have faith.'"

Peter places a little girl on his shoulders because she cut her foot the day before and it hurts her to walk. He gives her a piggyback ride all the way to the sports hall. His physical strength continues to amaze me. When we arrive, Peter goes to the vestry to put on his alb and stole, and he begins hearing confessions. I remain outside watching the people arrive, while Theresa and some other women sweep the sidewalk. The band rehearses its music, and the elderly rush to find a seat. From a distance, I recognize some characters that are becoming familiar: the old man with a hat and an iron leg, the toothless madwoman who is always drunk, the fat man who is the usher, the elderly woman who has a stump instead of a foot, and my little girls from the dining room. What an assembly of miracles here in Akamasoa, which is itself a miracle!

After Mass, we have the typical Sunday lunch: we eat in the dining room, Miss Bao says grace, there are songs, and more than thirty children join the usual bunch eating on the floor, sitting on the woven mats. After our nap, it is time for soccer at the stadium, where Peter runs like all the boys aged between fifteen and seventeen. He runs up and down, touches the ball, gets away from his marker, and even scores a goal from outside the penalty area. The Reds, commanded by Father Opeka, are winning after the first half by a resounding six goals to nil. Peter comes off the field, and Gregoire and I go in to play for the White team. If it is difficult for me to run at low altitude, I cannot even begin telling you how difficult it is this high up, but I give myself the pleasure of twice kicking the ball into the nearby goal.

TWO

FAMILY VALUES

Today I heard the rooster, but I slept in until nine o'clock. I'm not sure if this is because of yesterday's soccer game or because it is a holiday. I hear a great din outside—vendors are selling bicycles that arrived from France not long ago. Many people crowd in front of the television room, which is next to my house. Forty bicycles are being sold (most of them secondhand) for much less than market value, but ultimately they must be paid for, because that is the spirit of the organization. The potential buyers try them, check to see if everything is in working order, ask a neighbor for his opinion, and make up their minds. They go inside to pay and ride back home, full of pride and satisfaction. This way of distribution continues during the following days, bringing with it some problems and squabbles, particularly involving those who cannot afford the bicycles.

"When something new is introduced, problems always arise. We would love to satisfy everyone but, at least for the time being, there's no way we can do that," Peter tells me later.

After lunch, I meet Father Peter in his office again, and we renew our conversation. I suggest that we talk about the problems in families and in the community.

"The family is of prime importance in society. Through the years, it has gone through different types of crisis, but none as great as the one it finds itself in at present. In the past, when most people lived in the countryside, the environment helped because all family members had to cooperate to obtain their sustenance. They were quite isolated from the rest of the world, and they remained together. But these days, with more than half the world's population living in cities, the situation is different. The family is exposed to outside influences, and this weakens its ties. Some influences are good while others are not.

"Take television, for example. Television enters homes and takes up its position in the family midst. Everybody wants to have it, in order to be up-to-date with the news and to enjoy themselves; that's understandable. But at the same time, viewers are constantly exposed to programs that undermine family values. Those who produce these programs do so to entertain people, but without meaning to, they are destroying the family, being disrespectful, and mocking it. The last time I was in Argentina, I couldn't believe what I was seeing and hearing. There is so much violence and immorality, with plots that show no respect for anything at all. In the long run, this destroys people's subconscious, especially affecting children, because gestures and attitudes are repeated in real life.

"All the marriage breakups and unfaithfulness that appear on TV are considered to be normal. The truth is that when a family breaks up, it's a tragedy, and the ones who suffer most are the little ones. In these programs, there are no values, only problems, shouting, teasing, anger, and turmoil. The family must set limits for society, in order to stop itself from being invaded by certain elements. The problem is that today, in liberal societies, there are no limits; everything is considered to be art.

"The virus of consumerism is also responsible for the crisis in the family because it penetrates from every angle. Consumerism implies that possessions make you somebody. Certain things are a must if you want to attain a certain status. So then, when you don't have a job, or if you have one but there is never enough money to satisfy these fictitious needs, problems arise in the family. Young people want to have fun, wear certain brands of clothes, do what their friends are doing, and all this is expensive and generates problems for their parents. Today, it seems like our worth doesn't depend on who we are but on how much money, how many clothes, houses, and cars we possess.

"In a way, consumerism leads us to pretend. We must appear to be rich, strong, intelligent, fashionable, or important. In truth, families should not even be concerned with appearances: family life should be lived with whatever it has, whether it has a little or a great deal; it should be lived with sobriety, honesty, and truth. We live in a world of pretence and sham. We pretend to be fair, good, open, and compassionate. The number of people who pretend is growing day by day, so those that continue to follow truth and live in truth are very restricted."

"What other symptoms characterize this family crisis?" I inquire.

"The absence of limits is another problem. In a society, family, or community where no limits are set, there is a risk of self-destruction. Nowadays, the best example is the way in which children are brought up, especially in consumer societies. Often, they are given whatever they want. No limits are set in the belief that they will become stronger that way, but the complete opposite is the case. They become weak and stumble at the smallest adversity. Here, on the other hand, we strive for children from marginal families to regain the hope of being able to overcome their marginalized state. We try to convey to them that, with effort, values, and objectives, you can get ahead in life. When a child misbehaves, he or she is punished and the parents are called in. Sometimes, we speak very directly in a loud voice, so as not to show any sign of weakness because parents don't understand that young people need limits."

I ask Peter what it was like in his own family.

"My father would always say: 'In this family, no one deceives; no one steals—neither within our family nor outside it.' There were no double standards, with a set of values within the family and another one outside it. We had to show respect to family members as well as to other people. When we arrived at any house to work, the first thing my father would tell me was that I mustn't touch anything there. When he had to tell me something, he was very direct.

"Today there is very little emphasis on values such as honesty, respect, sincerity, and truth, despite the fact that Christ said the truth would make us free. The absence of moral values is also responsible for crises in families. I know that being honest with the family is sometimes painful; you must learn to tell the truth at a very early age, because once you are an adult it is more difficult. You have to tell the truth and try to live it. Being sincere is the opposite of pretending. There are families that make a pact of silence: 'Mind your own business, and I won't interfere in yours. We live together in this house, but we all lead separate lives.' If parents say this, the children will behave like this too. That's not a community; it's a group of people that are together simply because they have to live under the same roof. When this is the case, it means they have wasted their time, and the children have not been taught to tell the truth. For a family to exist there must be a community; and for a community to exist there must first be love."

I am fascinated by what Peter is saying. Time goes by, and fortunately nobody interrupts us.

"There are different types of love: between friends, between a husband and wife, between brothers and sisters. These are all different kinds of love, but they all come from the same source. Fraternal love in a community, like the one we have in Akamasoa, springs principally from our faith in God, because God makes that kind of love possible. In a family where God is not present, it's more difficult, but it's not impossible if values and truth are being sought. All of us, even if we don't believe in God, know that when we speak the truth, we have the same point of reference; we are committed to not lying, not deceiving, and not pretending. Whoever lives in truth can live in a community. We cannot monopolize truth, saying that if we don't have faith in God, we cannot reach truth. Faith isn't the sine qua non for a family or a community to function; otherwise we wouldn't be able to live in a society that includes nonbelievers. However, if we believe in truth, everything will originate from that point: respect, dialogue, justice, and sharing."

I become a little like Pontius Pilate and ask him: "What is truth?"

"Christ didn't reply to Pilate, thereby suggesting he should look for it. Certain requirements need to be met in order to find it. If you are a person, a human being with a soul, not an animal, you must look for it. Christ was right when he didn't give any answer because in that context it wasn't worth it. The best answer he had was to remain silent. He says the same thing to all of us: search for truth, make the effort because he who searches, finds. Christ used few words. I have seen houses here with tiny doors, through which a lot of people can squeeze because they make an effort to take things calmly, with patience, without pushing, and in the end, they all fit in."

꧁

That evening we have a farewell celebration for Carole and Gregoire, who are returning to Paris tomorrow. The girls in the dining room prepare a show, and then Peter addresses some farewell words to them. "What you have seen here is what we are. When you return home, try to remember the thousands of children of Akamasoa who walk barefoot and live near the landfill site but who inwardly are very far from that place."

THREE

ACTION AND CONTEMPLATION

The rooster began crowing at a quarter past five and did not stop until six. At a quarter to six, he got into a duel with another rooster for two or three minutes, and I had no choice but to get up.

The issue of just wealth distribution is a never-ending story. How can we achieve this? Putting everything in the state's hands for it to distribute is an experiment that has already failed. Letting the strengths of the markets dictate this has not changed the situation either. What about something halfway? How should we do it? It's a dilemma for mankind that will only be resolved when hearts change and start sharing, something Peter stresses so much.

"God created the world with a natural order; that's why man should aim for a harmonizing order because harmony is what brings peace. Conflicts begin when that harmony is broken. There are conflicts that are sparked by our way of life, the way we think, and the way we express ourselves, and these conflicts can somehow be contained. But when they are of an existential or economic nature, when some people prevent other people from living, then the conflicts become violent. The world produces two times more food than it needs, and still there are millions of people starving. This breaks the harmony. We should consume only what we need, and the rest should be put at the disposal of others."

Half past six finds me seated at my desk. Through my glass door, I can people arriving at the fountain. Lining up, yawning, taking the sleep out of their eyes, with their colorful assortment of buckets, they are waking up to a new day of work and study. They are people like me, with two hands, two feet (although many are barefoot), with straight or curly hair, with eyes that admire the beauty of the valley, with mouths that wish others a good morning, hiding their sorrows and showing their happiness. Yes, there is happiness, even if the children have noticed that more water has been added to their midday ration because an official in Brussels put an end to the aid.

"The basis for harmony is respect for the other person; we shouldn't abuse or demean our neighbor; we should make him feel accepted. If rich countries knew how to share their surplus fairly, people wouldn't be marginalized," Peter has told me. "Here, when we receive aid from abroad, it makes people feel that they are not alone, that they are part of the human race. In conclusion, to attain harmony what is needed is acceptance of others and the sharing of wealth."

I go outside. It is seven o'clock in the morning and school is waiting for the children with its doors open, benches empty, blackboards clean, and kitchens deserted. I don't know where Peter is, but I imagine him praying in his room, asking God to transform hearts, to infuse them with new blood, awakening those in the European Union who decided to cancel food aid for Madagascar—opening their eyes, moving them to erase what they had decided; instilling in them the need to share until the people in Akamasoa become self-sufficient. There is a date—a year, a month, and a day: June, 26, 2006. It is not so far away. They must give them that opportunity; the people deserve it.

I do not know what I can do for them myself, beyond writing this book. Should I take the spirit of Akamasoa to my own country, even though I am not a missionary, nor have I ever laid a brick on a wall in my entire life? Reality questions me: What am I doing for those who have less, for the outcast?

❦

Today I visit the primary, middle, and high schools with Miss Fillette. When we enter a classroom, the children stand up and greet me with a "Bonjour, Monsieur." Then they sit down, and cannot stop looking at me, giggling among themselves. Who is this foreigner roaming the town? What does he want to find out? Yes, as you can see, this is where we study, sitting at wooden desks; we have copybooks, pencils, and chalk for the teacher to write on the blackboard, even though you cannot even imagine what it was like in the beginning.

Miss Fillette says, "We started with nothing. We had a classroom where we brought children from the landfill site just to entertain them, play, and sing songs. Later we started teaching. We didn't have any desks, so they would sit on the floor. Then we started giving them food rations, the number of classrooms increased, and we prepared a program of studies and hired teachers."

At the middle school, the young boys come over to greet me, although their gazes have lost some of their innocence, and they have begun thinking about what their future will be like, what is in store for them. Next I go to the high school. I am lucky to be able to talk to a Spanish teacher who studied the language at the University of Antananarivo. This good man allows me to join the final year class, which they call "terminale." I am able to ask the adolescents if they will study at the university and what career they will choose. Just like in Argentina, it seems more difficult for the boys to choose their vocation; girls have more clarity of vision in this respect. One says she will be a journalist, another will study law, and yet another will be a social worker. How marvelous! The results of the program can be seen, heard, shared and enjoyed.

Afterwards, we get on the bus with Gregoire, Carole, and eleven of the girls from the dining room. We set off towards the airport because today the French couple will return to Paris. The new outing awakens the songs that do not stop until we reach our destination. At the airport, everybody recognizes Father Peter. Some greet him, and others make remarks among themselves. Yes, Father Peter, the one who takes care of the poor, who appears in the newspapers and on television, who has formed a community of love that can clearly be seen in the way the girls share the chips, pretzels, and soda I have bought for them without fighting or arguing.

❦

On the way back, the girls seem tired and are quiet, so I take the opportunity to continue talking with Peter. I ask him to describe the main problems within the community.

"The problems are related to coexistence," he answers.

"Is coexistence easier when there is a leader who is respected, as is the case here?" I ask.

"In a certain sense it is easier, provided that the leader takes responsibility for interpreting and defending the wishes of the entire community, as long as he listens to them, respects them, and treats them as equals. In this way, they will be able to accept that there is someone who will make a final decision. There will always be jealousy, envy, and competition, but these things must be talked through and solutions must be found. Problems will always exist—they will never be completely removed from the heart of man—but they can be diminished by prayer, the Word of God, and meditation. These tools allow us to dominate problems and keep them under control."

"Any leader risks becoming authoritarian, arrogant, and vain. How can this be combated?"

"In my case, I can only combat it with prayer and Christ's example. If I consider myself a Christian, Christ is the example of what a leader should be like. The one who is at the head is the one who works the most. He has to listen, motivate, make decisions, and encourage people to forgive."

I as if the members of the community never criticize the leader, how can he discern if he is acting well? "People, above all children, are a great help for me. When the children come to me, it means that they can still perceive a certain amount of humility in me, because if they were afraid of me, something would be wrong. This is also true of the elderly who do not hesitate to approach me. If people don't say something with words, they say it with gestures. As a leader, you have to know how to interpret these gestures because flatterers also abound. You must act all the time with the strength of prayer, and you must also be self-critical, because you can do things wrong too. God knows what is going on, and when you pray, God speaks to you. Your own conscience also indicates if what you are looking for is for your own benefit or that of others. When you are near God, when you read the Gospel and really want to follow him, you cannot become blind or silence your conscience.

"When an enterprise of this nature is undertaken, it cannot be done superficially because there are thousands of lives at stake, which is why you must think in terms of a long-term effort. You must have conviction and inner strength, and this cannot depend on your frame of mind. Leaders can't bring their personal problems to the project.

When helping the poor, you must maintain your initial enthusiasm and effort. It is true that there are ups and downs but your inner strength is nourished by helping the poor, looking them in the eye, and visiting them. All this gives you more stamina, renews you, and raises your spirits if you are disillusioned. You have to put yourself in the poor person's shoes and realize that you too could be in that situation. That causes you to react and take pity on the person."

"Peter, what is compassion?"

"Compassion is not a vague sentiment; it's something that spurs you to act, to love, and to help others. Compassion, from a certain point of view, means getting closer to the other person. It doesn't imply being in the same situation, but helping to set him free from his problems. It's offering him a hand and filling him with the hope and conviction that he is not alone. For instance, if you see someone in a swamp, you don't have to get in the water with him, but you stretch out your hand to pull him out."

Peter toots the horn at a cart blocking the way and then continues with what he was saying. "You must strive to forget your own problems and even yourself. Otherwise, you will always feel a little resentful when you are not loved enough by others. You must try to love others more, and in that way you solve your own love crisis. Continuous, constant, everyday effort is needed.

"You never reach the summit, but life is like that—it's a continuous, effortful walk, always trying to create something better and searching for truth. We can only perceive a part of it, and at that point a great happiness will awaken in us, with the conviction that we are on the right path. I really like what the Epistles of Peter, James, and John say about this because they are short, clear, and to the point. They wrote about their own reactions when faced with Christ and the road he showed them. To someone who knows nothing about theology, I recommend starting with these epistles. It's difficult to discern the road to God, but there comes a point when you feel it; you have an intuitive feeling that you are on the right path. And when you find it, you feel an inner peace that only God can give you."

⤐�֎⤏

In the afternoon, I accompany Peter on his rounds through Manantenasoa. When we pass the neighborhood of Lovasoa (in Malagasy: "the good inheritance"), we see a lot of people crowding around the front of a house. Peter stops the pickup and gets out. He makes his way through the throng and reaches the door of the house. A woman cries: "My two sons are beating each other to death; the youngest one is on the upper floor and wants to hurl himself out of the window." The woman cries; she bites her lips. Peter calms her down and enters the house. I follow him. A young black man, strong and muscular, is on the first floor, sitting on a chair and hiding his face in his hands. Peter approaches the man, makes him show his face, and recognizes him. It is Heritiana, a quarry worker, whom he congratulated a short time ago for his work. He is drunk, with bloodshot eyes and a mouth that twists down at the sides as he dribbles. Peter says: "You are coming with me right now, and the fight is over this instant."

After talking to his mother, we take the man to the pickup, while the neighbors watch with curiosity and murmur among themselves. Heritiana climbs into the truck with difficulty. I sit next to him, and together we head for his neighborhood, Mangarivotra. On the way, Peter realizes that if Heritiana arrives home in this state, he might beat his wife and his children. So Peter decides to go for a drive in the woods near the Holy Family grotto, to provide Heritiana with some fresh air and some time to sober up. When we arrive, Peter tells him to sit under the pine trees, while we prune the lower branches of the trees. After a while, he calls Peter over. With difficulty, half-stuttering, he tells Peter that his quarry tools were stolen and that since then he has been drinking cane liquor because he cannot believe his friends could have stolen what he needs to survive.

Peter observes him. He thinks about what Heritiana has said, and he sees that he is sorry about drinking and fighting with his brother, but he tells him that he cannot understand how he has not found a way to solve his problem without turning to alcohol. Heritiana continues stammering some words. He tells Peter that he used to have four children but the youngest died in the 2002 epidemic. He says it was the doctor's fault; he believes the doctor failed to give him the proper treatment because he was from Akamasoa. When he told them he worked at Father Peter's quarry, they did not want to treat him because the doctors were on dictator Ratsikara's side and they knew Mompera was on the new government's side.

According to Peter, "Now that he is drunk, he has the courage to talk about his sorrows." They continue talking until the afternoon slips away and nighttime fills the woods with darkness. Heritiana seems to be calmer and less drunk, and I can see that his lips have stopped trembling. We set off for his home, a wooden hut where his wife and his three remaining children live. The door is open, and a small lantern is lit inside. Heritiana's wife is sitting on the bed with the children who are eating some rice she has warmed up on the brazier. Heritiana asks Father Peter for some money to buy new tools: a mallet, chisels, and pins. Peter tells him that if he is willing to continue working and to drop the alcohol, they will help him. Heritiana answers with an "Oui, Mompera, I promise."

FOUR

NUMBERS AND STATISTICS

The day begins in Peter's office at half past seven on the dot, following a frugal breakfast. However, an unforeseen meeting with his assistants delays our conversation. "There are so many problems here that if you put them all inside a computer it would catch fire."

The twenty-year-old man from Antolojanahary that Father Rok took to the hospital is back with a terminal diagnosis: "Kidney failure—no remedy," and the good friends of Akamasoa are wondering what they can do. In addition, yesterday a conflict broke out in the workplace at Bemasoandro because one of the workers (a scoundrel who has already been in jail several times, says Peter) threatened to set fire to the houses if the foreman did not give him more money. They have already asked the gendarmes to summon him. A woman with two daughters, who practiced prostitution and was expelled from Akamasoa, is demanding help because she has AIDS. There is a priest in the waiting room who has come to ask Peter for material help for his parish, and a deputy will pay him a visit at nine o'clock. Everything falls on him as if he were a social welfare minister.

Peter apologizes and tells me to return at ten. At ten o'clock I come back, but as soon as we start talking about his visit to Argentina in the 2000, the telephone rings. While he is talking on the phone, he hands me a little picture of the Virgin of Luján. On the front, below the image it reads: "Mother, listen to your nation's clamor." On the back, Peter had a biblical quotation printed:

> "The Lord's Spirit sent me to take the good news to the poor."
> Pedro Opeka, Vincentian missionary in Madagascar
> Silver Anniversary of Ordination, the Jubilee Year 2000

To celebrate his twenty-five years of priesthood, he also celebrated Mass in the Slovenian school in Lanús, Argentina. Marija, his mother, wrote: "We feel so privileged that God has settled his gaze on our humble family by choosing you. You are God's bricklayer. May your hands never cease blessing and your mouth never cease announcing his Word."

Peter hangs up and tells me there are problems with the sale of bicycles in Antaninarenina. "Let's go." We get in the white pickup and off we go. On the way, he stops the truck next to some children. He opens the door and calls a little girl called Jeanette. He lifts her up into the pickup, gives her a hug, and kisses her. When the girl turns around to look at me, I notice that she does not have a nose. I drop my gaze because I cannot look at her. She inspires compassion and repulsion at the same time; a strange sensation, faced with two black holes mounted on a cavity between the cheekbones, with the skin stretched due to the scars, as if she had been stitched up with a sewing machine. The girl's long hair is disheveled and her eyes are gorgeous, but I dare not look at them because my stomach turns at the other sight.

"A rat ate her nose at the landfill site when she was a baby. I baptized her," Peter says.

An old man, with a hollow eye and almost toothless, comes towards us. Peter says: "This elderly man is one of the finest persons that can be found here." Yes, I understand, but I cannot look at him either—it is hard; it hurts; I cannot do anything for him. Nor do I know where to hide when faced with such misfortune.

When we continue, I ask him how he can put up with these things. "The more you look misery in the eye, the more strength you obtain to continue struggling for them." And he adds one of his phrases that make a deep impression on me: "He who sows in sorrow shall reap in joy."

Later, when Peter has resolved the disagreement regarding the sale of bicycles, explaining that a certain quantity were sent to each neighborhood according to its population and that, God willing, more will soon arrive, we again meet Jeannette. When I see the little girl, I pluck up my courage, walk towards her, and look her in the eye, just above those two black holes and the tangled web of scars, and stroke her hair. She smiles; at least it is a step forward, even if I do not dare kiss her on the cheek.

"Pain and evil form part of life. We see many people suffering, and we ask ourselves why somebody else has to suffer, not us. When I see another person suffer, I think it could be my turn someday, and I ask myself what my reaction would be. Would I continue doing good to others, or would I wallow in self-pity, start crying, and asking for sympathy? We cannot answer these questions, but we can start getting ready spiritually. We live in an imperfect world. Evil exists, as does imperfection."

"But doesn't it get you down?" I ask.

"It depends on how you were brought up. If you were born into a family where there was joy and respect, you carry these with you in your spirit. For somebody who is born into a family where there was a lot of verbal and physical violence, it's harder to be happy and optimistic because he or she will always carry the weight of that childhood. But genuine faith always brings optimism. A Christian must necessarily be optimistic. Faith is a grace from God that must be nourished by our daily life, sincerity, and effort, but above all, by devoting our lives to others. The surest way of experiencing God and his happiness is through our neighbor. When we take our brothers and sisters into consideration, when we help others, we find meaning in our lives. The more we shut ourselves in, the further we get from God."

❦

This afternoon, I get together with Miss Bao to talk a little about Akamasoa statistics. We have a good laugh when she lists the names of the villages and towns. I really try to spell them correctly, but I find it practically impossible. The only one I know by heart is Andralanitra, which is pronounced "And-ja-lanch-a."

Numbers are always cold and very rarely show what lies behind them, but I take down what she says anyway: 2,923 families or family groups (almost 60 percent are women alone with their children), 15,560 residents (16,000 together with those in the Welcome Center), 8,409 pupils distributed as follows: 7,324 in kindergartens and primary schools, 765 in middle school, and 120 in high school (which shows very clearly how seriously education has been taken since Peter took pity on them and said: "If you are willing to work, I am going to help you").

Miss Bao laughs again when she tries to explain that "sages femmes" are midwives (she indicates with gestures the swollen belly and someone who tries to make it go down), and that the "aides-soignants" are the paramedics. We discuss the cash flow, including income and expenses. On the right-hand side are the expenses for education (staff, stationery, teaching materials, food, repairs, and construction work) and health services (doctors, paramedics, mid-wives, dentists, social workers, and hospitalization). She explains that the state has started contributing a small amount and that it currently finances the salaries of three doctors, the dentist, and twenty teachers.

"Only twenty out of eighty-nine?" I ask.

"Yes, but at least it is some progress."

It is true that the former government did not help at all, as though the children studying here were not Malagasy. Then there is the cost of building houses (materials, labor, land), furnishing the different workshops (furniture, mechanical, crafts, and embroidery) with materials, and paying the salaries of the drivers and those in charge of the organization.

On the left-hand side is the income. First, donations: clothing, medicine, and money. Then income raised by Akamasoa itself: school fees, sale of medicine in the dispensaries, participation in housing projects, the quarry, the sale of furniture, crafts and embroidery, compost preparation, agriculture, water supply contributions, the sale of books, and collections. Lastly, there is the state contribution that I have mentioned above.

I analyze the numbers and calculate what will happen if the European Union's measure is not reversed, even though Guy told me during last Sunday's Mass: "Perhaps it might help us achieve self-sufficiency quicker." There would be a definite imbalance. Then I calculate what will happen when they stop building houses. The world is governed by numbers, data, graphics, and projections, but behind it all there are human beings that live very comfortably, comfortably, reasonably, badly, or in misery. Despite globalization, individuals are increasingly cut off from each other. Someone who is considered poor in Norway, where the average income is $40,000, would be very well off in Argentina. And whoever is not well off in Argentina would be well off in Madagascar.

Differences between extremes that sound unfair break the harmony and cause resentment. Peter explains, "Resentment arises when people are forgotten, when such differences exist. The state must warrant social peace, justice, and human rights. NGOs and the Church offer help because they cannot let people die just like that, but it must be the prime responsibility of the state and of those who hold power to enforce laws that guarantee social equity and economic justice. "Resentment grows with time and is difficult to get rid of. When people look at you suspiciously and with resentment, you must react and build bridges. You have to lend them a hand, because they are incapable of helping themselves or have lost hope.

"The initiative should come from those who are more educated and are capable of understanding. Life in society is very complicated; when I address two thousand people, I know that not all of them understand me the same way. When I talk to them about help, some may understand that it refers to concrete help, while others see it as ongoing assistance. The most important thing is to start building that bridge. Doing this cannot be explained mathematically. It is in your soul, your spirit, and your heart. It's your intuition and your love that will guide you to choose the right words and gestures to approach the poor. You must surrender everything in order to get closer, and there is no material reward for offering your life in that way—only a profound happiness."

FIVE

FACES OF MADAGASCAR

Madagascar seems to go from one crisis to another. Two weeks ago, there was Cyclone Gafilo, and now it is the economy. Everything started at the end of last week when gasoline and gas oil prices went up. As an Argentinean, I have firsthand experience of this kind of crisis, and I know that increasing fuel prices by 30 percent leads directly to an inflation peak and devaluation. When I arrived, 9,000 Malagasy francs were equivalent to one euro, while today that figure has already risen to 12,000. An economic crisis is on the doorstep, along with political instability. Last night, three persons of Merina ethnicity were assassinated near the coast, and according to what Peter says, when the tribal fights break out here it is a serious problem. Meanwhile, former president Ratsikara continues his work of destabilization while living in Paris.

⚜

At midday, I go with Tojo and Viviane to the primary school canteen: a great shed, where 2,500 children have lunch on weekdays. I've never seen anything like it in all my life. The yelling was deafening, but it got even worse when I went inside and started taking photographs. They all wanted to have a photograph taken and, thanks to the digital camera, I was able to show them what they looked like. "That's me!" shouted one. "And that's the teacher," said another. I leave when the men began bringing the steaming hot pots from the kitchen and a great silence falls over the group.

"I dream that the children here will be good people and that, if they become leaders, they will in turn be able to encourage others and give them hope. If the world were full of leaders who transmit values, love, and joy, it would be completely different. Happiness for me is something very important, but it isn't only a moment, it's a state. Momentary happiness is only entertainment, while happiness of the heart is something completely different. It is something you seek and achieve with time. We have to learn to be happy people," said Peter.

In the afternoon, I accompany Peter to the dentist again, and then we go up to Manantenasoa to see how the construction of the new group of fifteen houses is progressing. Last week they had no roofs, but this week half of them are already covered. These are two-story houses meant for single families, with a living room and kitchen downstairs and a large room upstairs that is usually divided into two with a partitioning wall. The bathroom is outside, in keeping with Malagasy custom. Later on, we go to a neighborhood of temporary wooden homes, where the people have been waiting for almost ten years because they trust Father Peter and Akamasoa.

"We still have to build 400 houses. I hope that by the end of next year, not one of these old houses will remain. However, we will still have to find a solution for the temporary neighborhood of Andrala-nitra if the state donates the lands, as well as solving the water supply problem, enlarging the schools, and finishing the hospital..."

While Peter finishes the list, I look at the wooden hovels. No, I would not be able to live here, right next to my neighbor, listening to what they are saying or having them listen to me. I would not last even a few hours, with the summer sun heating the corrugated iron roofs, making the room into a furnace; feeling the drafts entering through every crevice at night, or the rain soaking my bed due to the leaks which they must surely have. I can only imagine what winter would be like, wrapping up as best I can, breathing the smoke of the small brick brazier where the rice is boiled, delousing my children, smelling poverty all over the place, killing flies, listening to shouts, laughter, and complaints. Peter tells me: "As long as the population grows and the economy does not, this will never end." I can see Peter, faced with other people's misfortunes, accepting more and more people, more women on their own. He has a compassionate soul and could never be able to tell them to leave, to manage as best they can on their own, that he has already done enough.

Peter looks into the distance and, pointing to a new neighborhood of broad streets, green vegetable patches, decent houses, clean sidewalks, and street lights, asks me: "Isn't that neighborhood beautiful?"

I reply: "Of course it is, Peter. It's a great contrast between the poor who are waiting, and those who have recovered hope as a result of the effort you have all made."

We leave that place and go to the dispensary, accompanied by Theresa. The young man with kidney failure is lying there, terminally ill, and the doctors have given up hope. Peter greets the man who must be his father; he is slowly eating a plate of rice. The man asks Peter if he can baptize his son before he dies. Peter listens to him, while I watch the young man who will die in a few days. How hard all this is, Lord! What am I doing here? I do not belong to this world. My world is a world of big, comfortable houses, with well-dressed children, where we only see fragments of this other world on television. In my world, poor people are only remembered when we give money to beggars in the attempt to appease our conscience.

We go out into the corridor where the doctor confirms the diagnosis, saying, "He doesn't have much time left." I try to put on the bravest face I can. For Peter, this is an ordinary occurrence; it is what he sees every day: life, sickness, and death prowling around the villages.

We go down to Andralanitra in the pickup. When we arrive, a woman who has walked over three hours from the other side of town approaches Father Peter carrying a child in her arms. She tells him they have nothing to eat. Peter looks at me and says: "I simply cannot solve the problems of every single person." However, he tells her to accompany him, and I am sure he will find a way to alleviate her suffering.

The Welcome Center statistics fail if you take into account the thousands of cases that are not recorded. How many have I seen in the last fortnight and a half? Hundreds. I become stronger as the days go by; there is no point in crying when faced with misery. "All those experts come with their advice—they should concentrate on creating a better world instead. Sometimes, people come to us with such an arrogant attitude that we tell them if they are going to help us in that way, we don't want their help. We have to become aware that whatever we give doesn't belong to us. We have to work very hard to make people understand this. It is every generation's job to invite their fellow men to share their human, spiritual, and material wealth. The number of people on this planet is growing, so we must share more; we cannot simply wash our hands, pretending we don't know."

During dinner, I ask Peter if he will baptize the young man. "Well, it depends whether the baptism is requested by the young man, because one cannot give a sacrament just like that."

I frown with doubt, and Peter adds: "When Jesus cured the paralyzed man, he first asked him: 'Would you like me to heal you?' If the boy asks me to baptize him, I will do so."

Afterwards, everyone roars with laughter when I tell them how I misuse the Malagasy words. For example, "thank you very much" in Malagasy is "misaotra betsaka," but I say "ni laucha ni rata," which means "neither mouse nor rat" in Spanish. Peter laughs like a child, and that makes me feel better after the afternoon we have just had.

⚜

At night, the faces of the people I've seen flash before me, preventing me from falling asleep. Heritiana's bloodshot eyes stammering with remorse, Jeannette's face which breathes differently, Charline eyeing her small world, the elderly man with a hole for an eye, the woman crying with her baby in her arms, and the elderly woman with the broken arm. I try to replace these faces of misery with the Asian smile belonging to Rina, who has combed her hair in ten braids today, Claudine devouring a piece of chocolate, Viviane who has returned from burying her grandfather, restless Natasha who dances continually, dreamy Tojo who inquires about Argentina, or that smile that very occasionally I manage to get from Miss Bao.

The dark or copper faces return to fill the darkness with their features. Figures of women breastfeeding with completely dry breasts, farm laborers splitting the earth open with their sweat, men working like mules pushing carts up a slope, children carrying loaded buckets, peddlers, or men shunning their responsibilities to indulge in cane liquor. Oh, Madagascar! Forgotten island between Asia and Africa, floating in poverty, floating in the sea of fatality. Come and see it, powerful and mighty people of the world. Open your eyes and start telling its story. Tell everybody about the number of people who walk barefoot, those who are dirty, smelly, hungry, and undernourished. Then make your way to Akamasoa, where Peter will explain how to free the people and make them stand on their own feet, even if the expressions on their faces suggest they are condemned to live in the marshes of fatality.

SIX

THE NEED FOR PURIFICATION

Five o'clock in the morning: Father Rok knocks on my door. I get up, open the window, and tell him I am already awake. "Merci, Père Rok!" Today is the first Friday of the month, and like every first Friday for the past nine years, Mass is celebrated at six o'clock in the morning at the grotto of the Holy Family. We go on foot. I walk hand in hand with little Annie, Marcial's daughter. A girl called Pulini and Viviane also join us.

The road is longer than the one I take on Sundays to get to Manantenasoa, and we have to climb even higher. It is still dark out, but a diaphanous streak of light reveals an overcast sky. It is quite cold. I joke along the way. "Je suis fatigué (I am tired). Why don't we stop here and celebrate Mass?"

We arrive at the pine trees planted by Peter ten years ago, which surround the grotto at the top of the hill. There is a small stone altar and tires for seats on the sides. It is full of people. Michel and Christine (a French couple who are Peter's friends who come every first Friday) are already there. We greet one another affectionately, and they invite me for lunch on Sunday. My friend, the elderly lady who has a stump for a foot, comes over to greet me. We hug each other, and I massage her back as a sign of affection, even if we cannot understand each other. She lets herself be pampered, smiling and leaning against my chest. She wears a handkerchief on her head, a bright-colored sweater, and a long, orange skirt that covers her legs right down to her heels. She carries a crutch in her right hand and a rosary in her left.

Peter and Father Rok concelebrate Mass. The grotto is oval-shaped, and the walls are painted with images of the Holy Family of Nazareth. They emphasize, yet again, the importance of work: Joseph is depicted putting up a wall; Jesus is cutting stone; Mary is weaving some rush matting. The message is always present: You have to work to make progress. At this moment, I remember Alojz Opeka, Peter's father, and his stay in the concentration camp; I think about his mother's farewell, giving him her blessing, entrusting him to the Holy Family, and hence the special devotion that was transmitted from the parents to the children.

Peter's homily speaks to me: "Don't be afraid of spreading the Good News. Struggle for truth like Christ did." After Mass, we drive down in the pickup with Father Rok, little Natasha sitting on my lap. I stroke her hair and steal a smile from her, sharing affection.

Later on, I manage to hold a conversation with Peter, and we talk about Argentina. "When I left in 1968, Argentina was a different country. There was happiness; there wasn't so much insecurity. Today, there's a complete lack of respect for life. Those who impose the law are bullies—whoever refuses to obey is killed, making it difficult to defend a just cause. Physical strength is all that counts. It's a lot like Old Testament times."

"What solution could there be?" I ask.

"I think Argentina must be shown the way by example, because words are no longer enough. What is said must be put into practice, and lived day by day. The political class must cleanse itself. The Church must cleanse itself. All the leaders that hold power and have some degree of responsibility must also cleanse themselves, since Argentina didn't end up in its current predicament just like that. Many people have shunned their responsibilities for lack of courage and valor. Many remain silent and don't say anything. Not getting involved allows violence and immorality to gain ground. These spread incredibly fast, while religious and moral values and faith spread at a much slower pace. Evil, the easy life, easy money, and power gained through lies move much faster."

"What is your opinion regarding the 2001 crisis?" I inquire.

"The crisis established important precedents. People today demand more courage, truth, audacity, transparency, and morality. People need leaders, leaders who are willing to sacrifice their lives for the country. This is a difficult thing to ask for. Christ said there is no greater love than to give your life for your fellow men. Being a leader today in Argentina in a way that will bear fruit requires courage, honesty, and the willingness to completely give your life for the people. The number of people in Argentina who no longer believe in a spiritual message is very large. They have become violent and have taken justice into their own hands. Moral values have become muddled."

"How can we achieve purification?" I ask him.

"It is important to try to encounter the reality of the poor. I believe that is the key. If I were separated from the poor, there wouldn't be any sense to my priesthood. It's true that I could preach the Gospel, but the ones who convinced me to go even further were the poor; they were the ones who invited me to live the Gospel radically.

266

I think that a society which attends to the poor, bearing their reality in mind, is saving itself and giving values and a sense of direction to its existence. If the nation worried more about them, it would purify itself, create more jobs, and experience more peace. Many violent and anarchical places, ruled by the law of the jungle and referred to as "nobody's land," would calm down. The phrase 'nobody's land' made a great impact on me."

"How do you interpret it?" I ask for clarification.

"It means that if we don't exist for them, they think you don't exist for us, either. It implies that the government has forgotten many Argentineans due to prejudice or lack of dialogue. That is why so many Argentineans took up arms, and today that violence kills innocent people. I don't know how to remedy that. Too much time has passed. The citizens were abandoned. No one reached out to them.

"The mission of the Church, stemming from the Gospel, is to reach out to the poor. Christ was born among the poor and lived among the poor. He didn't have any place to rest his head. Neither Medellin, or Puebla, or any liberation theologian invented that. Today Argentina, which calls itself Roman Catholic, is violent, sectarian, and disunited. Still, we must not dwell on such a negative picture. I believe Argentina will begin to recover. This crisis can bring new hope, new changes, and new leaders. Let's hope many will appear. You have to risk everything for the poor. My recommendation for all Argentineans who still believe in Christ would be to take out all their spiritual weapons, use all their strength, and live out their convictions. Don't be afraid or embarrassed of what you are. As Pope John Paul II said: 'Let us not be ashamed of our faith.' The ones who should be ashamed are those who created today's Argentina, those who attacked spiritual values and ransacked the country. They are the ones who should stand in shame, not those who would like to live in solidarity, fraternity, communion, and happiness—which was what Argentina was famous for and what made her stand out. I haven't seen that recently. Violence has devastated everything. Here too in the landfill site, the Malagasy were destroyed because misery destroys man. Today, after fifteen years, we have turned the situation around. Argentina can do likewise. It is possible that the arrogant and selfish Argentina, which didn't make room for the humbler Argentina, the one with people of goodwill who believe and help, will be cast aside."

"What about the importance of sharing?" I ask.

"Yes, sharing is fundamental. Argentinean farming land is rich; there is enough to feed all of Africa! Our selfish and negative tendencies—which end up destroying the family, society, the country, a whole civilization—must continually be transformed into more positive values of happiness, hope, and morality. Man can only become truly himself when he lives in truth and with joy. However, Argentina has spiritual and human reserves. The people harboring these reserves should make themselves heard more often, demanding that the ruling class be more honest, transparent, and true. The Church should assist them. The Church should make its voice heard in the media more, because it is through the media that public opinion can be influenced. Nowadays, public opinion is influenced more by people who are not searching for the truth. It requires imagination to find ways of reaching people, talking to them, and presenting a message. I trust Argentina's young people. I believe they will have the imagination and the evangelical courage to proceed and fulfill their mission."

In the afternoon we have the Stations of the Cross. I ask for permission to carry the cross. I have never done this in my life, but I now do it in this remote hamlet in Madagascar, without understanding a word they are saying except when they mention Jesus, Mary, or recite some of the prayers that I already recognize. Yanine, a fourteen-year-old adolescent, helps me, telling me when to advance and when to stop. Later someone tells me it was the first time a vahiny (and a layperson as well) carried the cross in the village.

Once we arrive at the chapel, Ernest, Tojo's father, requests a round of applause for me because I carried the cross. I think that if I compare my cross with theirs, I do not have much to complain about. I have everything I need, yet they are rising up from material misery, from the poverty of a garbage dump. However, I think they have surpassed me in terms of dignity.

SEVEN

THE THIRD WAY

The next morning I arise at eight o'clock. It is drizzling, a very fine rain which seems to anticipate my departure, making the flowers complain and the streets, which would prefer a downpour to get rid of the dust, curse. The rainy season is over and the weather will become drier until the winds bring the black clouds—and with them precious rain to water the seeds and fill the cisterns.

Peter is in a meeting with his assistants. Last night, two representatives from Antolojanahary (the village in the countryside) came with bad news. There is no more rice, and it will be two months before the next harvest. Food has run out, and the 1100 schoolchildren cannot wait. I am on the porch next to his office, contemplating the school playground, watching how the storehouse workers get their wages paid in food. The way they are organized and the way they handle problems that crop up every day fills me with admiration.

❦

When his assistants leave, I enter his office. I want to ask him his opinion on today's world, although there must be other things on his mind. However, as Peter is extremely patient with me, I take heart, and he does indeed show his good will by replying: "After the jubilee year 2000, we thought the world would be more united and would act with more solidarity, promoting friendship among nations. Today, in 2004, we can say the euphoria of the third millennium has evaporated and we have regressed. It seems to me that this is surprising to all of us. At the same time, we are living a new conflict we hadn't even imagined before, a conflict between believers and nonbelievers, between those who see man as a means and those who see him as an end. It's a conflict between those who say all progress should be centered on man and those who say there should be no limits, even if man has to suffer."

"So there is contempt for believers?" I ask.

"Respect for all religions is very important. They hold the wisdom of many centuries that cannot be swept away in a matter of a few decades. Religions have helped people find meaning in their lives, giving them a reason for their existence. Today, this great economic progress wants to get rid of religion by promoting consumerism and the mentality of instant satisfaction. Much harm has been done, and some people have resorted to fundamentalism. We have all gone rather astray, as if we were lost, looking for new roads, but the past must not be indiscriminately destroyed or forgotten. This conflict will last a long time. I believe that was why Andre Malraux said that the twenty-first century will be spiritual or it will cease to exist."

"What about the third way?" I ask.

"After the fall of communism, prospects of a 'third way' emerged, but so far, nothing has come of it. In my opinion, this third way will be found in the great religions of the world. Every religion must undergo a certain amount of purification and adapt to the times while keeping its values. This progress cannot be anarchic. Christ was for progress. He brought a new spiritual and moral kind of strength. He never said that what existed before was wrong; he said the law had to be respected, but he also promoted the necessary changes. The faith of every generation will have to undergo some kind of purification according to current discoveries and the progress achieved.

"Faced with these discoveries, people of faith have something to say. But these days they are often ignored. There is no dialogue, or insufficient dialogue, between scientists, philosophers, and the heads of different religions. Scientists say: 'Why should we ask the religious, if what we are doing is empirical and material and has nothing to do with the spiritual?' However, man is not only material but also spiritual. Dialogue is necessary. Finding the best path is a task for different generations. The third way passes through the religions, which respond to man's thirst for the transcendent. It is a shame that Europe, which is about to adopt a new constitution, should expressly omit the word 'God.' Europe is what it is today thanks to Christianity, which gave individuals the freedom to say 'I believe' or 'I do not believe.' Why doesn't anyone in Saudi Arabia say that he or she doesn't believe in Islam, or that he or she is an atheist? They dare not. It was Christianity that defended freedom of conscience in Europe. Other religions will eventually follow suit, but it will take time. But for now they are trying to remove God from society."

Peter pauses to let me relax for a second before continuing.

"It was known that communism wasn't going to last because it was a system which sought to oppress man, his conscience, and his soul, as well as physically oppressing those who didn't subordinate themselves to the state. However, capitalism cannot claim victory for the fall of communism; it too should cleanse itself. Both systems destroy man. One crushes the person, while the other undermines a person's roots; suddenly you are standing up, but they have cut off your spirit."

"How can this situation change?" I ask.

"With an economy based on solidarity, which treats the individual as the center of the system and the end in itself. I don't have any formulas. The only thing I know is that here, with just a small amount of money, we gave people education, healthcare, housing, jobs, and meaning, and they changed; they became peaceful. What we have done for 16,000 people could be done for many more. We must strive to share all the time. Nobody should be excluded from human progress, which is glorified to such an incredible extent. What glory can world progress achieve if we are creating more and more and yet an increasing number of people are excluded from it? We have to humanize capitalism, placing man at its center as the social doctrine of the Church teaches. That is what the medieval religious communities did; they proposed alternative lifestyles. There must be courage to create new communities and promote spiritual renewal. To attain all this, it is necessary to have a lot of evangelical strength and audacity like Christ had. We must aim high.

"Renewal and change are possible, but for this to take place, man has to purify himself and accept in his heart that he is a created being. Man has to believe in something because he is a dependent being. He must accept that the purpose of his existence cannot be himself; the purpose of his existence is the One who created him. Those who believe this must work side by side with those who have other options. Even if we have different beliefs, we have to work together to reach the truth. In pursuing that objective we will unite, and we can become friends, coexisting in respect and tolerance—which doesn't mean indifference. The number of people who believe in truth, as we do, may decrease with the passing of time, and we will be persecuted, because evil is more attractive than truth."

"Peter, what is your message for young people?"

"Young people should seek the truth and only the truth, because this will make them free. They should have the valor and courage to pursue it with sincerity and humility. They should leave their own nests and the security with which they have surrounded themselves. Truth can only be found with humility. Christ says that whoever wishes to become great must be prepared to serve. Coming into contact with poverty and its reality makes the quest for truth worthwhile and fills life with purpose."

⁂

We conclude our conversation and head for Manantenasoa. Peter has called a meeting with the elderly people in the room next to the sports hall. He wants to discuss the way they will ration the food supplies. I am not smoking, because I have run out of cigarettes. "It's good for you, and it's a small sacrifice for Lent," Peter tells me.

We enter a room crowded with people. As usual, I scrutinize people's faces carefully. They all greet Mompera. Madame Louisette is at his side. People are sitting on the floor or standing next to the doors. Peter begins talking, and they all fall silent. He explains the problem that has arisen because of the ending of the European Union's food-aid program. "We will have to start rationing the rice and beans," he says. I observe an elderly man leaning against a wall next to some bags. He is wearing a small straw hat, he has sunken eyes, and the wrinkles on his face suck in the skin around his cheekbones, as if it were plummeting into an empty hole that serves as a mouth. His gaze is lost on his walking stick, which is resting on his right foot, but he conveys something to me that is impossible to describe in words. Is it the peace gained by keeping hope alive when confronted with adversity?

"We will try to help all of you, but we will have to carry out a selection process because poverty is not the same in every case. Some of you have more resources than others because you either have a job or collect a pension. The state should provide at least a minimum of assistance to all of you, but it doesn't. Consequently, we must be fair. Those who are older than seventy and those with fewer resources must be given priority," Peter continues.

When he finishes talking, a man thanks him for having come to explain the situation. Peter tells me later, "It was pure praise; they always try to be cordial and convey everyone's respect."

Afterwards, a woman stands up and asks that every person receive equal help. Very few people applaud her. Then another woman, who seems to be voicing several people's opinions, stands up. She says, "Miss Theresa has already made a list of those who are in most need, and it must be respected. The elderly and those who have the least resources must come first." A great round of applause ends the meeting, with the decision approved by the majority. "This is how decisions are made here," Peter comments.

On the way back, I ask Peter to drive me to a place where I can buy cigarettes because there aren't any in Manantenasoa or in the adjoining market. What a vice! I seem desperate, and Peter does not understand me. He turns onto the highway and stops in front of a store that appears to sell them. I get out in a hurry, without realizing we are on the edge of a ditch. In an attempt to avoid the ditch, I slam the door on my left hand. Bang! My thumb stops me, reminding me with pain that it is still jammed in the door. Peter worries when he sees my face, but fortunately I have not lost my thumb; it is only a cut that bleeds in torrents. The pain runs up my arm, seizes my shoulder, and descends to my foot. Peter turns in the direction of the dispensary at Manantenasoa. I curse the cigarettes and stare at the open cut and deep wound which looks a little like poverty to me. Thanks to the Akamasoa project, there is a dispensary here with disinfectant, pieces of gauze, and adhesive tape. I bandage it, even though the nail has darkened and my thumb looks like a red pepper.

In the afternoon, after reading some articles in Spanish about Father Peter, I hear his voice calling me from outside. "Jesús María."

"I'm coming," I reply. I climb into the pickup. "How's that thumb?" he asks me.

"Better, improving. Perhaps it will be a mark to remind me of Akamasoa," I tell him. My scar will be a souvenir of my visit to this place, so I won't forget the dispossessed, the forgotten, the rejected, and the poorest among the poor. We return to Manantenasoa. This time, Peter has called the men to tell them about the need to remain united in this time of crisis. It's a crisis in the country, with the government being harassed by its opponents every day, and it's a crisis within Akamasoa because of the food aid having been cut off, resulting in the need to ration food.

We enter the sports hall, which is full to the brim, and Patrice says it will be easier to hear Peter from the neighboring patio, as there is a problem with the microphones. The meeting is for the purpose of reminding everyone that we are a family, we are brothers and sisters, we are a nation. Peter tells the crowd that everything is in their hands, and they must respect one another and remain united.

Peter talks and the 800 men listen, sitting on the stairs, while the afternoon slips away and I try to keep my mind off my swollen finger. After half an hour, Peter stops talking and listens to what the assembly has to say. An elderly man in a white straw hat and a walking stick in his right hand stands up and addresses the people. He says Peter is a man of God—that he came here to help them and he has the right to say these things because he helped them when no one was interested in them. "He has no family here, we are his family; he loves us and respects us; that is why we must listen to him. I've been here for the past thirty-two years, and I know what it was like here. There was nothing. The government brought the first families here, and five people died practically every day. This place was hell. Father Peter says he planted a small seed, and from that small seed a great tree has grown. We can all see it. The priest says we must love and respect one another. Who isn't ready to receive a message like this?"

A round of applause follows and the old man sits down, proud of what he has said. Then Patrice draws the meeting to a close saying: "We have nothing else to add; it is clear that every one of us has to make the effort within our own families and neighborhoods." The assembly closes with prayer and a thanksgiving song that resonates in the sunset.

<hr />

Afterwards, Peter shared his thoughts about the meeting. "If the people left with some food for thought, I am satisfied. I spoke above all about unity, truth, work, and responsibility towards their families, especially their children. I said that we must defend what we have constructed and be very cautious in the face of the politicians, because very serious things are going on now. I begged them not to let themselves be deceived. We must defend what we have constructed for our children, and if something happens, we must get together to discuss what position we will take. At a certain moment, I felt that unity very clearly. How good it was to see them all together!"

EIGHT

PALM SUNDAY

Sunday is already dawning, the last Sunday of my stay in Aka-masoa. I get up to the sound of water running outside, and it sounds like hope. I brush my teeth, take a shower, get dressed, and go out to breathe the air that today is not so laden with smoke or smells; it's as if the waste dump is resting too. I walk to the dining room, feeling that under the stone there is an earth groaning with labor pains. I say good morning to Olga; I listen to her voice and see her eyes gleaming with good health today. Janina gives me a palm leaf, which represents an olive branch. I drink my coffee, eat two pieces of bread, go out, and greet the inhabitants of this small community, which forms the spiritual and executive heart of Akamasoa. Peter had asked me before I came to stay at least until Palm Sunday, so here I am. A day full of images, smells, tastes, encounters, and emotions lies ahead.

⊱✦⊰

Peter asks me if I will go up on foot to Manantenasoa. Of course, I will. It is very good for me to move my body, fill my lungs with oxygen, and let the blood circulate from my head to my feet. Claudine and Viviane walk by my side, reminding me of my two daughters who are of the same age. Mrs. Fanja, the lady with mental problems who has been staying in Akamasoa for the last four days and receiving a plate of food every day, escorts us. Fanja speaks French fluently. I ask her what her problem is. She says that her husband left her and now she is being followed by many enemies.

"What kind of enemies?" I ask.

"The ones that want to harm me."

"Who?"

"The soldiers."

"Which ones?"

She falters, avoids my look, opens her mouth with that cluster of teeth piled up in the middle, one on top of the other, and stammers a sincere answer: "Something is wrong with my head." I tell her she must go to hospital. She nods. "I will go tomorrow."

"Are you sure?"

"Oui, oui," she replies, with her gaze lost somewhere inside her mysterious lunacy. I know she will not go. Viviane confirms my suspicions. Every so often, she arrives, stays for a few days, and then leaves.

We advance, crossing the highway. The red soil of the road sticks to my feet. Viviane carries Father Peter's bag with his vestments and all the necessary things for the Mass. I try to help her, but she laughs and does not let me, because she knows I will get tired very soon. I breathe. Peter, with his group as usual, is about half a mile ahead of us, out of sight near the top of the hill. Tojo carries an umbrella to protect herself from the sun; her head hurts as it does every single day, and she did not sleep well last night.

I ask Mrs. Fanja her age. "More than thirty," she answers cleverly.

"Do you have any children?"

"No, because the enemy...."

We pass the large sports hall and climb up to the Holy Family grotto surrounded by pine trees. I ask them to stop for a minute. The girls push me to continue, but I pause to contemplate the valleys that surround us. That intense green combined with the lighter shade of the rice fields, the wildflowers, and down below the landfill site that "one day will leave this place," according to Father Peter.

We walk past the grotto. Thousands of people are already going up, with their palm leaves in their hands. We get to the highest point, just above the quarry, reminding me of my visit there with Father Rok. There is complete silence now; not a stone is stirring. We go up to the shed, next to which the prayers for the blessing of the branches will be said. Peter will read the Gospel passage that talks about Jesus' triumphal entry into Jerusalem riding a donkey, amid the clamor of the crowds. From here the villagers, climbing up the hill with their green palm leaves, look like a legion raising the sword of dignity.

The tourists can be distinguished by the color of their skin. The majority are French nationals who live in Antananarivo. I wave to a couple and they reply by raising a hand. I look for some shade under the eaves of the shed. I scan the horizon again. What a beautiful place! Now the multitude is crowding round while Father Peter is putting on his alb and the red stole of the day. Holy Week has started here in Manantenasoa, this place of hope.

I take dozens of photographs—of Peter, the valley, and the crowd. Peter takes a bucket of water and sprinkles the multitude, using his hand. The loose drops shine in the light of the radiant sun that is rising over the hills. Hosanna! Glory to God! Father Peter moves his hand into and out of the water as if it were an oar. Now he walks through the crowd, and the young altar girls, also dressed in white with red capes on their shoulders, make way for him. The stole is red, the chasuble is red, redder even than the earth, as red as Christ's blood, which is waiting for Good Friday to leave his body and spring from his heart. As red as the Resurrection fire, lit on the Sunday dawn by us, his disciples, who are still afraid in the upper room.

The procession descends towards the sports hall. The band accompanies us as usual, with a mandolin, two accordions, and both a large and small drum. The songs rise to the sky as if the hill were breathing music. Thousands are going down the slope, black, copper, and white people together. Thousands of bodies with feet cracked by the passing of time, frizzy hair, and teeth lost in the track of misery. But there are also thousands of hearts full of hope, struggling to get out of the swamp, with effort and sacrifices but also with dignity. "How beautiful upon the mountain are the feet of the messenger who announces peace," are the words of a song that very much fits the occasion.

Yes, Peter is a messenger of peace! Padre Pedro Pablo Opeka, a priest, bricklayer, soccer player, herald to the poor—of Argentinean and Slovenian origin but of Malagasy heart! He was nominated on several occasions for the Nobel Peace Prize; he was named "Knight of the National Order of Madagascar" in 1996; he was selected as an officer of the "Ordre National du Merite" by France in 1998. Italy chose him as "Missionary of the Jubilee Year 2000," and Kiwanis International, headquartered in the United States, presented him with the World Service Medal in 2005. These are but a few of the many honors that he has always humbly accepted in the name—and for the benefit of—the poorest of the poor. Together with Mother Teresa, whom he deeply admires, he is one of the brightest humanitarian lights in the world, a man with a heart of gold, incredible leadership ability and perseverance, and the striking appearance of a modern Moses, with his long prophet's beard and the large hands of a bricklayer.

⤜❧⤛

We enter the sports hall; it is brimming with people. It's amazing, especially considering that the celebration today will last almost three hours. The long Gospel of the day is read. Peter is the narrator, and a few of his coworkers read the other voices: Theresa, Miss Bao, and Mrs. Emma. During the homily, Peter asks the people to remain united during these times of economic and political adversity in Madagascar. "Don't let yourselves be fooled. There is strength in unity." Then he asks them: "Who can we say who we are? The Jews didn't believe that Jesus could be the son of God, but he used to say: 'If you don't believe in me, at least believe in my work.' Jesus broke the mold. God is like that—humble, simple; he talks from the heart.

"Who cannot see the work of God in Akamasoa? Some French people visited yesterday, and they were amazed at all our work. And you, the beneficiaries of the work of Akamasoa, what do you have to say? We are all children of humble people, myself included. My father and mother left everything behind for their faith: their land, their oxen, their home..."

Peter tells them how his family settled in Argentina. "These are my origins. Don't be afraid or ashamed of saying where you come from, because God resurrected you, and we can see God's hand here today. That is why we believe that Jesus is God's Son."

Next come the songs, followed by the consecration. Christ who makes himself present, twinkling in the fire of an imminent resurrection. It is time for the Our Father, and we hold hands to sing it together, swaying from side to side. The sports hall moves like a soft breeze, accompanied by the palm leaves that are raised high in the air, like a wave of harmony bringing inner peace. We partake of Communion, sharing the bread in an atmosphere of love in this place of dignity and hope.

I return to my seat, next to my three young friends from Akamasoa. Peter says a prayer after Communion. I cannot stop looking at him—his eyes closed, his white beard, the alb, the red stole, his hands. A special light radiates from him. Peter tries to imitate Christ, and that is what has made the deepest impression on me. Peter refers everything to Christ and his Gospel and tries to be consistent with what Christ says.

I say to myself: "This man is a saint," and I start crying. "He is a saint, and I have had the privilege to meet him," and I continue crying. I do not mind, even if Tojo and Viviane notice and later ask me: "Why were you crying so much after Communion?" Something transports me; everything is blurred. I imagine this same multitude together in heaven, where there will be no poverty, no crying, no landfill sites, no girls without noses, or elderly people without eyes, where there will be no more bedridden people, no more prostitution, no drugs, no missing teeth—and no more cracked feet because we will be walking on white clouds and we will all be cleansed of vices.

Although my sobbing is like an endless stream, there is no remedy because joy cannot be held back. I see them all in heaven, forming an immense choir of angels, all the same, without any differences in race, creed, or condition. When I finally stop crying, I wipe my eyes and dry my hands on my trousers. The Mass ends. Peter asks me to climb onto the altar and—in front of this immense crowd—he says good-bye to everyone on my behalf. He grabs my arm and asks me to say something, handing me the microphone. "Thank you very much," I say in Malagasy.

Suddenly, there is a round of applause from the children, young people, adults, and elderly people. I add in Spanish for Peter to translate: "I will always carry you in my heart."

⁂

We go outside, and I leave with Michel and Christine, who have invited me for lunch at their home. When I return in the afternoon, there are prayers in the chapel, and the song they dedicate to Mary in Spanish fills me with happiness: "Mientras recorres la vida, tú nunca solo estás, contigo por el camino, Santa María va... (While you walk through life, you are never alone; with you along the way, the Virgin Mary goes...)". I do not know how long it has taken them to learn the words, but I can imagine that it was quite a significant amount of time. Their language is completely different from ours.

During dinner, I ask Peter why he never goes to Michel and Christine's. He replies: "I don't accept many invitations, not even from Michel and Christine who are my best white friends. I visit them once a year. I've learned that if I go to the other side too often, I neglect this side. If I live with the wealthy, I neglect the poor and my words become like a monograph on poverty, an explanation of poverty instead of a lived experience. I'm not here to be a diplomat but to work with those that have the least."

NINE

FAREWELL IN THE SMALL CHAPEL

Half past four in the morning: I get up before the alarm clock that Peter has lent me rings at five o'clock. I get up before the rooster sings, before the bells of the church on the other side of the valley ring, and before people start fetching water from the fountain. Peter is expecting me for Mass in the small chapel in his house. We climb the stairs in darkness. At the top, he turns on the light. The small chapel is on a balcony that Peter has enclosed with glass. It contains a small table for the altar, the cross, the image of the Holy Family carved in wood, the Sacred Heart, a small picture of the Virgin Mary (a present from his mother), a photograph of Mother Teresa, one of Abbé Pierre, and another of the Pope. Father Peter lights a candle, puts on his stole, and the ceremony begins, this time in Spanish.

It's just the two of us alone, at dawn, with the altar between us, and the chalice, the host, and the Gospel. Everything I have experienced makes itself present all of a sudden, as if this world had become mine. I must admit that I do not feel like leaving. I feel well here, even if it is not Mount Tabor. Naturally, my own family is expecting me, but I could bring them here, pitch a tent and stay here, helping Peter, trying to give others a little of what we have but receiving much more from them—so much affection, so many smiles, and so much hope despite the material poverty.

"In the name of the Father, the Son and the Holy Spirit." Amen. Peter

Paul Opeka is standing in front of me, celebrating his daily Mass, praying for my return trip, for the book, for his parents and his brothers and sisters. I pray for him, his assistants, and for all the inhabitants of the villages of Akamasoa. The shared prayer is sincere, surrendered to the other person's gaze, which can be sensed despite the diaphanous light in the room.

He asks me to read the first reading. It's Philippians 3:12-16, subtitled: "The apostle makes an effort to achieve perfection." In that passage, Saint Paul indicates that perhaps the goal may never be attained but one must always continue trying—"Forgetting what is behind." I think of the song that goes: "Hoping against hope." It must be because the good people of Akamasoa have emphasized it. Forge ahead, even if it is difficult, even if it hurts, devoted entirely to God's will.

Then Peter reads his favorite Gospel passage, Matthew 5:3-12 on the Beatitudes. "Blessed are the poor in spirit, for theirs is the kingdom of heaven. Blessed are those who mourn, for they will be comforted. Blessed are the meek, for they will inherit the earth. Blessed are those who hunger and thirst for what is right, for they will be filled. Blessed are the merciful, for they will be shown mercy. Blessed are the pure in heart, for they shall see God. Blessed are the peacemakers, for they will be called sons of God. Blessed are those who are persecuted because of righteousness, for theirs is the kingdom of heaven. Blessed are you when people insult you, persecute you and falsely say all kinds of evil against you because of me. Rejoice and be glad, because great is your reward in heaven."

Silence falls after this declaration of evangelical radicalism. The world goes in the complete opposite direction, diametrically opposed to such a message. Afterwards, Father Peter consecrates the bread and the wine; I kneel down, he sings. We hold hands for the Our Father. I feel the strength in his hands, hands that encompass, that embrace, holy hands. "Let us go in peace."

What else can I tell you about this encounter? Nothing. Words are of no use. The man who is looking at me is made of flesh and bone, but he has something else fixed in his gaze, something out of the ordinary, a deep mystery that is linked to his complete and utter surrender to others. This is what makes him different.

◦✦◦

After Mass, around nine o'clock, I say good-bye to Miss Bao, Theresa, Viviane, and Tojo, who are leaving today on a spiritual retreat. Three kisses on the cheeks, kind words, good wishes, and a desire to meet again in the future. "Let's hope it is soon," they say, and I must admit I was moved to tears again.

I enter my home, walk through the dining room, climb the wooden staircase that creaks under my feet, arrive in my bedroom, have a sip of mineral water, take my trousers off the nail hammered in the white wall, gather my things together, and pack them in my suitcase. I take the sheets off my bed, fluff up my pillow (which seems more comfortable now), and go downstairs after closing the window, which at this time of day brings me greetings from the landfill site.

During the time I have left, I flip through the folder of newspaper clippings and notes that Father Peter has lent me. I look for something else for the book, a grand finale with which to complete the farewell that fast approaching. I read something Father Opeka wrote on February 16, 1998, in the district of Los Nogales, near Madrid, Spain, during a retreat. It is entitled: "God, Christ, and the Holy Spirit!" It is handwritten in Spanish and it seems like a good summary of his spirituality.

"I must continue living my evangelical commitment day by day in order to create the conditions of life that may liberate the poor from an inhuman life. I must speak with audacity and clarity in defense of people's dignity—above all, of the oppressed.

"Hostilities and trials must not disorient us. We must not fear anything or anybody. We must keep the peace and be calm under any circumstances, good or bad. In every situation, we are called to be brave and show courage, to offer hope and solidarity everywhere. I must get rid of all unnecessary things and share all worldly possessions.

"It's my goal to instill a mysticism of fraternity, courage, and spiritual values into the Akamasoa people—above all into the young. We are all responsible for whatever isn't working well and for the injustice which hinders so many people's lives.

"I strive to defeat mediocrity and the easy way out. I desire to make every daily gesture significant and give it transcendental value. I choose to resist selfishness and accept sacrifice as the path that must be followed so I am more readily available to help the poor. I will be an instrument of dialogue, of unity, and of God's love. I want to live like Christ did, so his kingdom will come. I feel the fire of the Holy Spirit, who is a source of constant renewal and makes everything possible, together with Mary who helps us in this daily struggle."

Before lunch, I give Claudine my medal so that Mary will protect her. I ask her to continue studying even though it is hard, and I tell her not to leave Akamasoa. Afterwards, it is time for the lunchtime ritual: the bucket of water, the white soap, the towel, the two cats, grace, and the food. Fideline, Pierrete, Honorine, Jean-Jacques, Maurice, and Father Rok are all present. I thank Jean-Jacques for his history and geography lessons, Maurice for the visit to town, and I tell

Father Rok I will pray for Slovenia.

When we go outside, the little girls and the teenagers run towards us. They all want to accompany us to the airport, including Olga, but in the end only thirteen fit in the minibus. They wait until I board, showing affection in the form of farewell hugs, while I recite Hemingway's saying: "Two friends are equivalent to two stories that unite."

Life is like a river with many piers where you can tie up your boat. Some of us are more nomadic than sedentary, and we rejoice when we know different parts of the world and keep them in our life's albums. I know that this project, these people, and this place will not be just one more stop in my eternal search. Peter will continue with his daily work, coming and going, seeking solutions, and I am sure we will meet again.

Standing in the check-in line, I tell him about the hidden pearl that I found in the folder he gave me, referring to his notes from Los Nogales. He tells me to give his regards to his family. "Tell my father to remain strong so that we can meet again, and don't forget to tell him about the Holy Family grotto; and greet my mother, who I hope is well after the fall she had the other day, and tell her to distribute the presents as she thinks fit; tell my brother-in-law, Carlos, that I miss his good wines and tell Jorge that I will soon be there to accompany him to the Boca Juniors stadium."

Then the warm embrace; I thank Peter for everything I have received in these days, and I tell him how good it has been for me to take this trip, to share hope with him. Later, and before I get lost in the boarding lounge, I turn around to look at Peter one last time, surrounded by the little girls, with his raised hand, his thick white beard, and those transparent eyes that have said everything to me better than words ever could.

EPILOGUE

On Thursday, April 22, 2004, ten days after my arrival in Buenos Aires, I find out about an interview Father Peter gave to the most important newspaper in Madagascar, Midi-Madagascar. The journalist gave it the title: "Think of the Poor and Put an End to Sterile Arguments, Father Peter Says." In the interview, Peter mentions that the Malagasy political class is playing around with the feelings of the poor, and he strongly criticizes the fact that the European Union cut off food aid.

The day after the article was published, the European Union ambassador called Father Opeka to tell him that Brussels had decided to maintain the food aid until the end of the year. Indeed, the aid continued to arrive during 2005, but was cut off during the first eight months of 2006, forcing Akamasoa to purchase at least ten tons of rice for the schools every week. This produced an imbalance in its accounts that delayed the construction of permanent housing. Together with rising oil prices, which had a detrimental effect on Madagascar's economy and caused unemployment levels to rise, this has delayed the organization's self-financing goal. Nevertheless, Father Peter and his helpers continue to work hard in the hope that they will some day achieve it.

Meanwhile, the European Union has promised to restore the food aid program until 2008.

ACCLAIM FOR PADRE PEDRO

"Padre Pedro, or Father Peter Opeka, is a prophet and a mason of God. A modern Moses, he taught the destitute how to unite their strengths, insights and wills to create a better world. About 17,000 of the poorest of the poor who have been rescued from slow death on the trash hills of Antananarivo, Madagascar, now live in seventeen villages and over 8,000 youngsters are being cared for and educated for a better life in schools which Pedro, their parents and benefactors have established. Over 5,000 participants, mostly children, pray, sing and dance each Sunday at Father Pedro Opeka's Mass, celebrated in the spacious multipurpose hall."

—Excerpts from Paris Match *magazine, June, 2005*

"Padre Pedro Pablo Opeka is a priest, bricklayer, soccer player, herald to the poor—of Argentinean and Slovenian origin but of Malagasy heart! He was nominated on several occasions for the Nobel Peace Prize; he was named "Knight of the National Order of Madagascar" in 1996 and was selected an officer of the "Ordre National du Merite" by France in 1998. Italy chose him "Missionary of the Jubilee Year 2000" and Kiwanis International, headquartered in the United States, presented him with the World Service Medal in 2005. These are but a few of the many honors that he has always humbly accepted in the name—and for the benefit—of the poorest of the poor. Together with Mother Teresa, whom he deeply admires, he is one of the brightest humanitarian lights in the world, a man with a heart of gold, incredible leadership ability and perseverance, and the striking appearance of a modern Moses, with his long prophet's beard and the large hands of a bricklayer."

—*J.M. Silveyra, author, Buenos Aires, Argentina*

"In 1997, Prince Albert of Monaco (now His Royal Highness Albert II) visited Father Opeka's Akamasoa (Community of Friends) to personally dedicate a new dispensary, a school, and a junior college which had been built with Monaco's generous help for the children of Akamasoa, the future leaders of poverty-ravaged Madagascar. These children of trash people have become academically competitive with those from capital city's well-to-do families!"

—*Editor, "Two Messengers of Hope—Prince Albert and Father Peter,"*
Pourtant C'est Vrai (Nevertheless It Is True), *November, 1997*

"A bricklayer's son, Pedro began teaching the poor how to work hard, to make bricks and build family homes, and in this way strengthened in the people the consciousness of their own worth. Today, the Akamasoa boasts seventeen impressive villages. Almost every family has its own home (which it gradually pays for in small installments), while working hard and following the rules democratically established by the delegates of the entire Akamasoa community. The settlements have all the necessary infrastructure: schools (which, according to the most recent report, are attended by over 9,400 children, from kindergartens to high schools and junior college), dispensaries, shops, churches and a huge multipurpose sports hall. The inhabitants of these new communities hope to become self-sufficient and independent of foreign aid as soon as possible, while multitudes of other poor are waiting to take part in this unique journey to hope, with dignity and hard work."

—*Cardinal Franc Rode, Rome, Italy*

"Within the context of the celebration of the 60th Anniversary of the Universal Declaration of Human Rights, St. Mathhews Foundation honored Pedro Opeka with the first Cardinal Van Thuan Prize, Solidarity and Development 2008, for the Akamasoa project. The award was bestowed by Pope Benedict XVI and presented in his name by Cardinal Renato Raffaele Martino, President of Pontifical Counsel on Justice and Peace, and Cardinal Tarcisio Bertone, Secretary of State, in the Paul VI Audience Hall, Vatican, on December 10, 2008."

—Pontificium Consilium de Justitia et Pace,
Rome, Italy, December, 2008

"On December 16, 2008, Msgr. Alojz Uran, Archbishop of Ljubljana and Metropolitan of Slovenia, presented Pedro Opeka with the Cyril and Methodius Medal, the highest honor the Slovenian Conference of Catholic Bishops can bestow. The medal was awarded in recognition of Pedro's exceptional accomplishments in missionary, educational, and humanitarian work among the poorest natives of Madagascar. Thanking his benefactors, Pedro spoke with deep conviction how, with God's help and human commitment, poverty can be defeated."

—Drago K. Ocvirk, "A Friend of Garbage People,"
Misijonska Obzorja, *February, 2009, Ljubljana, Slovenia*

"Like Blessed Mother Teresa of Calcutta, Pedro has lived and worked with the poorest of the poor, bringing new hope and new life to those who had been neglected and forgotten. For this reason we are pleased to name Don Pedro one of our *Inside the Vatican* Top Ten people of 2010.

—Dr. Robert Moynihan, editor, Inside the Vatican,
Urbi et Orbi Communications, New Hope, KY, February 2011

"Social scientists and religious, social and political leaders will greatly benefit from studying Peter Opeka's organizational genius. They will be able to witness how he motivated the destitute and demoralized. He taught them to become self-reliant and productive members of increasingly self-governing villages, living in individual family homes (not in city blocks!). He brought once demoralized adults to the ethical level when in times of economic crises they voluntarily voted to minimize their own portions of rice so that the children would have something to eat."

—*Edward Gobetz, PhD, Professor Emeritus of Sociology,*
Kent State University, Kent, Ohio

"This book is a heartwarming, inspiring account of challenges and triumphs in Pedro Opeka's exceptionally successful struggle to help thousands of extremely poor residents on the Island of Madagascar. We also learn about Pedro's mother's life in Italian refugee camps, his father's suffering in Teharje death camp, and his miraculous escape from death in a communist mass grave in Slovenia, and we observe young Pedro's adventures as a shoe salesman in Harlem, a star soccer player in Paris, a hitchhiker in Morocco, Africa, and so much more. This is a thoroughly absorbing story—a classic!"

—*Mary Therese Volk, PhD, JD, lawyer and former*
Associate Professor of Classics, University of Arizona

"I was not previously familiar with Padre Pedro. His story is amazing and inspiring."

—*Robert Ellsberg, Orbis Books, Maryknoll, NY*

"I am delighterd that the inspirational story of Padre Pedro, the internationally known humanitarian Peter Opeka, is now available in

English and thus also to American youth who have as Peace Corps volunteers so nobly served the less fortunate in many poor countries. They will admire and be inspired by Pedro's idealism, commitment, and contributions to human dignity and peace."

—*Breda Loncar, educator, editor of SAT, and retired principal of North High School, Eastlake, Ohio*

"Father Peter Opeka is also an excellent model for neighborhood organizers. I love his emphasis on individual responsibility, respect for moral values and healthy living habits, and hard work as the means for self-improvement, self-reliance, self-respect, a higher standard of living, and human dignity."

—*Peter Osenar, former CEO of Emerald Health, Inc., and former Group Executive Vice President of AmeriTrust Bank, Cleveland, Ohio*

"Visiting Father Peter Opeka in Madagascar was one of the most unforgettable experiences of my life. He is one of the greatest missionaries and humanitarians of modern times who has given thousands of formerly destitute "trash people" a new lease on life through work and dignity and has provided for their children a good education, daily meals, and the assurance of a better future. He created a veritable miracle of Madagascar."

—*Joze Kopeinig, Rector, Sodalitas and Editor,* Dialog, *Tainach-Tinje, Austria*

"Father Peter Opeka, CM, is accomplishing for Madagascar what Mother Teresa accomplished for India."

—*Dr. Anton Stres, Archbishop of Ljubljana, Slovenia*

"Padre Pedro's life, his sacrifices on behalf of the poor in poverty-ridden Madagascar, his determination that no child should ever be hungry and without education, and his leadership in the struggle for human betterment, brotherhood, and peace are a wonderful source of inspiration. Please count me a supporter of Pedro for the Nobel Peace Prize."

—*Jerry M. Linenger, MD, PhD, astronaut and author of the best-selling memoir,* Off the Planet: Five Perilous Months Aboard Space Station Mir

Journalists, editors, publishers, filmmakers, religious and civic leaders, and benefactors who may wish to contact Padre Pedro can reach him at:

akamasoa.bdf@moov.mg

or write to:

Father Pedro Opeka
B.P. 7010, Antananarivo 101
Madagascar

The authorized US address for tax-deductible contributions is:

Catholic Missions Aid, Inc. (for Opeka)
17826 Brian Avenue
Cleveland, Ohio 44119

ABOUT THE AUTHOR

Jesús María Silveyra was born in Buenos Aires, Argentina, in 1954. He has a university degree in business administration and a long career as a writer and collaborator in different media.

He has published several works of fiction: *Stefan's Notebooks* (1992); *Peter—The Story Never Told* (1994); *Mary's Eyes* (1996); *The Apostles* (1999); *Gregory and Hemingway* (2000); *To Die with Glory* (2002); and nonfiction: *The Martyrs of Algeria* (1997); *Opening the Heart: Confessions of a Pilgrim to Medjugorje* (2001), and *The Way of Mercy* (2003).

In 2003 he met Father Peter Opeka while the missionary was visiting Argentina. The magnetism of his figure and the force of his mission made a deep impact on Mr. Silveyra. The idea of taking the long trip to Madagascar to see Father Opeka's projects in person, to experience the transforming power of hope lived by thousands of people in a place called Akamasoa, originated from that encounter. This book is the account of a personal journey that has become a testimony of the blessings lived in the twenty-first century, without superfluous words or empty promises, but simply with the power of faith in a God who promised his kingdom to those who work in the name of peace.

PHOTO SECTION

The poorest of the poor scavenged the trash deposits of Antananarivo to find something to eat or sell or lived in extreme degradation in city slums.

Padre Pedro rescued countless thousands of the poor in Madagascar and taught them how to work, make bricks to build homes and schools, how to live in dignity.

Once despised as trash people, the poor natives have learned to work as bricklayers or to cut stone blocks in the quarry, or become farmers, carpenters or metal workers.

Women making piles of gravel for house and road construction, or planting trees, working in rice fields, making dresses and souvenirs and so much more.

Work, education and decent housing (in photo below, temporary at left, permanent at right) have brought dignity to thousands of residents of Akamasoa villages.

"Give us this day our daily rice!" Over 7,000 children must be fed each day and survive the worst of natural disasters and economic crises when the poorest always suffer the most.

In 2008, over 9,400 children attended schools from nurseries to junior college and were academically competitive with those from higher economic classes.

Prince Albert of Monaco (now His Royal Highness Albert II), a friend and generous supporter of Padre Pedro and his humanitarian projects, visited Akamasoa in 1997.

The delegates gathered in Akamasoa Assembly discuss and establish the community's goals and rules which are implemented by native staff and members of Akamasoa villages.

The first great inspiration of Pedro were his Slovenian refugee parents who settled in Argentina, while writers like author Silveyra helped spread his message of hope.

Father Rok Gajsek from Slovenia (at left) has for many years been an invaluable assistant of Pedro, who is shown below on one of his many visits of the sick.

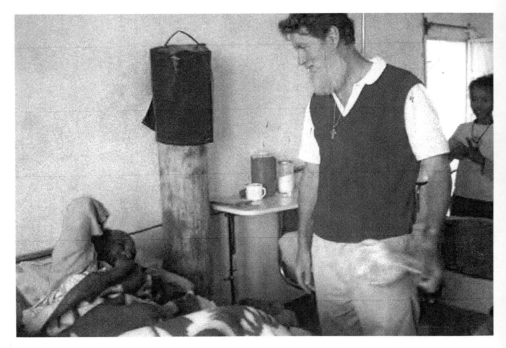

A small sample of books in various languages which have contributed to international awareness of Padre Pedro's "miracle in Madagascar."

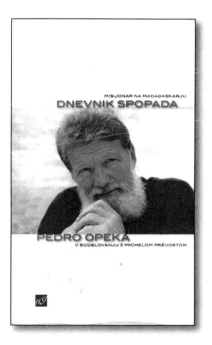

Among many forms of recognition, Pedro was awarded Cardinal Van Thuan Prize by Pope Benedict XVI, presented by Cardinal Martini and Cardinal Bertone in 2008.

Pedro's sisters from Argentina in Rome and Msgr. Alojz Uran, Metropolitan of Slovenia, presenting Pedro St. Cyril and Methodius Medal, the highest recognition of Slovenian Bishops.

Author Silveyra with children before the Sunday Mass in the multi-purpose hall in 2004 and photo of Pedro, the "Prophet and Mason of God," as published in *Paris Match,* Jan, 5, 2005.

The quarry that provided construction materials for Akamasoa has also served as a natural "cathedral" where thousands have celebrated newly-found hope, dignity and peace .

Kiwanis World Service Medal,
awarded to Padre Pedro Opeka
by Kiwanis International Foundation
in 2005

CPSIA information can be obtained at www.ICGtesting.com
Printed in the USA
BVOW011804310512

291387BV00004B/6/P